LIKE A
BANYAN TREE

The Story of an Undeterred Optimist

Eric Severn
with the Anand Family

LIKE A BANYAN TREE
The Story of an Undeterred Optimist

By Eric Severn

Inspired by Interviews with the Anand Family

Copyright © 2023 Rajesh Anand and Brijesh Anand.
All Rights Reserved.

See more from the author at:
EricSevern.weebly.com

Note: All quotes are common phrases from Baij Nath Anand that his children often heard him say, although he may not have been the first to come up with the phrases. Photographs are contributions from the Anand family.

Contributions from Southern States, LLC made this book possible. It is being published in celebration of the new building at Southern States that is named in dedication to Baij Nath Anand.

Library of Congress Control Number: 2023906849
ISBN: 978-1-7358507-6-4

Book Published in Portland, OR, USA by
ZIEBEE MEDIA
www.ZieBee.com

CONTENTS

Thank You Note | iii

Foreword | v

1. Origins and Birth | 1
2. Refugees in September | 17
3. Conflicts and Desire, Conflicting Desires | 63
4. Stories, Fathers, and Labyrinths | 113
5. Avinash and Love, Reality and Fantasy | 153
6. Joy | 179
7. Discontents and Content Discontentment | 191
8. Waiting at the Train Station | 231

Family Tree | 249

Glossary of Non-English Terms | 256

Photo Index | 257

Author's Afterword | 259

> *"Fix today,
> and tomorrow
> will fix itself."*

THANK YOU

This book presented the unique challenge of writing about someone from a different culture and time than my own. The structure of the book—to address Baij Nath and how he lived—was my way of trying to meet that challenge. Rather than attempt an authoritative voice on who Baij was and the India in which he lived, I wanted to approach him and his world as a dialogue, and I wanted to let his life and the questions it raised for me enter into conversation with my own life.

In doing so, I learned how Baij lived, but I also learned about how I want to live. It is my hope that this translates into insights for the reader as well. Writing in the second person also served as an ongoing reminder to me that stories are always a kind of conversation, and at best they can serve as a means for curiosity, openness, and understanding.

This book wouldn't exist without the time Baij's children took to tell me stories about his life. For their time, generosity, and openness, I am hugely grateful. Like Baij, his children are also storytellers. I am also grateful for my partner, E., who is a skilled editor in her own right. Throughout our many conversations about Baij's life, she has been instrumental in helping me focus my own at times disorganized thoughts about how he lived. Her feedback and thoughts on the book's structure were invaluable. My former teaching colleague and now close friend, Nancy Koppelman, read every single page of each draft and provided astute comments along the way. This guidance was also essential to my writing, and I am indebted to her for it.

Lastly, I am grateful for Baij, for how he lived and what he gave, and for the strange fact that his life touched my own.

~Eric

HOMER LEWIS & ASSOCIATES, INC.
ARCHITECTURE

B.N. ANAND COMPLEX
SOUTHERN STATES, LLC

FOREWORD

I believe that when someone starts a business that survives and prospers over time, the founders of that business deserve a site of recognition. When I came to Southern States in March of 1996, the company was already over 80 years old. Founded by the Mitchells on February 29, 1916, the family brought their legacy of success to Hampton, Georgia. Just over a decade earlier, they had moved from New England and provided electricity to the South by starting Alabama Power Company as well as Georgia Power Company, which today is Southern Company.

Through the growth of Southern States, they also grew the city of Hampton. They used their resources to build infrastructure like modern sewer and water systems throughout the town. They also donated to community organizations, such as The Boy Scouts.

By the second year into my job at Southern States, I wanted to honor the Mitchell family's success and legacy, as well as recognize their community contributions. So, I had plaques made of our founder, W.E. Mitchell, and his biography, and I had them installed in the lobby of the main building at 30 Georgia Avenue. To pay tribute, I invited all the surviving members of the Mitchell family who were still in the Atlanta area to join us during the dedication ceremony.

This building is now called the Mitchell Building by Southern States employees, and the dedication inaugurated our tradition of naming key buildings and campuses after those who have contributed to forming what the company is today. Following the Mitchell Building was the McGarity Building, named after my predecessor Tom McGarity. We then expanded to 30 Oak Street to house our Power Switching Division HQ. We named this the Spencer Complex after Sash Spencer, Tom's partner and then my partner after Tom retired.

We have now expanded a few miles north and built a new site at 1029 US Hwy 19/41, in Hampton, where our Service & Mobile Solutions HQ is located and being expanded. In naming the new division headquarters the B.N. Anand Complex, I want to recognize my father, Baij Nath Anand, and honor the values he instilled in me, which are now embedded in the core values of Southern States LLC.

His story is one of human triumph and optimism. Along with the B.N. Anand Complex, this book is meant to commemorate his memory and influence.

Raj Anand
President & CEO
Southern States LLC

LIKE A
BANYAN TREE

The Story of an Undeterred Optimist

*"Be the hand that gives,
not the hand that takes."*

1

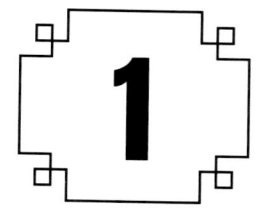

ORIGINS & BIRTH

In a small village called Chokkar Kalan a boy is born. His first memory, the one he will tell his own children about decades later when he is a grown man, goes like this: He's in the courtyard, playing alone, his mom and dad occupied somewhere off stage. I imagine this scene taking place on a quiet afternoon, maybe a kite hangs somewhere overhead, or wind rakes fallen leaves into a whisper, or a voice, unremarkable, passes in a neighbor's familiar complaint about a routine burden.

The boy is two years old and his name is Baij Nath Anand, Baija to his parents—a term of endearment—and he is aware, this boy, almost preternaturally so. His child's eyes big and brown and wildly receptive to the world, his world, which is India—one day to become Pakistan—a world to which I have never been but try to imagine: The flat roofs of brick-and-mortar houses clustered tightly in the middle of a flat landscape. Green fields farmed for wheat, maize, and sorghum. Peepal trees braiding shadows across the tall grass. It's 1920, or somewhere thereabouts. And the boy sees a snake.

Or maybe he hears it first, scales edging along the dirt, the rough glide like fine-grit sandpaper. He doesn't cry. He isn't startled.

Undisturbed, he lets the snake coil up his arm, around his leg, against the soft baby flesh of his toddler's neck.

And so here he is, protagonist and snake, a dramatic moment that, veering in one direction rather than another, could cut the whole narrative short—a dead end before it even begins—and in the wink of an eye the boy would never become the man, and his story would never have made its way to me and then, following that thread, the coil, my own story, who knows, could have found some other dramatic kink, drifted toward some other conclusion, some other end. And like that, life would be different, circumstances shifted.

But the boy lives. Lucky for me, the writer. Lucky for his family. Lucky for the countless people who crossed his path and to whom he offered his help. Lucky, too, for his children. And of course, lucky for the boy, who gets to remain the protagonist, at least for a while.

Our lives begin at birth but they begin all over again with our first memory, and then they begin again and again with each revision of the stories we tell. But let's say, however spurious origins may be, that Baij's story begins right here, in the courtyard, with a cobra, hood out, twisting around his small frame. And let's say Baija smiles, even laughs, his first dance with death a child's game.

What to make of this? Maybe nothing. Pure chance, dumb luck, inconstant moon that life is. And yet, origins and snakes are hard to resist, their symbolic importance as seductive as ever. The thing is, there is always a snake in the shadows. That's the primary fact of being here, in this world. And whether this life ends before it begins, say, in a small village, before the third birthday of a boy named Baij Nath, Baija to his parents, or later, after a long life full of stories he will tell his children and then, incidentally, his children will tell me. Nothing can change the temporary nature of being alive in this world.

So what do we do when the snakes come?

Play, perhaps, as Baij did.

Or, of course, become hysterical, as I would.

I should tell you about how this book began, its own origin story of sorts. The email from a former grad school professor came in August of 2021: *I found you a nine-month writing gig below as a ghost writer.* I scrolled down, only half interested. *I'm writing to ask a favor on behalf of a former student of mine*, it read. *He's an Indian American businessman, very humble, well-read. The family has been successful here in America, and his brother wishes to dedicate a building and a book to the life of their father. They are looking for a journalist to ghost write the project. I think they would pay well for the right person; timeline is about nine months and would involve oral histories, written sources, letters, and etc. I promised him I would ask around, so if you know any writing teachers or writers who might be looking for this kind of gig, let me know.*

I sat in the kitchen of my small, sparse apartment in Seattle, read the email once and then read it again. A heatwave had settled over the city and the box fan crammed into my kitchen window fecklessly blew hot air. Everywhere everyone seemed to be waiting for something—the global pandemic to end or surge, the next martyr or saint or villain to spark another political conflagration, the four henchmen of the apocalypse, the new Everlane store at the University Village Mall to open.

I had been waiting too. For the last four years I had been sick with a mysterious illness that tore through my life after my dad died, as if the two were causally connected. I had been waiting for the grief and the illness and the loss to pass so I could step back into who I used to be, start teaching again, start writing again, get my life back on track and start making sense of how it had gone so far off the rails in the first place.

But when earlier that spring my illness began to lift, I was still left with a life in upheaval. The migraines had departed, the dizziness had steadied, the vision in my right eye had slowly filled in, and the near constant muscle spasms that shook my body like the crack of an electrical current right before a light bulb blows had eased. But I still had nightmares about emergency rooms and the inconclusive looks of doctors. I still had panic attacks and flashbacks so powerful that sometimes I'd find myself paralyzed in bed, trying to will my own death. And I still felt the shame of having been sick, of having been so scared, of having had friends slowly pull away, of somehow feeling like it was my fault. But more than anything there was the shame of helplessness, the shame of living a life I felt I still had no control over.

Haze from the most recent forest fire turned buildings in the middle-distance piss-yellow. I looked out the window and typed a response to the email. I just wanted to see. I was curious. Who wouldn't be? Plus I needed a job. Besides a mattress, my only piece of furniture was a lawn chair from Fred Meyer. I was nearly out of money. The previous summer I taught creative writing on a short contract at a small liberal arts college and managed to save a little, but I was approaching a fiscal cliff that my habitual austerity measures alone couldn't resolve. I had rent for two more months before free fall.

And then there was E. After being sick and single for four years, I had met someone. And she was a reminder that a job is never just a job. A job is picking up the check on a date, it's being able to invite a woman over to your apartment because you have more than a lawn chair, it's a sense of self-worth, it's companionship and coffee in the morning and a gift you give with a little note: *This made me think of you.* This is how capitalism gets you.

E. was a clinical psychologist and she was smart and insightful but said she wasn't ready for a relationship. I didn't know where our story would go or if it would even go anywhere at all, but I wanted it to go somewhere. For four years, I hadn't wanted anything but my health. Now I wanted E., maybe even needed her. I'd be lying if I said I wasn't also thinking of her when I reread my email once and then hit send.

The next day was hot, just like the one before it and the one before that. I was sitting in my lawn chair by the stove drinking lukewarm coffee. My phone dinged. It was an email.

Hello Eric,

What would be a good time to talk about the project. Looking forward to it.

Brij

I made up some arbitrary times to make it seem as if I had a busy life, and then wrote that I was available today after 5 p.m. and then tomorrow until noon.

Brij called later that evening. Out my window the sun was low with an angry red on the horizon. My phone rang once, twice, and then after the third I picked up. I don't know what I expected, exactly. Probably I didn't expect anything, but then the voice on the other end was warm and inviting, and though I didn't know who Brij was, not even the most basic facts, like age for instance, I could tell he was older, fifty at least. There was an intensity to his voice, something studied and careful, thoughtful, and after he introduced himself and asked how my day was, we were both silent for a moment. For some reason I suddenly felt very young.

I started to ask about the project, stopped, started again. Brij cleared his throat.

"Let me tell you what we are looking for," he said, and then proceeded to give me the situation. He had three siblings. Brij lived down in Portland, Oregon, a few short hours from me, and one of his brothers, Raj, lived in Atlanta, Georgia. He had a sister, too, Rashmi, living in Delhi with her husband, and Ajesh, the youngest brother, lived in Lucknow, an old Islamic city in Northern India where they all were raised. I repeated the names to myself knowing I would still forget them: Brijesh (Brij), Rajesh (Raj), Rashmi, and Ajesh.

Their father had been an extraordinary man, Brij said, and I thought I heard a slight inflection of irony mixed in with sincerity as he began to sketch the briefest outline of this man's life. He was born in a small village in Pakistan shortly after World War I. He had survived Partition, fled Pakistan with his parents in his late twenties, and then returned, only months later, the newly drawn border still rocked by political upheaval and genocide, to rescue his sister and her husband.

His name was Baij Nath Anand, and as Brij spoke about the man I realized that this was a conversation about a life completely foreign to my own. What registered from what Brij told me was a series of hard facts, but a life is more than facts. Baij was apparently selfless, charitable, kind, duty-bound. He had lost everything as so many who survived Partition had, but against the odds he became a prominent lawyer, moved to Lucknow, and started a family. He had passed away in July of 2001. This project was in dedication to the man, his memory, who he was.

As Brij told me these things I kept thinking, but where's the dirt? A man has to have some dirt, some ugliness, and if he doesn't, where's the story? Where's the protagonist? Brij paused, as if picking up on what I was thinking.

"But of course, part of your job would be to humanize him. We're his children and so of course we think he's extraordinary. What child doesn't love their father?"

I could tell he meant it as a rhetorical question, dangling there for me to agree with. I wasn't sure how to respond. I waited a beat, two.

I didn't love my own father. How could I? I hardly knew him. I met him when I was twenty-one, and saw him only four more times after that before he died when I was thirty-three. Most of what I think I know of him I've invented out of the stories passed down from my mom and his other children.

After our shared silence Brij cleared his throat again, and I tried to laugh off the awkwardness.

"So at first this was my brother Raj's idea," Brij continued. He explained that Raj owns a successful electrical power infrastructure company and is expanding its Hampton, Georgia campus with a few new buildings, one of which is dedicated to their father. Raj wanted to have something written about Baij's life by the time of the building's completion, something to hand out to family and friends. When Raj mentioned this to Brij, Brij had the idea to make something more involved. Why not a book, something longer, something more literary? He told me how he asked one of his former writing instructors if she knew anyone, which was how word got back to me, circle complete.

"So," Brij said. "What do you think?"

I didn't know what to say. I didn't know anything about India other than what I had learned from a post-colonial studies seminar I took in graduate school. I didn't know anything about fathers other than the empty spaces where my own should have been. I wasn't even sure that I could write my own story anymore—the way illness and loss and trauma had confounded my own sense of narrative—let alone the story of a man I knew nothing about, who lived in a time completely different from my own, had a world-view that couldn't be more distant from American individualism. I imagined myself lost in research, confusing names of cities and people, maps of India and Pakistan pinned up against my wall with thread connecting one village to another like some absurd *Homeland* episode. I didn't even have a desk. Also, what if they didn't like what I wrote, but because they had paid me I had to keep revising it? What if this turned into some weird iteration of Steven King's *Misery*, except I'd be stuck revising a story about an *extraordinary* father that I'd never have, living over and over my own father's perpetual absence?

I took a breath, tried to think. I didn't want to be mercenary but the other part of it was that this would be full-time work and then some. I didn't have to remind myself that I needed a job. Again, I thought about E. Of course I did. I took another breath.

"I'm definitely interested," I said.

"Do you think you'd be able to do this?" Brij asked, as if he could hear the doubts ricocheting around in my mind. There was something almost consoling in his voice.

"Definitely," I said. I had to bring up the issue of money if we were going to start seriously thinking about this, but Brij was quick to pick up on my hesitancy, said we could talk in a few days and discuss compensation.

So, that was that. We hung up.

That night I slept fitfully. It was hot and I woke up sweating. After I took a cold shower, I stood in the kitchen, in front of the box fan, dripping water onto the floor. It was 3 a.m. and outside I could see the lights of the city, and I imagined all those people and wondered how many of them really felt okay. I wanted to feel okay. I wanted to feel like I knew something about something again. I stood there thinking about my former self, how before I got sick, I'd pace in front of a lecture hall filled with students and make sweeping claims about the contemporary literary landscape, saying obscure things like, "Every story is about a story that can't be told," and "The third person simply isn't sustainable anymore." I'd say these kinds of things with great conviction.

I missed that conviction, but at the same time I felt embarrassed at the thought of it. What do we really know anyway? Nothing. We're written on water, or however the saying goes. From nothing and into nothing. You can't really say anything about anything.

I began pacing around my small kitchen in great strides, towel around my waist, traversing the length of it back and forth, back and forth. I wasn't even sure if I wanted to be a writer anymore. After my experience with illness, I saw how petty the literary world was. Writers are bickering, back-biting, self-aggrandizing, insecure, and power-hungry people. I know because I was one.

I had to let go of all that when I became sick. I lost my ability to read. No matter how hard I tried, I couldn't get my eyes to track words. They'd swim all over the page. I couldn't hold an entire sentence in my head, couldn't follow a thought to its logical conclusion. I remember that first year of my illness a neurologist who administered a cognitive test, alarmed by the results, looked at me very seriously and said he wouldn't be worried if I were an eighty-five-year-old man. But I wasn't an eighty-five-year-old. I was thirty-three years old and had ambitions and plans. I was going to write novels, publish more short stories and essays. I had memoirs whispering in me.

Though I was no longer sick in the way that I was, I still had real doubts that I was the writer I used to be. I still had days when I struggled to read for more than thirty minutes, and there were also some days when if I looked at a computer monitor too long, trying to write, I could feel my vision beginning to shift, my depth perception start to go, that weird and horrifying sense of aphasia returning. I worried that if I took on this project and failed at it, it would confirm what I had been afraid to finally admit to myself. I was less than who I used to be, and I would never return to the writer I was.

Or worse, what if I returned to exactly who I was? It wasn't just that I was afraid of realizing I no longer had the capacity to be the writer I used to be. I was also afraid that I didn't know how to be a writer without prioritizing publishing—my work, my ridiculous opinions—over lived experiences and the real relationships in my life. It's so easy to mistake being a thoughtful, sensitive writer for being a thoughtful, sensitive person, especially because stories are about human interactions. I know how seductive this is. I've conflated the two myself. I wanted to wash my hands of all of that. I wanted something less contingent on the opinions of others. I wanted something more honest.

And yet, there was something I had learned from stories that I couldn't let go of. Characters develop. They change. I kept wondering, could I develop? Could I change?

I took the job.

Brij and I negotiated compensation. Things moved quickly that first month. He put me in touch with his siblings to do interviews about their father. He had also emailed two documents, large PDFs that pertained to Baij. Raj had written the first document, an account of his own life: *Ice Cream Boy, American Man*. I liked the title, which I learned was suggested by his daughter, Shelly. A classic Bildungsroman. The second document was more academic, written by Raj's daughter, apparently her thesis at Wellesley College: *Oral Narrative and the Post-Partition Indian Identity*, a heady title.

I skimmed the first document on a hazy August morning. A hard glare caught my computer screen and words skipped around on the page, a reminder that I was still up against the occasional migraine and dizziness. I felt the prick of anxiety. I made a cup of coffee and put on some Gregorian Chant to clear my head. I stood by the kitchen window, and I could feel the heat radiating through the glass. How much of my life had been spent in front of windows, staring outside, waiting for the phone to ring, for the knock on the door, religious revelation? Nobody's coming, I told myself.

Later that day I went down to the Kinkos at the end of my street, confirmed that printing two documents of seventy-five pages each cost far more than I could afford, and then I had them printed anyway. A stack of paper in my hands, I walked along the canal to Wallingford, and then to Gas Works Park. Windless and hazy, smoke bunched up on the horizon, and even though it looked far off you could still smell ash in the air. I found a bench and sat down, started to read.

At first, *Ice Cream Boy, American Man* was hard to follow, something about Raj referring to his own childhood in third-person threw me, but then I fell into his story and by early afternoon I had read half of the document. Certain passages had a kind of candid honesty and economy I appreciated. I read one sentence out loud because I liked how it sounded: *"For three days he rides his bike around the veranda, singing as he tries to go faster and faster."* The sun slipped behind a tree and mottled the pages as I pushed on.

After reading all of it, my first impression of Baij mostly had to do with the kind of father he was.

He was the kind of father who once made Raj return a coin where he had found it on a bus, however unlikely it seemed that the owner would ever find it. He was the kind of father who came home from his work and narrated his day to his children because he wanted them to understand and be curious about the world. He was the kind of father who lectured his children about the difference between legal justice and moral justice because he wanted to impart to them the value of fairness, but also because, even as a lawyer himself, he wanted them to understand that there was something about a human life and human suffering that couldn't be easily measured in the balance of legal strictures, that sometimes thinking morally meant considering what it is to be human in broader ways than what the law allowed. He was the kind of father who tried to instruct his children by providing examples they could emulate. I appreciated all this and also felt the contrast to my own father.

According to the stories I know about him, my own father was a man of extremes, both charming and violent, sensitive and selfish.

There are the stories about how he'd drive down to the bars right before closing. Stone sober, he'd wait outside for the biggest man he could find. I still can't decide if he was looking for someone to hurt or someone to hurt him, or if the difference even matters, and I still feel a twinge of shame when I catch myself imagining that his desire to fight came from his own ache of having to choose between his wife and my mom, with whom he was having an affair, and who by then must have been pregnant with me. But maybe we never even mattered that much. Maybe all he wanted was the thrill of a fight, of fists against bone, the delight of drawing first blood.

But there's the other extreme, too. The stories about his sensitivity, the letters my mother told me about, the ones he had composed to her during their affair, and the vulnerability and desire written in them. When I think of this side of my father I imagine his need and hunger, the boy in the man who would sneak away from his own wife and climb through my mom's bedroom window when she wasn't a mom yet, careful not to wake her college roommates, and I recognize this urgency in myself, how scary it is to know you need someone you can't have, how sharp that pain can feel, but most of all how selfish it can make you.

As I read more I realized it wasn't just my dad and Baij who were different. I also became aware of what felt like a distinct difference between Baij and myself: Raj had written that his father "had one overarching belief, a belief in which he never wavered in his life; it was a belief in his own ability to accomplish whatever he set his mind to."

In part I understood this to mean that Baij was a man who wasn't burdened by his own history, and this was also foreign to me. This was a man who grounded himself in the present. This was a man who set his sights and acted. This was a man who knew what he was about and moved accordingly. In short, this was a man who couldn't be more different than I am. Hemingway said there were two kinds of people in the world: those who can sleep at night and those who can't. If I was the kind of person who couldn't sleep, my early sense of Baij was that he slept like a baby. We were made differently, in this sense, Baij and I, and I was curious about this difference.

But I would learn in the coming weeks from his children that there was something about Baij that I also very much related to. I could understand the value and joy he found in reading, in education. While it's hard not to think of Baij's story beginning with the snake, it's also hard not to think of it beginning again with his education. That Baij was able to get an education, and a very a good one at that, was an against-the-odds kind of situation.

Not that Baij didn't have advantages. He was a lucky boy, all things considered. His grandparents on both sides were prominent people, especially on his father's side. Landowners, they had warehouses and stored grain for the local farmers. They were money lenders. They were pillars in this small community, and when Baij's father, Lakhsmi Das Anand (Lakhi), married Baij's mother, Gyan Devi Chadha, they were already in a good position to do well for themselves.

By the time Baij was four or five, the young couple had moved into one of Lakhi's ancestral homes. In a village of otherwise small houses this home stood out, not for its size but for its windows, large panes that I imagine spanned floor to ceiling, giant windows, especially to a boy, that caught morning sun and then in the dying daylight sent motes of dust kaleidoscoping into dizzying patterns. The House of Glass. This is what Baij called his childhood home, and by all accounts it was one of the finest homes in the village.

But this is no penthouse on the Upper East Side of New York.

The limitations to the life that Baij was born into are extensive. This was village living, and this meant labor and serious toil under the harsh sun in the summer and brutal cold-snaps in the winter. Disease was common. There was no plumbing. In the morning, still half-asleep, the men and women would wade out into the tall grass to relieve themselves, the men yelling as they cut into the fields so as not to surprise the women, hidden in their own crouch under tall foliage, pissing on hard dirt. Once, as a young man, Baij saw a man dead or dying in the street, overcome by illness. The idea of opportunity, education, upward mobility, were all circumscribed by significant material limits.

And yet, Baij thrives.

According to what Baij told his children, his second memory goes like this: It's the first day of school and Baij's grandfather, Radha Kishan, is going to walk the boy across the street to the schoolhouse. It can't be more than thirty yards away, but for a child, it's a whole adventure—other children, the mystery of a teacher imparting knowledge, the world opening into all the complexities of social interactions.

His grandfather takes his hand, and they step out of The Glass House. Early morning light softens the hard edges of brick-and-mortar houses, their shadows creating pockets of air still cold from the night before.

Nervous but excited, Baij and his grandfather make the journey from one side of the street to the other. There's the distant voices of men in fields, of work and labor, and it is replaced by a rush of child voices as they enter the schoolhouse, kids sitting on a large jute mat while in front of the classroom the teacher prepares the day's first lesson. Baij stands there at the precipice, clutching his grandfather's hand, uncertain. And then his grandfather reaches his own hands into his bag and pulls forth fistfuls of batashas, little white sugar candy, and offers it to the class. It's a happy memory, the way the children crowded around, taking candy, all smiles.

But more importantly, this is the start of what will be a lifelong love of learning for Baij. From the start he enjoys school. He likes reading, and easily finds himself lost in books. But it isn't just books. He is curious. He likes to arrive early at that one-room schoolhouse, looks forward to the small joy of being the first child there, the reward of rolling out the big, jute mat the children sit on during class, and those first moments alone with the teacher, a chance to talk. I imagine Baij's curiosity and hunger filling that early morning space with eager questions both irritating and endearing, the teacher trying to mark papers while fielding a storm of the boy's breathless inquiry.

During those early years, Baij reads constantly. In the evenings he reads by candlelight, until his father yells at him, annoyed with his son's interest in books, already their sensibilities diverging into what would become a lifelong contention.

"Put that book away," I imagine Lakhi snapping.

"Let him read," his mother counters. "He isn't bothering anyone."

"He's bothering me," Lakhi retorts. But this doesn't stop Baij. Candlelight out, he sits by one of the big windows, book positioned such that the pages catch a sliver moon barely in view and he gropes along, sentence by sentence, finishing books and starting new ones, willful, determined, even then, at such a young age.

But this early love affair with knowledge is continually punctuated by interruptions and obstacles. The primary school in Chokkar Kalan only goes up to fourth grade, and Baij blows through them all with ease and speed, already sharp, already a quick study, easily impressing his peers and his teacher, too. Finished, he wants more, and this would mean moving to another village where there is a secondary school.

His father won't hear of this. "Why do you want an education. You have everything you need right here."

But Baij doesn't have everything he needs, and Lakhi can't understand this. He turns to his mother, Baij does. He tells her that he wants to live with her parents, his maternal grandparents, in the neighboring village, where he can finish secondary school. At first she doesn't say yes but she doesn't say no, either, and he keeps working on her, follows her around the house, pestering her. "Please," he begs her, his pestering overwhelming. The Glass House is already full of so many competing needs, his two younger sisters—Sarla and Toshi—and his older sisters—Prakash and Rambheji—making their own demands on Baij's parent's time.

So eventually Baij's mother agrees, and they come up with a plan. He and his mom will go visit his grandparents in the neighboring village, and then when his mom comes back without him, she will simply tell his dad that he refused to come back, a story Lakhi would easily believe, already knowing how obstinate his son could be.

It's the start of many moves Baij makes for education, his trajectory roving in pursuit of further schooling. He lives with his grandparents for three years, finishing fifth, sixth, seventh, and eighth grade, and then he attends Sanatan Dharam High in this same village. He reads constantly, his appetite for knowledge growing the more he learns. Then his grandparents move to Gujranwala, a larger city, further away, down south, and this interrupts his schooling again. So he stays behind in Lalamusa. Hoping to finish high school there, he asks one of the teachers if he can live with him while he does, and the teacher says yes.

This episode in Baij's life must have felt like a dream. It must have been everything a young boy who wanted an education could hope for. During the day he goes to school and then in the evening he comes home to his teacher, the lectures and topics they went over in class continuing into the evening, Baij asking questions, ever curious, ever eager to know more and more.

Over dinner teacher and student talk, and maybe it's here that Baij learns to not just appreciate books, ideas, study, but conversation, the joys of dialogue, of banter, and the playfulness of language and discourse. I imagine him with his high school teacher, living in the same house, the same way that I think back on my first mentors, how I idealized them, hung on their every word, read whatever they recommended. And read Baij does.

In the afternoons, between school and coming home, he rides his bike out into an open field. Under the shade of a tree, he props his book on his bicycle seat, and he stands there, poring over whatever books he can get his hands on, whatever books his mentor has or recommends, be it history, medicine, or poetry. And it's then that he begins to realize something about himself. He has an incredible memory, photographic, the way he can read a page and then recall almost the entire thing, word by word.

So, like clockwork, Baij reads every day after school. The same field. The same tree. That same afternoon breeze stirring the grass. He stands there, hardly moving save to turn the page of whatever book is in front of him. He does this so often the villagers begin to talk.

"It's an apparition. An evil spirit. A jinn."

They say it's a devil.

They say that the man in the field has lost his mind.

But they are wrong. Baij hasn't lost his mind. He is finding it.

Then comes another move.

There's political upheaval in Chokkar Kalan. The State's Chief Minister makes money lending illegal, and this effectively destroys Baij's parents' and grandparents' livelihoods. They move to Gujranwala, where his maternal grandparents are already living. This time Baij moves with them. He's so advanced that he finishes eleventh and twelfth grade in one year. High school, done.

There would be more education to come, college, three degrees—one in History and one in Economics, both from Panjab University, as well as a Master's in Oriental Language from Aligarh Muslim University—all punctuated with work. He works jobs at railroad stations, jobs filing insurance claims, periodic office work, at one point he will teach high school and then eventually take a position as a professor of Persian poetry, and Urdu, a language he falls in love with, its sweet linguistic texture a subtle music he will always gravitate toward.

And it's this period of Baij's life that I understand most, these early years, and his love of language, of poetry, of the way words can captivate and bring the world closer and then blow it open again. It was the love that I had lost when I was sick. When I think about Baij's childhood, of his beginnings, of the way he would follow the moonlight across his room to read, or when I think of him as a young boy, against the odds, moving from one small village to another just so he could keep reading, keep learning, I recognize a shared value, but I also recognize the thing that I saw slip away, that desire to learn and read and write. It all reminded me of a loss I wasn't yet over, that still felt close and uncertain. And yet, at the same time, it also reminded me of how much I wanted to salvage what I could, how much I wanted to reclaim as my own what I loved.

So what is an origin, a birth?

It is a snake that winds out of the shadows. It is the words we use to tell the stories about that snake. It is the stories of how it came for us but didn't strike, or did strike but how we lived nonetheless to tell the tale.

Origins are birthed from language that is hard won, culled from the forbidden books pursued beneath the fading moonlight under the roof and governed by the law of our father's house. Origins are loss first and then rebirths later. Origins are arbitrary but no less meaningful for the human will they require, the desire to say, this story begins right here. They are failures and they are those places where we attempted to begin again.

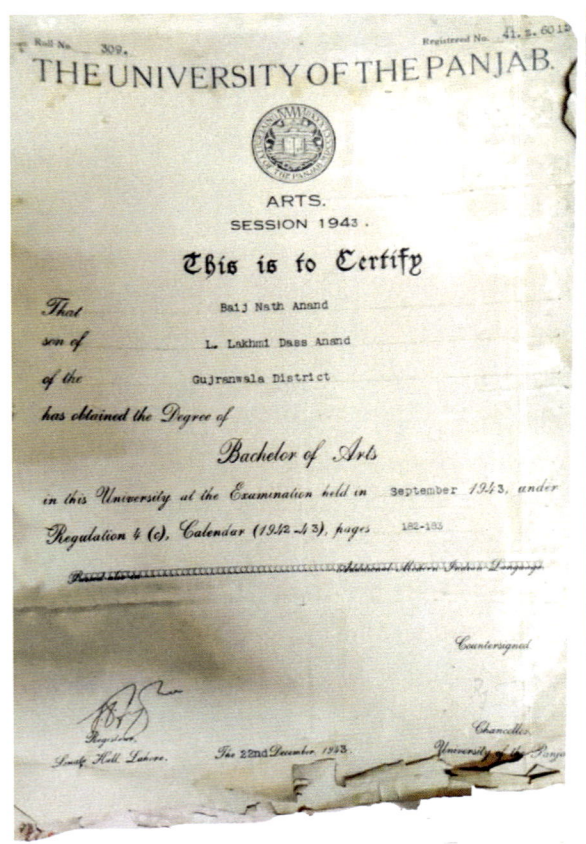

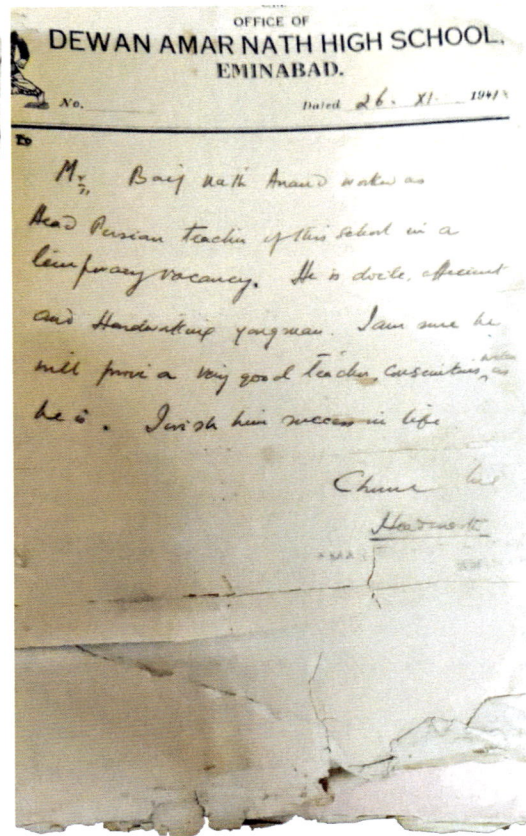

Clockwise from Top Left: A certification from the University of Panjab for Baij's Bachelor of Arts, 1943. A letter from Dewan Amar Nath High School describing Baij as "head Persian teacher." And a certificate from University of Panjab for completion of Intermediate Examination, 1941.

Origins & Birth

2

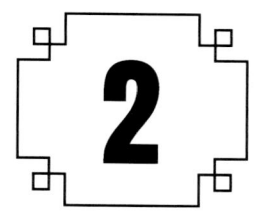

REFUGEES IN SEPTEMBER

But how do you begin again after you've lost everything? This is what I would ask you, Baij. If I could bypass the interviews and research and ask you one question, I'd ask:

How did you start over and then set the past aside and move forward?

And so I am asking you, Baij, how did you do it? I can't help but think about the parallels between our own lives but also the differences, the drastic, material and circumstantial differences.

In September of 2021, the heat wave that had settled over Seattle finally broke and I was just starting to rebuild my own life. In August of 1947 you had lost everything, the genocide and political upheavals of post-Partition India just getting started, the monsoons refusing to come, to bring relief from what had been a hot and unusually still summer.

In September of 2021, I started interviewing your children, began asking questions about your life, the kind of father you were, the work you did as a lawyer, and I learned things about you. You enjoyed food. When it was sunny you always wore sunglasses. You liked Safari hats. Your dental hygiene routine was unusual, to say the least, the way you'd brush every single tooth individually, taking five, ten, fifteen minutes in the morning. I learned that there was a period in your life when your youngest son, Ajesh, was studying law so that he could take over your practice, and during this period the two of you would drive to court together in your blue, tag UPD 8411, Hindustan Ambassador, a car based on a British model and affectionately called the "King of Indian roads."

You would tell stories about your childhood during these drives to work, and this image stays with me—a father opening up to his son, idling somewhere in the old city of Lucknow, the smell of gasoline, traffic fenced in by the weathered minarets of mosques, and you loved these old mosques, loved Islamic culture generally. You were a Hindu with a real respect for Muslims, even after everything you had seen. I learned that this was the kind of person you were. And I also learned that in August of 1947, your life would swerve completely off course and alter your trajectory entirely.

So in September of 2021, when I received the first paycheck I had received in years (I bought a desk, a few plants, a new pair of shoes!), when I read about Partition and Hinduism, when I was trying to turn my spare apartment into a home, when I was trying to build a new relationship with a woman I was just getting to know, E.—in late August she finally said, "maybe I'm starting to soften and come around to the idea of trying things with you"—when I was excited and scared to feel like I might start living again, when for the first time in what felt like forever my basic needs were being met enough to start to think about my other needs, my other desires, when all this was happening I thought about how in September of 1947, you had lost it all: Your job teaching at Hindu College, Gujranwala, your home, your country. You were living in a refugee camp. Your basic needs were all that mattered. Where would you live? What would you eat? Disease and death were all around you.

In September of 2021, I was just starting to figure out how to live again, and in September of 1947 you were trying to figure out how to survive.

But it's that morning on August 18, 1947, when you and your family escaped what would become Pakistan that has stayed with me most.

You were twenty-eight years old and life was what it pretends to be—predictable. Gujranwala was such a marvelous city to you that later in your old age you would joke that there was a switch, somewhere hidden in the city center, and when flipped it magically cleaned the streets, scrubbed tile and stone.

So you liked it there, maybe even loved it. A professor, you were highly educated, had attained your goal and then some. You were making a good living and so your family—mother and father, and two of your four sisters, nine-year-old Sarla and eleven-year-old Toshi—were living with you. You had already eclipsed your own father as the provider. Not that this was a surprise. Your father, Lakhi, couldn't be more unlike you, his disdain for work, his love for tobacco, his hookah. And you were political. Disillusioned with Gandhi, you had gravitated toward the RSS, but in a time of rising tensions and rumors—Hindus pitted against Muslims and Muslims pitted against Hindus—you were one the of the holdouts, believing Partition wouldn't happen, that there was another way. You talked about a shared sense of belonging, an India universal enough but not pandering to religion. And there was your optimism, too, your belief in humanity.

But your Muslim friends worried for you. In Gujranwala, The Muslim League had become increasingly extreme, and your Muslim friends urged you to consider it, to think about leaving. So it couldn't have been a complete surprise, what you saw that day. You were wearing shorts and an undershirt. Broad shouldered, dark hair pushed back, a high, handsome forehead, you must have been the picture of equanimity, a cup of tea by your side and a newspaper unfolded in front of you. This was the routine that you followed every day before you made your way to campus to teach, and that day wasn't any different. Except that it was.

The smoke from a burning house only a few blocks away caught your attention, or maybe first it was the smell, not just of wood burning but of something different, the smell of melting plastic and rubber, entire households incinerated and paint torched. Or maybe it was none of this, maybe that whole morning, before the killings and rapes and beatings even started, maybe there was something in the air, a palpable tension you could feel, something you were alert to but couldn't yet name.

Once you realized something was wrong, I imagine you decisive, in control of yourself, no sign of panic, not yet. Your mom is in the courtyard milking the cow, and you tell her first. And then once inside you alert your two sisters, along with your dad. They try to pack, not quite understanding the situation.

"Now," you say. "We need to leave now," and then you tell them about the smoke.

Your sisters, already dressed, take very little. Your mom has the foresight to grab her gold jewelry. Your father, hardly dressed, seizes his hookah. Outside you can hear shouting, a woman screaming. Gunfire. You take your degrees from the wall and roll them up tightly so they fit naturally into your hand.

That first leg of your escape is cinematic, almost breathtakingly so.

On the roof of your house, you lead the way, leaping from one rooftop to another, your family close behind. It's hard not to imagine this from up high, a birds-eye view, slowly zooming out. First you, your degrees gripped tight, then your father and mother close behind, your dad cradling his hookah and your mom has both your sisters by the hand.

Slowly the larger scene unfolds. The smoke of homes and temples a few blocks away, and then the streets, the surrounding perimeter a bottleneck of confusion, Hindus trying to escape, Muslims closing ranks, your city of magically swept streets soon to be littered with corpses. It's a scene repeated again and again on the Pakistan side of the border, and on the Indian side the opposite, Muslims trying to flee while Hindus and Sikhs close in. Nobody is exempt.

You and your family make it to the police station where you assume you'll be safe, where you assume that there will be order. And there must have been a shift in your thinking here, a horrible realization of how deeply your world was about to change, had already changed. The police are Muslim and they give you directions to a designated area, a park several blocks away, where Hindus who want to leave Gujranwala can gather and where there will be transportation to leave the city. You're suspicious of this, your foresight razor sharp as ever.

After you find a place close by for your family to wait, you alone follow the directions the police gave you. The streets are crowded. You hear windows breaking, the splintering of food stalls overturned, tension already breaking into pockets of rioting. You move fast, down an alley here, cutting a street corner there. It's hot, the sun eclipsed though magnified by smoke. You turn a corner and get a clear view of the park. The killings are so orderly and clinical it leaves you frozen, a brief spectator. The Gujranwala police surround a group of Hindus, shooting men, women and children with such precision they fall almost before you hear the sound of gunfire.

I don't imagine you telling your family what you had seen. Instead, you wordlessly hurry them to the Gujranwala train station. But it's packed, bodies wedged shoulder to shoulder, unmoving, and when you catch a sliver of a view of the platform through the crowd, your stomach sinks. There are no trains. There is just panic and gunfire drawing near, and then there is the screaming, what you will describe later simply as "the sound of death."

What unfolds next is a series of escapes, almost too many to plausibly account for.

First it's the water tower.

When you saw it at the train station you must have known it was your only chance, and you must have felt the gamble too, knowing it could be full of water, given there were no trains to refill. But it was empty, and as you and your family climbed in, and as you slid the lid back over your head—gunfire closer now—it must have hit you as fast as the hot air inside that small space did: Dying of thirst in a water tower wasn't just an irony but a real possibility.

Time passes. The darkness inside as dark as the darkness of closing your eyes in a dark room. How much time? First minutes. As you adjust your body against the bodies pushed tightly against yours—a sister's arm, your mom's foot, your dad's back upon your shoulder—those first minutes come with relief, amnesty from the horrors you could still hear.

But then minutes give way to hours, your thirst a hard gravel in your throat with no sign of the violence outside giving way. Then hours fold into half a night, an entire night. You try to sleep, adjusting into each other, finding momentary positions of comfort—your head resting on someone's shoulder, one of your sisters back leaned up against your chest—the repetition of minor adjustments leading to the repetition of minor discomforts becoming more and more uncomfortable. Your bones are hard against hard surfaces. And the thirst. And the smell of your bodies, of bodies relieving themselves in a tight space.

Night gives way to day and still the violence can be heard outside.

Then day to night again and the gunfire and screaming are just noise now. Was it a full day, two, three? How could you tell, with the darkness swallowing whatever light slipped through the wooden slats?

But it's the thirst that drives you to gamble again.

You inch the lid back, peer out onto the platform. Night again, and somehow there is a lull. You push the lid back and lead the way, your family following as

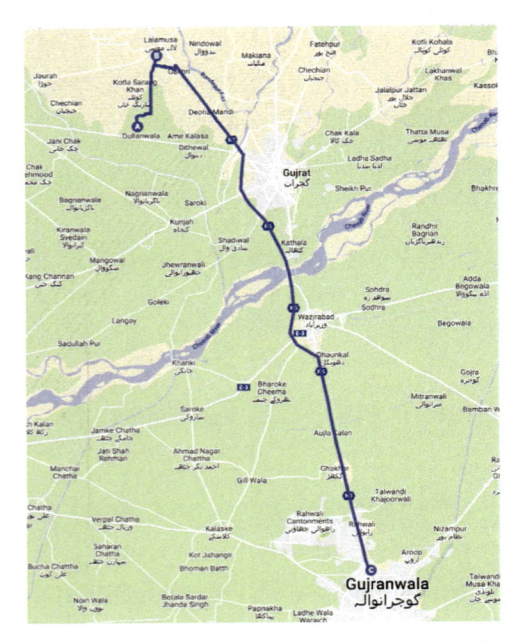

Left: This shows Baij's first train ride, the night of his family's escape, all within Pakistan. The points marked are as follows:
A: Chokkar Kalan
B: Lalamusa
C: Gujranwala

Below: A map showing Baij's route from Gujranwala to Lucknow. The points marked are his stops, as follows:
A: Starting from Gujranwala
B: Lahore
C: Amritsar
D: Haridwar (Here, the family lives for a while)
E: Dehradun
F: Batala (here they live for several months)
G: Delhi (a short stay)
H: Lucknow (where Baij settles his family)

This whole trip covers approximately 1925 km (1196 miles) from Chokkar Kalan to Lucknow, with 1852 km (1150 miles) traveled on his journey from Gujranwala to Lucknow.

Refugees in September

always. It's a gamble but it must have felt like fate, the timing, the way a train arrived, just in time.

The train takes the five of you to Lalamusa station, and at Lalamusa station you board another train, this one to Lahore, knowing that once there you will have to go further to cross the border into India, and knowing too that each station, each stop, will be a risk.

Still you aren't prepared. What's normally a two-hour train ride stretches into a lifetime. You and your family share a car with Muslim pilgrims from Afghanistan. They hadn't yet heard the news of Partition and the reason for the violence. At the first stop in Deva Juliana station when Muslims storm the train looking for Hindus to slaughter, these pilgrims fiercely guard the door to your car, a strange moment but not entirely uncommon of Muslims keeping Hindus safe from Muslims.

You watch the slaughter of Hindus from the car window at each station, men quickly decapitated, stabbed, women raped, but it's the babies that leave you speechless, that rip something out from under you, the sound they make when thrown freely into the air, the horrible thud, strangely soft, when thrown against the brick wall of a station building. After the first two stations you no longer look. Hiding under the seat with your family, you cover your ears and count the stops as they go by: Gujrat, Kuthala, Wazirabad, Ghaukal, Ghakhar, Kamoke, Muridke, and Shahdara. A two-hour train ride stretched into an eight-hour death trip. "The sound of slaughter" is simply how you will recall it later.

When you get to Lahore you are hollowed out, unhinged. You stumble from the train, tell your family to wait, and the smell of corpses, a wall of rotting fruit and shit, so thick you nearly vomit. You don't have a plan anymore; there is no map. You weave through dead bodies, piled three, four, five feet high, and in some places piled higher than you, faces contorted, mouths open. Somehow you find your way to the ticket clerk and somehow he is still there, still alive while his fellow clerk, a Hindu, gutted, lays sprawled on the ground next to him.

"God help you," the ticketing clerk says, and he tells you where to go, takes pity on you, tells you where to hide and wait for the next train. You come back to yourself, at least enough to trace your steps back to your family, to retrieve your mom and dad, your sisters, then to lead the four of them out into the open station yard, to the empty train car the station clerk promised. Once inside the car, you and your family wait. I don't know for how long, and I'm not sure that it matters. At this point time must have moved differently, an empty space between unknowns spreading out indefinitely. When the train engine finally arrives and hooks the car behind it and leaves the station, you lift yourself to the window and all you see is fire, the Lahore Station burning.

You don't know where this train is taking you, but you try to figure it out based on the rivers you cross. You count them one by one, the sound of a train crossing a bridge different than the sound of wheels rushing over tracks on solid ground. You count one river, two, three. You think you might be moving east. You pray you are. Then, somehow, daybreak, and the train slows, comes to a stop. You look out the window. You see a man with a beard, a Sikh. India. You are safe. You turn to your family, and in a dry whisper say: "God has saved us."

But your journey has just begun. You are in Wagah station, Amritsar now. When the train stops and you step foot onto the platform, you see the other side of the violence, bodies piled again in rows as tall as you, but this time the bodies of Muslims slaughtered by Hindus, and this isn't lost on you, how the blame falls on both sides. Your time in Amritsar is brief, then another train to Haridwar, where you have family connections, priests who have kept generations of records for the Anands, Brahmins who would know your family name.

It had been days since the water tower, and with no food and hardly anything to drink, it's still difficult for me to imagine how you turned down the food the priests in Haridwar offered to you. But you can't take from Brahmins. You can only give to them. So there you were, safe but starving, Haridwar a wrecked city, the sudden influx of displaced Hindus so big that the absence of Muslims—those who fled and those who were killed—hardly noticeable. You find a refugee camp, and finally you and your family are fed there.

I think about your life in the camp and it's hard to imagine what it was like. You owned nothing, had nothing. At some point your mom sells her bangles, her last real possession. With the money, you and your family buy clothes and enough food to supplement the slim rations at the refugee camp. But there are so many horrific details of camp life that you must have witnessed.

Details like how limited rations were. So limited that when a family lost a loved one to cholera or an infected wound, those families would be forced to choose between reporting the death or propping the dead body up under blankets so they could continue claiming the rations that were delivered by head count, at least for a few more days, before the smell gave away the lie.

Details like how a mother's engorged breasts indicated a murdered infant, or the way a young woman hiding her disfigured face—a sign of being doused with acid or disfigured, was also a sign of rape.

Details like seeing a Hindu mom whose baby had been slaughtered now breast feeding some other baby whose parents had also been slaughtered.

Details like how despite seeing so many women in circumstances like these, it would have been impossible not to notice that other detail, the utter lack of young women, an absence pointing toward the ghostly presence of the countless women who had been abducted.

And then there was the disease, the astounding death rate in the camps. Cholera, dysentery, pneumonia, measles. The numbers were staggering, and you must have seen this. In one camp of 150,000, around 500 and then 600 refugees would die in a single day. In another camp of 80,000, there were 200 deaths a day. In another camp of 80,000, there was only one doctor. One doctor for 80,000 people. And then there were the flies. Such a small detail but an important one. The way the wounded or those who were too sick to move would find themselves covered from head to toe in flies, a black, buzzing mass.

You would have seen all these things. You hated to see people suffer, but I imagine what bothered you the most was the senseless violence, the way it kept escalating, the cruelty, and what this said about humanity, the way people lose themselves in circumstances, get swept up in events, lose track of personal responsibility. On those days when you aimlessly walked the city of Haridwar, getting your bearings, thinking, formulating a plan, what you and your family would do next, how you could provide, keep them safe, you must have seen Muslims still being forced out of their homes, murdered, or beaten cruelly in the streets, all while people impassively watched. You had so much faith in the human capacity for choice, agency, to do good, but you also must have recognized the other side of it, the cruelty and violence, the dumb desire to inflict pain and cause suffering.

But there was always a choice.

You held firm to this idea. Even in the unthinkable trap of this situation, for you character was the ability to take responsibility for your circumstances, those little places where you aren't simply reacting to the world but acting in the world, choosing. The world didn't have a vendetta, it didn't owe you anything, it just was, and bad things happened all the time for no real reason. That didn't mean you couldn't still respond to what was handed to you.

Through all this hardship, you still read the newspaper every day. And you saw it there, too, the gloss and broad narratives with which Partition was being described, the political motivations and competing interest—the circumstances at large in which you were caught—and yet here you were, one individual, that tension between events and personal agency so acute. And still you believed in the human capacity to choose.

Weeks go by, and during this time you do something that amazes me. You create for yourself a job out of nothing. You spend your days at the Haridwar post office, and here you offer to be a scribe, to write letters for the displaced, for people who can't read or write themselves but are trying to get in touch with their families. You know six languages: English, Pushto, Hindi, Punjabi, Urdu, and Farsi, and day in and day out others narrate to you and you write down their stories in letters to lost family, ask their questions, put their desperation into writing. And I wonder how you contained all those stories on top of your own, on top of what you had seen. But you did, and you managed it all, making money for extra food for yourself and your family, spending each day at the post office writing the stories of others.

And then one fall morning you walk into the post office, and you see an envelope pinned to the poster-board. It's an unlikely scenario to say the least. You do a double take, still not believing it. You've seen the mess and randomness of mail during these last few weeks. Hundreds of chance letters pinned to the poster-board with no real hope of finding their recipient, and even those letters that have gone to the right place, the right city, by the end of the day they must have been covered by other letters or knocked to the floor or simply thrown away without second thought to make more room for more incoming letters. The numbers themselves are unfathomable enough. Somewhere between 10 million and 20 million displaced people during Partition, and untold numbers trying to find their family and friends through the post. But there it is, visible and alone on the board, an envelope with your name on it.

You reach for it and finger the dirty edges of the paper, notice the letterhead from a Batala College, a small university in a small city just on the Indian side of the newly drawn border. The post office must have been crowded; it must have always been crowded. The early morning sun falls through the big windows, and there's the smell of unbathed bodies, sweat, and illness all amplified by the heat that wouldn't break that September. In disbelief, you begin reading the letter.

The letter is from a Muslim friend, Fida Mohamed, with whom you haven't spoken in years, but you had been there for him when he was in need. It was a complicated situation. You had both applied for a teaching job at Batala College, and you both knew that Fida wouldn't get the job because he was Muslim. Even then, years before Partition, the lines between religion, already heightened and exaggerated by British rule and the political purposes expedient to colonialism, were beginning to turn more extreme, more antagonistic. In a mostly Hindu college it was unlikely a Muslim would get hired.

Your qualifications were impeccable, but you didn't need the job. You were already teaching in Gujranwala. Your plan was to apply, accept the position and then, at the last minute, decline the offer but recommend Fida in your place. Because it would be so last minute, the college would have to hire immediately, and because of your unimpeachable recommendation, you knew that the college would hire Fida, despite their prejudices. And they did. Your plan worked. You had gotten him his job.

Now he was writing you because he was fleeing Batala. As a Muslim in an Indian city so close to the border, his life was at risk. He was writing to tell you he was recommending you for the position he was leaving, the job you got him now coming full circle back to you. You stood there in the post office reading and rereading the letter. It must have felt like fate.

* * *

You tell your family, and their relief is palpable. Since you had all lived in Gujranwala, you had been the breadwinner, the provider, but this was even more true now, your two sisters and mother relying on you more than ever, and your father, stubborn, refusing to work. But there was another difference between you and your family that must have also added to your sense of duty. You were educated. You had access to a degree of opportunity they wouldn't have had otherwise. You must have known this, felt that in a situation of such chaos and so few opportunities, you still had something that could get you and your family ahead.

You take the job, and you and your family find yourselves on another train, heading west to Batala.

I've thought a lot about this train ride. I've thought about the relief of leaving the refugee camps. I've thought about how there had been another outbreak of cholera, and how each day you and your family didn't get sick must have felt like another day closer to when your luck would finally run out. I've thought about the relief of knowing that the college was providing housing and I've thought about how badly you must have wanted a home, shelter, some degree of privacy. I've thought about this and about how there were times when I was sick when I didn't have a home, when the cost of medical treatment after medical treatment that insurance wouldn't cover left me living on friends' couches, left me having to rely on whoever would take me in—all of my belongings stuffed into a reusable Trader Joe's bag—and this meant using people if I wanted a roof over my head. What I learned from this is that in so many ways, dignity is a privilege. What I learned from this is that in so many ways morality is a privilege. Having ethical standards for yourself so often means having the material means to meet those standards.

But with you it was different, and I've thought about this, too, how in a way that I could never imagine doing, you were able to maintain your dignity despite what was to come, the months and years ahead of refugee camp after refugee camp. I've thought about this and wondered if the hope and relief you felt heading to Batala was also colored with a sense of dread as each station ticked by—Saharanpur, Ambala, Ludhiana, Jalandhar—and you drew closer and closer to the border you had barely escaped.

And then you are back in Amritsar. The scene is now one of wasted aftermath. Where you had seen flames and bodies hardly a month ago, you now see the charred structures left behind. You see the blood from the massacres that stained the ground, haunting reminders of where the dead once lay, and you see more refugees—thousands of them—Hindus and Sikhs still fleeing Pakistan, and you see their desperation, these new citizens of a new India, their fate as uncertain as the new country in which you live.

It's a short ride to Batala, two, three hours, on a map, but over eight hours with the interruptions of a country in upheaval. Eventually, you and your family arrive, and when you do you are met with something so grim and dark it's hard to imagine how you and your family responded. When you get to the house that the college has promised to provide for you, you find the recently slaughtered bodies of dead Muslims, the previous tenants. I can only guess that the house was assumed empty, that the occupants were assumed to have fled, but in fact had been killed in their homes like so many others. How this was somehow overlooked, how the college didn't have a better sense of the lodging they were providing you is a mystery, but it's hard not to speculate about more sinister connections.

Like so many of your stories, the writer in me gets hung up on technicalities here, questions, not the "what," exactly, but the "how." How did you and your family handle this moment? I know you must have taken charge because that was your role, what you always did, and I know eventually that you were assigned new housing for your brief stay in Batala. But that night, what did you do? Did you remove the bodies yourself, clean the blood, light incense, and scrub the stains with a jute brush, on your hands and knees, using the ash that you had been using for soap since you fled, the black, foamy water turning brown from the blood? Was this how it happened?

What I do know is that whatever it was that needed to be done, you did it, and because of this I can't help but imagine you pulling the bodies out of the house with your own hands. It's a scene that defies logic, but you were living in a world that defied logic. This is the thing about genocide that is so hard to understand. It takes the familiar and turns it upside down. The rules of engagement no longer apply. This is a truly foreign country in which you lived.

Your time in Batala is short. Even after you had relocated into new housing, you knew that your family couldn't stay in that city. You understood something about Partition, even in the early stages. The violence wasn't going to just stop. It would go on and on, and you were right: it did. The best you could do was get as far from the India/Pakistan border as possible. You made a list of the cities where you thought you and your family might be able to live. You narrowed it down to four: Dehradun, Delhi, Jaipur, Lucknow. You'd start with Dehradun. There was an old World War II Prisoner of War Camp for Italians there, and you had heard it was being used to house refugees. You thought you and your family could stay there. Then you planned to visit Delhi, Lucknow, and then Jaipur. These cities all had the potential to create a life, a place to settle and grow roots.

You are in Batala for a couple of months, and you would have left sooner if it weren't for your older sister, Prakash, the married one was who was still in Pakistan. The dramatic scenarios in your life during this period don't stop. You keep getting thrown into one conflict after another. Prakash sends you a letter, and in it she details the danger she and her husband and their four sons and three daughters face. They live in the city of Hafizabad. She wrote to you that the city was becoming more violent, that more and more Hindus were being murdered, that she was worried for their own safety. It isn't even a question whether you will go or not. It isn't even a question of how you will cross the border again.

There is only the fact of your duty to your sister.

You had made friends with a Sikh during your brief time teaching at the College, and he also had family in Hafizabad he wanted to help. After receiving your sister's letter you go to him, and ask if he wants to accompany you back into Pakistan.

He must have had questions, asked about your plan, if this was even really possible; he must have hesitated, at least a little, and if he did it must have been your certainty and conviction that convinced him.

You and the Sikh leave at night. You don't tell your family. You know that if you do they won't allow it, the risk being what it is. You pack some bread, and then later that evening you and the Sikh are on a goods train, heading back to Amritsar. In normal times it's a short train ride, but these are not normal times. The journey that should have taken two hours at the most drags on, first six hours, then eight, veering off course to avoid train stations that are no longer operating, taking alternative routes to avoid bridges that have been blown or stretches of track that have been decimated. The train trundles at a snail's pace. It must have been December by now, and it was already cold—the winter of 1947 would be unbearable. You could feel it in the air even then, while you and the Sikh sat on top of the train, the inside of the cars sealed off and carrying cargo.

*This map shows the countries of India, Pakistan, and Afghanistan.
Each blue pin marks one of the stops on Baij's journey.*

LIKE A BANYAN TREE | 31

The night is obsidian black. The cold air wraps around you. The two of you begin to doze off. You catch yourself falling backwards, jerking awake, suddenly and distinctly aware that if you had fully fallen asleep you would have fallen off the train onto the tracks, crushed by the wheels. Your companion is also nodding off. You reach your hands out to him and take him by the wrist.

"Sleep," you tell him. "I'll hold you. And then I'll sleep. We can take turns."

He nods at you and as he begins to doze you feel the weight of his body grow heavier. It takes work, sitting cross legged like that, his wrists in your hands, keeping him steady enough so that he can sleep while not drifting off yourself. I imagine you reciting Persian poetry to yourself to stay awake: Sheikh Saddi, Azuri Samarkandi, Zauk, Zafarnama. I imagine the dark sky above giving way only periodically to low city lights in the distance while you whisper Urdu. The remarkable irony of being fortified by Islamic poetry while you venture into a country that wouldn't have you because of your own religious background, another object lesson of the many contradictions of Partition.

And then it is your turn to sleep. The Sikh takes your hands in his, holds your wrists tight, and finally you close your eyes. You could have dreamt about anything, or maybe you didn't dream at all. But I like to think that you see yourself as a boy again, standing under a tree, reading, or just lazily swimming in the Chenab as you so often did, gliding into a deep breaststroke, and then rolling onto your back, weightless and free in the current as the train pushes forward.

You were known for always having a plan, to meet life on life's terms, to look at a problem as an opportunity. When you get off the train in Amritsar, you find a military convoy based there. Since the massacres began, shortly after Partition, both sides—the Pakistani army and the Indian army—had been sending military convoys to escort refugees back across the border safely. This must have been in your mind since you left Batala, knowing that if you could find an Indian military convoy you might be able to cross the border with them, retrieve your sister and her family and then return safely with the same convoy. And maybe you even knew that the majority of these convoys on the Indian side were composed mostly of Gurkhas, Nepalese soldiers who knew almost nothing about Pakistan, would speak neither Punjabi or Urdu, and that because you spoke both, maybe you could ingratiate yourself, make yourself an asset. Maybe you knew that because you grew up on that side of the border, knew more about it than they would, the terrain, the roads, the culture, you could convince them that they needed to keep you with them.

After you and your Sikh companion somehow insinuate your way into the military base, after you somehow manage to meet with the general, whose comical name you will recall for the rest of your life—General Bakhshish Chimni—after you tell him what you want and that you can help, it isn't just that you convince him to bring you; you have this man who was educated at Royal Military College and Sandhurst Staff College, who was an Officer in the British Indian Army, practically insisting that you come along, practically imploring you. Somehow you made yourself indispensable.

But there is also another connection the two of you share and this matters. General Chimni was born in Gujranwala. There's comradery in this, maybe even a shared sense of loss. Wanting to go back into Pakistan took courage. It was fearless. And to a man like General Chimni, a war hero in the British Burma Campaign, that must have made an impression. But when he learns you had also lived in Gujranwala, I imagine him appraising you quietly and recognizing something of himself in your need to return to home, to help the people who mattered to you.

You simply say: "My sister needs me."

So you and the Sikh cross the border in the midday sun, stuffed in the back of a military bus. Halfway to Hafizabad, at one of the stops the convoy had already planned on making, you're at the front of the bus because the Convoy Officer in charge is asking for your advice, input, and help with translation. This happens again and again, so much so that by the time you're in Hafizabad, it's the Officer in charge who is deferring to you, asking how best to navigate the tangle of Hafizabad streets, sections of the city you thought would be safe and others that wouldn't. But this is how it goes with you, or so your children have all said. You had this remarkable ability, a kind of social brilliance and charisma. And you had this laugh, this booming, warm laugh that people couldn't refuse, and I wonder if even then, despite all the tension of being back in Pakistan, you were able to laugh, to find that warmth and share it.

The plan was to stay in Hafizabad only long enough to pick up the Hindu refugees who had been waiting, and then for you and your companion to pick up your respective family members. Like the cities you had seen on the other side of the border, Hafizabad is no different, though instead of desecrated mosques, you see desecrated Hindu temples, entire Hindu neighborhoods that look like ghost towns.

There is some uncertainty about what happens in Hafizabad that day, but here's what I know. At some point your companion insisted he go to his family without the assistance of the military convoy. I know you protested this, saying it was too dangerous. I know that later that afternoon, after you had gathered your own sister and her family from the gated neighborhood that had been all Hindus but now was practically empty, after you and your family were safely back in the military convoy and then went to pick up your companion at the designated street in Hafizabad, he wasn't there. I know you waited, and likely convinced the Convoy to wait as long as it possibly could wait, but your companion and his family never arrived. You could only speculate about what had happened, and those speculations must have been drawn from what you had already seen, the butchering and brutal murders, the forced disappearances. When you recount this story to your children, you will distill these speculations down to a phrase that for some reason, to me, is almost more haunting than what may or may not have happened.

You will simply say: "He didn't make it out."

But there's something else about this trip that stays with me. Prakash's husband's name was Sita Ram, and he owned a wholesale and money-lending business. You would later refer to him as the most miserly man you had ever met. As collateral, his clients would often leave behind jewelry, whatever they had that was worth the money they needed to borrow. When you arrive to help them, Sita Ram has trunks full of this gold jewelry, at least 200 pounds. He has the collateral and the gold they had accumulated over the years. And he has more currency than he alone could carry, so he sowed what he could inside his jacket, and then made his sons and daughters do the same with what was left. They are so weighed down with their wealth, that when they walk from the house to the bus, they waddle awkwardly, laboring under their riches.

You and Sita Ram argue about this. To you it seems unethical, the fact that he is taking what doesn't belong to him. In response, Sita Ram insists that any of his clients who haven't returned to collect the collateral they had left behind were probably murdered or displaced, lost in the chaos and upheaval like so many others. Still, you want him to leave it behind. If they do return for it, you argue, they probably need it now more than ever, much like your mom had needed her own bangles to sell for food.

Sita Ram still refuses, and the entire way back to the border, the two of you argue about this, you firmly maintaining that it isn't right, that he is taking what doesn't belong to him. When you get back to Amritsar the two of you are stalemated on the issue. From Amritsar your sister and Sita Ram and their children make their own way to another city where they have family, and yet in the months to come, you won't let the issue drop. Through handwritten letters, you will somehow convince Sita Ram to post classifieds in the Indian newspapers. Should any of his former clients happen upon them they could contact Sita Ram and retrieve what is rightfully theirs.

Of course, nobody does contact him, but it's the principle here that is remarkable. The fact that you had risked your life for your sister and her family, that you had made it in and out of Pakistan again, and despite all of what you had already seen, you never once lost track of what you thought was right or wrong, and that you still argued for it, despite everything.

In total, how long were you gone? Two, three days? I don't know, but when you get back to Batala, and when your mom sees you walk in the door, she demands to know where you were.

"Pakistan," you tell her. Explaining that you had to help Prakash, the letter, the danger she was in.

Your mom puts her hand over her mouth.

You step toward her.

And then she faints.

But your experience as a refugee keeps going, not even close to done. Dehradun comes next, a small city in the foothills of the Himalayas, 833 kilometers from the Pakistan and Indian Border. As Batala became increasingly violent, the urgency of leaving became more and more pressing. Sometime in early 1948, the five of you—your two sisters, your mother and father—get back on another train and head to Dehradun and into more unknowns.

There you and your family stay at the Italian Prisoner of War Camp that had been converted for refugees. The winter was pressing closer, and the temperature must have been dropping. You and your family were back to square one, back to zero, starting over yet again, and there was no electricity in the section of the camp that had been designated for displaced people. There was a lot to despair over: your teaching job not being what it promised to be, the once again close proximity to illness, and all the obvious hardships of refugee life.

But you never stop; you don't even pause to despair or wallow in your circumstances. The next morning you're up early, as always, the sun just deepening the Doon Valley with watery light. You decide to explore the camp, and as you move across the grounds you realize the beauty of this place, the day's first glimpse of the Himalayan foothills, a world enfolded into sloping verdure, quilted greens so dark they look black. I imagine you walking across an open field to the other side of the camp where another long row of barracks runs parallel to yours. This side of the camp is unoccupied—empty cells after empty cells, only recently vacated by the remaining POWs. You see one of the cell doors open, a triangle of sputtering light wedging out.

You push the door open further and the man standing inside holds a paintbrush in one hand and a palette in another. He looks at you and then applies another brush stroke to the wall.

You must have stood there for a moment, uncertain, confused. But then you step inside, curious as ever, and ask him what he's doing.

He keeps his eyes trained on his work. This is how I imagine him. He applies another stroke, dips his brush into more paint, examines his progress, and as he does so he explains that this had been his prison for the entire war. He was one of the last POWs to leave. He steps up to the wall again and there's the rough sound of horsehair against concrete as he fills in his mural with more color. He tells you that now that he is free, he wants to make what had been his cell the most beautiful place on earth. He wants to turn his suffering into art.

But there's something else, too. As you're standing there in his cell you realize: electricity. This side of the barracks has power.

Later that afternoon you, your mother, father, and two sisters, move your few belongings into an open cell with light on the other side of the camp. The other refugees must have seen this. By late afternoon the entire camp migrated across the grounds. You were like Moses, leading your people into the light.

Your time in Dehradun is short, not that it would have been a bad place to live, had the circumstances been different. In some ways I think that the picturesque city with two rivers forking around it—the Song and the Asan—might have suited you. In the summer months you could swim in these rivers, something you had loved since childhood, and there were universities where you could have taught. But the refugee crisis was still too acute there, and the living conditions in the old POW camp, while better than they were in Haridwar, were still unsustainable.

You still have your list of cities you want to explore, and you keep it in your pocket. You walk around Dehradun, fingering that list, curious about the city, thinking about the life you want. You weigh your situation pragmatically, considering if it would be wisest to try to settle where you are now or keep searching, aiming for what you want despite how much hope must have been dwarfed by immediate need. On those walks, I know you are thinking about your family, too. You were always thinking about your duty to them, what you had to do. And not just your mom and dad and two sisters, but the prospect of starting your own family, having children, and the kind of life you wanted to give to them. You wanted to give them a good life. *You* wanted a good life.

But what did a good life mean for you? I know that at some point during your time in Dehradun, you had the passing thought that you wanted to send one of your own children to the Doon School, one of India's most selective private boarding schools. There's something about the thought of you walking on that campus, pausing to stand in that expansive circular plot of grass, the perfectly manicured palm trees in the middle, facing the ponderous brick administration building in front of you, and seeing all those teenage students in their neatly pressed school uniforms. It throws into harsh juxtaposition all the parentless children at the refugee camp you saw every day.

These were the bare circumstances within which you lived, privilege on one side and extreme want on the other, and the idea that somehow you would craft a life out of the opposites you had been handed, that you could send one of your own children to this school was an almost impossible bar to meet. But I think the good life for you really meant the ability to strive. To try to meet high bars.

You would always tell your children "low aim is a crime," but to aim high meant to believe, and you did believe. You had a deep faith in personal autonomy. You believed in the universal human capacity to manifest one's will with the right effort, and the good life, for you, meant being able to strive. It meant being able to work hard and apply your potential to achieve what you hoped for. Your son, Brij, would later tell me that if there was one thing that drove you crazy, that made you furious, it was those times Brij didn't apply his natural abilities and intellect to do well in school. You couldn't stand wasted potential. And just as you wouldn't be able to stand wasted potential in your children, you wouldn't tolerate it in yourself either.

* * *

You made sure your family was settled in the refugee camp and had everything they needed and then you set out by yourself. I like this part of your story. I like the freedom in it, the lone man out in the world and on the search. You're on another train, heading south, maybe crammed into the back of a passenger car, bodies pressed tight around you, and though you've always been gregarious, social, willing to talk to anyone, I see you here as focused, pulled into yourself, considering and reconsidering your future. For months now you had always been with your family, in tight quarters, navigating one crisis after another. How could you have had any time to yourself?

But now you are alone, and I want to think that there was something restorative in this, something energizing in the train's momentum, the way the rolling greenery of the Doon Valley gives way to farmland, browner now, and flattening, and the solitude and satisfaction of watching the scenery change. Maybe you read a newspaper, looking up occasionally, or maybe you just sit there, an unbroken gaze out the window, breathing, while the train cuts across rice paddies, the still water flooding yellow-green rows flashing silver in the morning sun.

Your first stop is Delhi. It does not go as planned.

Right away, you are overwhelmed by the sheer number of refugees. The train station itself has more refugees than the camps in Haridwar. Modern Delhi would become a city rebuilt by refugees and seeing the streets and station flooded with untold numbers must have been hard to believe. There was also the fact that despite what you had seen over these last months, you were and always would be from a tiny village, and in contrast there must have been something about Delhi, this anarchic snarl of humanity that completely flooded your senses.

The volume of refugees in Delhi had also created another dynamic that was different from the other cities where you had lived. The number of mouths to feed, the medical care required, the resources necessary to keep them alive had strained this city to a breaking point, and because of this there was a palpable animosity between the locals and the refugees. You must have felt this too, seen it. It's hard to imagine that you would have felt welcomed in such an environment.

Still, you explore the city anyway. Maybe you take a rickshaw to see Delhi University, or maybe the local mosques—you still miss Islamic culture and Islamic art despite everything—but visiting these sights would have only left you with the feeling that this place could never be home. The Kingsway refugee camp across from Delhi University would have eclipsed anything promising about the college and so many of the mosques you could have seen would have been gutted and torched, the architecture that you so respected and loved vandalized and destroyed.

You stay the night, find a cheap hotel somewhere. It's winter now and bone cold. So cold that when you check into your room and find a refugee sitting in front of the door to your room, begging for money or food, anything, shivering, without hesitation you invite him inside. You feed him, share your dinner with him, and then strip the blankets off your cot and give them to him.

In the morning when you wake up he is gone, and so is all the money you have with you, stolen out of your coat pocket. You truly have nothing now. Just the clothes on your back. Down and out in Delhi. You try to draw on one of the very few resources you have, a good friend who owes you a favor, someone you had helped years ago when he was sick with tuberculosis. You helped run his business, helped look after his family.

You go to the post office and send him a wire, detailing your situation. You hated asking for anything, hated borrowing money, but you also know that he is doing well and is easily in the position to make the loan.

He doesn't wire you back. You wait around the post office all day, hoping to hear word. Nothing. This will be a betrayal you won't forget, even when, years later, he comes to you in need again, a favor for his son. You will do what you can for his son, but you will be cold to him. You won't accept his apology, and you will treat him with an air of distance. This is the other thing about you. Despite your generosity, your willingness to give, your empathy, you have another side to you, too. When you are betrayed, when someone breaks your trust, something inside you turns and can't be rerouted. You are impossibly stubborn.

You must have stayed in one of the sprawling refugee camps in Delhi. Without any money it's your only option, and these camps, like those in Dehradun and Amritsar, are bursting with contradictions and tensions, disease and suffering. Hindus and Sikhs who had been former landowners, the highly affluent, had driven their expensive cars across the border, and now have those same cars parked in front of dilapidated tents. The once rich now languish in their great coats, starving. Refugees who had lost their identification, who had held a prominent role in society are now reduced to having no past, no identity, no history, and are left trying to convince even the poor of their previous station in life. And as disease and starvation and violence increase daily within the camps, the question of government relief and support only becomes more pressing, and as it does a simmering resentment toward Prime Minister Nehru and the Congress Party grows. What good is being a free citizen in a country that lets you starve?

You feel the urgency of these questions, maybe even feel that resentment, but you don't let it stand in your way. You stay focused. You keep moving. Somehow you find a way in Delhi to make enough money to continue your journey. Maybe you translate letters again at the post office, or maybe you find some other means. Whatever it is, it's still barely mid-winter by the time you are on yet another train, heading to the second city on your list: Lucknow.

Things change in Lucknow, and this is one of those moments in your story that makes me want to slow down. I like to think that the winter morning when you arrive in Lucknow is all bright sun, a cold winter light that blanches everything it touches, washes everything clean. Is it possible to fall in love with a place at first sight, before you really know it? Not that you didn't know a thing or two about Lucknow. There was an anecdote that you had often heard about the city, a joke, and it goes like this: In Lucknow, two people wait at a train station. They're so polite and civilized that when the train arrives both people insist that the other goes first. "Really, you first," one says. "No, no, you first," replies the other. "No I insist," the first one says. "No, no, I insist." And on and on it goes until the train pulls away from the station without either one of them, both missing their ride out of kindness.

This is part of the reason you are drawn to Lucknow, part of the reason it makes it on your list in the first place. It is farther from the border, yes, and therefore farther from the violence of Partition, but also the rumors are true. It is a civilized city. The people are kind. This old Islamic city embodies a culture and a language you missed and respected. And also there's the history. This is part of what really draws you to Lucknow, what really captures your imagination before you even arrive. You were in love with Lucknow's cultural history before you even arrived.

Part of the Mughal empire during the 16th century, the Nawabs of Lucknow, Shiites and patrons of the arts, turned the city into a thriving cultural center. This period brought Hindu and Muslim culture together in a harmonious way, and the two traditions kept their autonomy but also found points of overlap and intersection. You must have loved the analogy used to explain this relationship, that of the confluence of India's major rivers—the Ganga and the Yamuna—two separate bodies of water rushing in their own directions and each flowing with their own energy but eventually merging as one, indicating the friendship and union but also indicating the separateness of each. You must have loved this idea because it encapsulated so much of what you thought humanity could aspire to at its best. A shared respect and a recognition of sameness and difference. The universal and the particular coexisting, contradictions and all.

To your delight, when you step off the train and find a rickshaw and ask the driver to take you into the city, the rickshawalla speaks to you in Urdu. It's this moment that you will recall, much later, to your children, as the moment you knew this would be your city. After the fall of 1947, with all you had been through, hearing the language you missed so dearly—for its sweet cadences, yes, but also for the world it invokes, a world organized linguistically less around the egotistical "I" and more oriented toward the communal "we"—hearing this language feels like home. This is your place and you feel it in your heart.

I don't know what you did on that first day in Lucknow, but I know that it was winter and I know that the winter of 1947-48 was cold, too cold for the scene I have in mind, but still I can't resist because I know you loved to swim.

So as I imagine it, you ask the rickshawalla to give you a brief tour of the city and he does, taking you past the old mosques, down narrow streets, and it's the first time since the eve of Partition that you've seen mosques that weren't vandalized.

It's early afternoon and the temperature is pleasant, not too hot but not cold, almost Mediterranean. You ask to see the Gomti River, that swift, deep body of water that snakes through the heart of the city, and I imagine that once you see it, there's only one thing to do. You tell the rickshawalla to let you out. The sight of it reminds you of your childhood, the lazy summer days you spent swimming, but it also invokes that muscle memory, that desire to feel the resistance of cold currents, to find your rhythm and glide, and you were good at it, had a powerful upper body and broad shoulders. As a boy you swam fast.

The rickshawalla drops you off at the Gomti River Front Park. You give the driver a generous tip even though you have so little money. You won't have it any other way. And then you walk across the street, over the patchy grass and dirt, under the cool shade of a perijaat tree, and then you are standing at the bank of the river, the sun in your face.

You take your shoes off, your outer layer of clothing. You wade out knee deep into the water and it is cold and sharp around your legs, the current strong. You stand there for a moment, smiling, feeling the sun and the hard edge of the cool water rising higher and higher as you wade further into the Gomti.

Then you dive. There's the powerful rush of water around you as you take one stroke after another, and it feels good to push yourself like this, having to strain your muscles and work your body after hours on a train, after months of being on the run, it feels good to feel yourself push against the force that is pulling you downstream but to feel the immediate progress of your efforts. You adjust into a clean and precise freestyle, slowly pulling yourself along, working harder now, turning your head on every third stroke to take in large gasps of air and then putting your head back down, eyes wide open, your vision clouded by the murky water, and inch by inch you make progress.

You do this until you are exhausted and nearly out of breath, and you would have kept going because even though you felt depleted, there's something gratifying in the challenge, in the slow and steady headway, but then, by chance, you hit a small eddy. And just like that, the current gives, slackens, and you float effortlessly, your body light now, weightless in the calm water. You roll over on

Top: Lahore Railway Station in the 1920s. Above: Charbagh Railway Station, Lucknow in the 1950s.

your back, and for a moment you let yourself go limp, lifted by the softly moving water. You are happy.

After you arrive in Lucknow you hardly rest at all. The year of 1948 is one of the coldest on record. Those first few weeks of January you camp with the other refugees by the train station, living in threadbare tents, warming your hands over small fires in the evening, and later in the night when you wake cold, the ground frozen beneath your thin dhurrie, the even thinner blankets failing you, you pull your coat tight around your body and watch your breath plume in the moonlight.

You write a letter to your family at the camp in Dehradun. You tell them about Lucknow, that this will be home, that you'll send for them soon, once your living conditions are better, more stable.

Refugee life in Lucknow is both similar to and different from what you've already experienced. Yes, the conditions are dismal, and yes there is still illness and suffering—that first week of January an infant dies because of the cold—but these aren't the mad and lost herds of people you saw in Delhi or those other cities where you had lived.

Maybe it's because Lucknow appealed to a certain kind of sensibility, or maybe because even getting to Lucknow, farther from the border than those other cities required at least some means, but many of the refugees in the camp by the train station were educated, like you, or if not educated then they came from families with money in Pakistan.

You were never one to judge or dismiss others because of their background, but I also know that you enjoyed talking with people who were educated, enjoyed the play of well-spoken conversation, and despite the otherwise difficult conditions at the camp, you immediately feel a shared sensibility with these refugees, and friendships quickly develop.

During spare moments—you were already busy looking for work, thinking of ways to better your situation—groups of you, mostly men but some boys, take walks into town, and on those cold afternoons, you all share stories not about what you had experienced during Partition—there is no need to recount the horrors you had all shared—but of your lives *before* Partition, of what you left behind, of what you still miss.

There is comradery in this, but there is something almost more important, too. It creates a shared story within a larger community, a shared sense of meaning and a way of situating your own experience alongside the experience of other refugees. Because of this, you quickly find yourself embedded in this small refugee community.

* * *

As winter pushes on and temperatures continued to fall, people you know, people who live alongside you in this small camp, begin dying, freezing in their makeshift tents or in their coats as they try to warm themselves by angithi fires. You want better conditions for yourself, that's a given, but you also want better conditions for your fellow refugees, and not just in a general sense—though you did want that—but for these specific refugees, your friends, your new community.

I don't know when the idea came to you, maybe during one of those nights when you tried to warm yourself by the fire, or maybe while walking with the other men in the group, but at some point it occurs to you that the Gun Factory and military barracks in Lucknow must be empty. This is the winter of the first Kashmir war, and all the Indian soldiers are fighting on the border. So you organize a petition, get signatures, rally your community to officially form the Cantonment Refugee Association. You have experience with political activism in the past. Before Partition you were a member of the RSS. There had been a time when you helped store weapons, hiding them under a trap door in your bedroom in Gujranwala, weapons that would eventually be used to help escort Hindus across the border once the violence had started. In 1941, when the British were hunting the freedom fighter Netaji Subash Chander Bose, you had escorted him from Gujranwala to Landi Kotal, where he would safely escape. In short, you are not naïve to the value of political organization, of numbers, and you understand that the political climate at this particular moment, the way the Congress Party had already failed the refugees in so many ways, is conducive to action.

You go to the Chief Minister, Govind Ballabh Pant, with your petition and you present the situation and the Gun Factory as a solution. He is a decisive man, Pant is. A former freedom fighter himself, he has one of those walrus mus-

CANTONMENT REFUGEE ASSOCIATION

Gun Factory Qrs.
LUCKNOW

No. _____   Dated March 23, 1950

I have known Shri Baij Nath Anand as Senior Vice-President of the Cantonement Refugee Association. He is an active and enthusiastic social worker. He has done much towards alleviating the sufferings of displaced persons both at Dehra Dun and Lucknow. He is a young man with amiable disposition.

(Chattar Singh Sethi)
President,
Cantt Refugee Association.

Right: A notice of refugee status, from 1950.

Below: A letter of recommendation for Baij from 1950.

Principal,
R.S.D COLLEGE

FEROZEPORE CITY.
DATED _____ 1950.

I have much pleasure in certifying that Shri Baij Nath Anand, M.A.M.O.L. worked under me at Hindu College, Gujranwala as a Lecture in Persian and Urdu from 1944 when the college was started till the August, 1947 when the College had to be closed on account of the partition. He was a very conscientious and hardworking young man with amiable manners. As a teacher he was a greatness and was liked very much by his students for whose welfare he worked very hard. He took a keen intrest in all college activities and was popular both with the students and the Professors. He was also the superintendent of the college Hostel where he took a fatherly intrest in the welfare of the students and at the same time maintained strict discipline. He bore a good moral character.

S. B. SenGupta
Principal,
R.S.D.College,
FEROZEPORE CITY.
(Formerly Principal,
Hindu College,
Gujranwala).

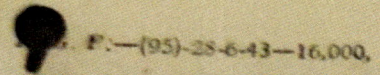

UNIVERSITY OF THE PANJAB.

Honours in .... EXAMINATION, 1943.

CANDIDATE ROLL No. 147 is hereby informed that he has passed the Examination and obtained 343 marks.

This post-card is issued, errors excepted, and being a notice only, the mere possession of it does not in itself confer any right or privilege independently of the proper certificate which will be issued under the Regulations in due course (about February next).

SENATE HALL, LAHORE:
Dated the 13. 8. 1943.

Asstt. Registrar (Examinations).
University of the Panjab.

This is to certify that Shri Baij Nath Anand s/o Shri Lakhmi Dass is a registered displaced person in this State. He is not in a position to pay the prescribed fee for the competitive examination to be conducted by the U.P.S.C. for recruitment to the U.P. Civil Judicial Service.

Magistrate 1st Class.
Dist. Relief & Rehabilitation Officer,
Lucknow.

Above: University of Panjab 1943 exam results.

Left: A stamped note registering Baij as a displaced person.

LIKE A BANYAN TREE

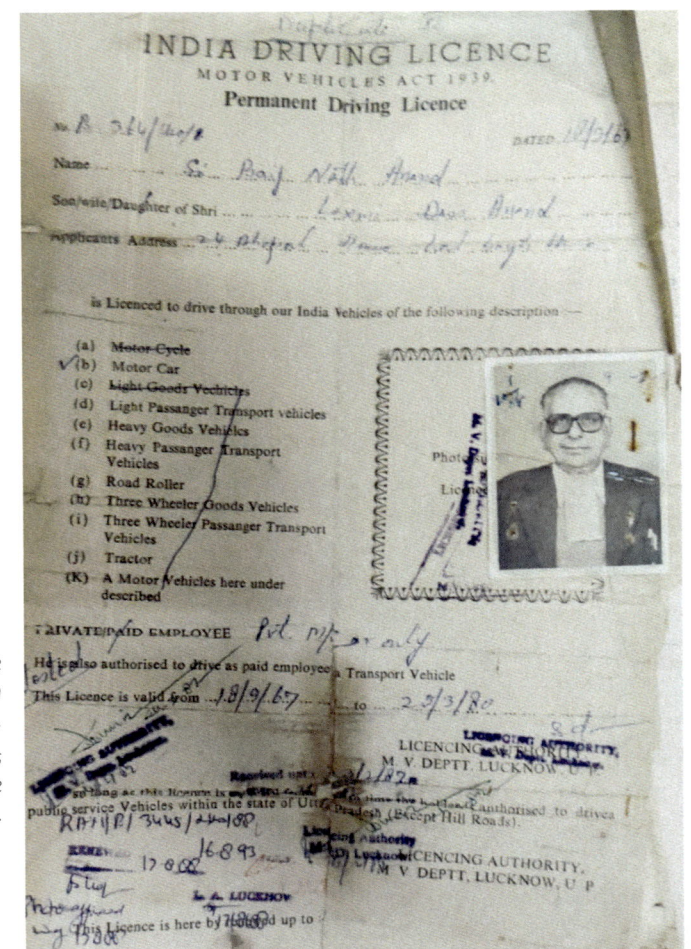

Top: Refugee paperwork from 1955.

Right: Baij's driving license form from 1963.

taches hanging over his mouth, and he nods as you make your case, sympathizes with your cause. Before the winter is out, the community of Lucknow refugees, of which you have become a leader, are living in the Gun Factory, occupying the barracks, the small 12x12 rooms. There's a communal kitchen, running water from a spigot, electricity. People are no longer dying from the cold.

You did this. You made this possible. Now when you walk around the grounds of the Gun Factory, your new home, your fellow refugees nod at you with respect and gratitude.

By the winter of 1948 you are thirty-one years old. In the last four months you have seen more than what most people see in an entire lifetime, and you will live as a refugee for nearly five more years. These are years of hardship and difficult circumstances, but that's not all they are. In other ways these are years of joy, rich in new beginnings and opportunity.

That winter you write a letter home, update your family, tell them about the Gun Factory. You also purchase a bike, a used and temperamental thing that I imagine had a slipping chain, pedals that resist your efforts but nonetheless get you where you needed to go. On the cold afternoons you ride around the city looking for work. At some point during the spring you get word that the Chief Secretary's office has clerical positions open. Although the legislative building, called Vidhan Sabha Bhawan, is an eight-mile bike ride away, you make the journey, your face red from the early spring warmth and your shirt damp with sweat.

You list your qualifications for the job—your education, the languages you speak, your work as a teacher—to the Chief Secretary as the two of you stand in his office. He looks you up and down, squints at you, takes you in. "If you can stay this healthy after six months as a refugee and you also have an education, you're hired."

He asks you if you can start the next day and you nod, and then when you're about to leave the office he stops you. But really, how did you stay so healthy, he asks, and you shrug, tell him that you come from healthy people. But you also have theories about your health, idiosyncratic but in so many ways in keeping with the eccentricities of your character. You're always eating spicy foods so that your body acclimates to the summer heat. You had read that foods that resemble parts of the human anatomy were beneficial to their correlates. Almonds for the eyes, walnuts for the brain, and eggs, you were constantly eating eggs.

Not that you can afford such variety in your food right now. When you start work the next day you bring three pieces of flat bread and an onion. This will become your routine for lunch. And this somehow sustains you for the entire workday, even with your 16-mile bike ride. True grit and then some. You write your family again, tell them come to Lucknow.

By the summer of 1948 you and your family—your father, mother, and two sisters, Sarla and Toshi—are living in one small room at the Gun Factory, and your days go like this: You wake up at 5 a.m. and you have a small breakfast, while your mother packs you a lunch of flat bread and on those days when you can afford it, a cucumber or an onion too. By the time the sun rises you are out there in the city heat, peddling your stubborn bike through narrow streets choked with cars and exhaust, and then the city opens up so that you are peddling out on the main roads, trucks blowing past you, trailing a backdraft of dust and more exhaust. Then you get to work and you write reports, sometimes translate letters, and return phone calls. It's monotonous work but you do it well and with extreme efficiency, an efficiency that gets you noticed. There's talk and rumors in Vidhan Sabha Bhawan that if you wanted you could have a good career working for the State, but you have other plans.

You enroll in law school, and in the evening, after work, you attend classes at Lucknow University, College of Law. It's fall now, and there are stories of you riding your bike from the Gun Factory to Vidhan Sabha Bhawan to work, then tacking on another six miles to campus, for those evening classes, still eating only a few pieces of flat bread, a cucumber. But now you make yourself wait to eat until your evening studies because you know if you eat during the day, you'll only get hungry again, that you won't last through an empty stomach, the pain too sharp, too distracting.

When you are done with classes you ride your bike home. It's like this every day of the week and every week you are clocking, on average, 100 pugilistic miles. By the time you get home your feet are raw and cracked—"horse hooves"—you tell your mom as she draws your nightly water so you can soak them. After dinner she rubs a balm of herbs and oils into your savaged feet, and I imagine you jerking them away at the first application, at the first sting, but then comes relief as she pushes the salve into the blistered folds.

The room you share with you family is crowded—your own dad obstinate as ever, refusing to work and spending his days playing chess with the older men in the camp, and your mom and sisters cooking. Despite all of this, sometimes you set off by yourself, and head to the Gomti River. In the afternoon heat, that first moment of diving into the water and feeling the hard current pulling you in one direction while your body strains against it until you find that cool eddy upriver is a perfect reprieve. I imagine that this is where you go when you need to re-center. The exhaustion of swimming upstream and then the release of finally letting your body unwind underneath a bare blue sky as you drift in a slow current helps you find your balance.

And then one evening it happens. It must have been the winter of 1949, and you are outside, crouched at the spigot, scrubbing dishes. You hear footsteps approach. You look up from your work, set your jute brush down. The footsteps grow closer, coming toward you, and then you see the silhouette of a man approaching, his outline filling in. He is an older man, your own father's age.

"I'm looking for the Anands," the man says.

You look up at him. You're wearing nothing but your underclothes. "Which one?" you ask.

"Baij Nath," the man says.

You stand up. "I'm Baij Nath."

Now the man looks you up and down, and in the dark you can't quite judge his expression, but he will recall this moment later, how he knew you would be a good husband because you weren't above doing the dishes, how you were humble enough to help, but that you also had a sense of confidence. You fold your hands together in the Indian gesture of greeting, unashamed of what you were wearing or doing.

"I'm Baij Nath," you say again.

He takes your hand. "I should have written first," he says. Or maybe he simply introduces himself: "My name is Khushal Chand Chadha. I have come from Allahabad. You don't know me, but your father's first cousin is married to my brother. She speaks very highly of you."

There must have been a pause here, a chance for you to put the pieces together, and then an explanation must have followed, the details. His daughter's name, Avinash. She needs a husband.

This is a marriage proposal.

* * *

Khushal Chand Chadha talks to you under the eve of the barracks. He tells you who he is and what he and his family have been through, and he tells you what they have lost. He talks in a quiet voice, precise words gathering momentum, a steady, refined cadence. He is a sensitive man, and as he talks to you, I picture him doing so with subtle gestures, mild movements, a flick of his hands here and there to articulate a point, hands that are smooth, the hands of a businessman, someone of means who before Partition was well-off. He tells you about Lahore, what he had there before Partition and what he no longer has, the ice factories he owned and the money he lost, all that he had to leave behind when, like you, he and his family fled Pakistan.

And I wonder if, at least in part, he tells you all of this to make clear to you what life could have been like for his daughter, Avinash, if it wasn't for Partition, and therefore the kind of husband she deserves, the kind of husband he hopes to find her.

I am cautious not to over sentimentalize this scene, mostly because I know that in so much of the world you lived in, choices were often made from necessity, and this marriage, too, at least in the beginning, must have been equally driven by circumstance, the immediate needs Khushal had for his own family, and yours too. But your marriage with Avinash, however informed by the immediate needs of your moment, nonetheless becomes a marriage of real respect and love.

You and Avinash marry on May 29, 1950, and it is on this day that you see your wife for the first time. The details around your wedding are so few. Most of the people who were alive to witness it are gone now, and those who were there were so young their memories are patchy. But I am told Avinash looked beautiful, that even then, as a young woman, there was something thoughtful and deliberate about her. She would have worn a shalwar kameez, and a dupatta shawl, and you would have worn a Sherwani.

It's hard to know for sure, but judging from Khushal's Shiksha to Avinash, it was a vastly diminished wedding from what it could have been, consisting of only the most essential rituals and traditions. Still, it must have been rich with what did take place, the meeting of the bride's family with the corresponding relatives of the groom's, mother to mother, father to father, uncles to uncles, aunts to aunts during the Milni ceremony; the exchange of garlands between bride and groom during the Jaimala ceremony; the Laavan Phere ceremony, the slow circling around the sacred fire seven times, the groom leading the first four and the bride the remaining; this, and more, but it's the Doli ceremony that stays with me the most.

On this day I can't help but think mostly about Avinash. To signify that she is letting her family go and taking on a new one, she throws a handful of rice over her shoulder in her family's direction, to wish them farewell, to say goodbye and to show gratitude for their care.

It's Avinash's life that is about to change the most, and it's hard to imagine, after Partition, after so much loss already, what it must have been like to then say goodbye to her family, to share the 12x12 room in the Gun Factory with a family she's never met before, in a city she's never lived. However exciting the moment must have felt to her, it also must have been a moment punctuated by question marks, uncertainty, and sadness, maybe even a sense of loss.

At the end of the wedding day Khushal gives you and Avinash a Shiksha letter he has written. The two of you read it together, a first shared moment of intimacy, a first tender moment of trust.

It reads as follows...

Avinash's Father, Khushal Chand, age 51 in 1950.

LIKE A BANYAN TREE | 53

The original letter written in Hindi.

Refugees in September — 54

A Father's Words & Advice for his Daughter

Take thousands of my blessings, my daughter as you leave me today
Take with you the love of your mother and father and your family's high values
We cannot give you much, take these few strands of this sacred thread with you
Take with you the garland of good behavior gifted by your sisters
May you be the queen of your husband and home, he is your love, life, prayer, kingdom and crown

My daughter, keep your high thinking always, live simply and get along with all
My daughter, earn respect of your in-laws and live like Durga, Padmini and Rukmini did
Marriage is a pure relationship of the soul, my daughter make it purer
You are the moonlight to your husband, your moon, my daughter shine brightly in your household
Sweet words, weighed well, should come from your lips like flowers of love
Your life to be an example, so the world says you are like Sita and Rama

This wedding would have been a grand show if we were in our own country
Huge gathering of our city's best, our celebrity would have been different
The music and song which sound hollow, would have a different tone
The whole occasion would be so different, if this city was Lahore

Go forward my flower, be happy and build on the love Baijnath has for you, my daughter
Your in-laws will sing your praises, take our thoughts out of your heart
Daughters go to the in-laws, this is the way of the world
Your father's house is no more yours, go build your own home my daughter
My heart is hollow to see you go, keep visiting like the cool wind
I will anxiously wait for your visits, visit often my daughter

Baijnath my son, deliver on the oaths you have given today
Treat Avinash like Rani Rukmani and become her Lord Krishna
Marriage and family is a highly respected undertaking, make it higher
Avinash, her heart like glass, do not hurt it even in error, my son
Blessings pour from my heart, may this couple be planted forever
May they grow like a vine, find happiness of marriage and family.

* * *

You and Avinash build a relationship together, but it forms slowly, as all good relationships must. There's the small, tentative gestures toward intimacy. You bring her food from the open-air market, treats, a small bag of Jalebi, a piece of sugared candy. At some point, Avinash mentions how much she loves ice cream, the way the cold, sweet taste reminds her of the ice factory her father owned. She mentions this craving late at night, too late for you to be reasonably expected to do anything about it. But you do—you stand up and dress quickly, and then you go outside, bicycle all the way to an ice cream shop, above which the owner lives, and you stand on the street corner, calling up to him something eccentric but earnest: "My wife needs ice cream," you yell. "It is dire."

Eventually he hears you, reluctantly comes to the window, meets you downstairs.

And when you return to Avinash in the 12x12 room with her ice cream, she smiles, thanks you shyly.

But you also talk to your wife. You confide in her. You treat her like an equal. You talk about the work you are doing for the state, you talk about your studies, justice, and the value of a justice system that is fair and balanced. You recite poetry to her, and you ask her about her interpretation, her take. "Life brought me here / Devastation will take me / I didn't with my own volition come / And I will not go with my own volition."

What do you think it means, you'd ask her.

Always thoughtful, she would take her time with an interpretation.

What do you think, you'd ask again, the eager boy standing in a one-room schoolhouse still in you, still breathless.

"I'm thinking," she'd say, and then later that evening, or sometime the next day, she'd tell you what the poem meant to her.

In the fall of 1950 Avinash tells you she's pregnant. And just like that, you will be a father. But there were other changes that would come too. You had been thinking about your job working under the Chief Secretary. Now that you had a child on the way, you had been considering more and more how the work you were doing would lead to the inevitable dead end. You'll graduate from law school soon and then you'll take your exams. The idea of opening your own practice is appealing to you, the freedom, yes, but also the financial independence, the ability to set a pay scale that can be adjusted to the needs of you and your family, as well as to the needs of your clients.

I like to think that this comes up between you and Avinash, that because you had come to value her opinion you share your thoughts with her. I like to think that on one of your afternoon walks together you tell her about the plan that has been on your mind, how you often have lunch at a roadside restaurant, this cheap and rundown place where many of the local Sikh long-haul truckers also take their lunch. You explain to Avinash that lately while you eat you had been listening to them talk and you had heard them express their grievances, one after the other, about the daily extortions from the local police, how they would pull the truckers over, write them a ticket for one false pretense or another, and how the truckers had no choice but to pay.

You tell Avinash about this and she listens intently, listens as you talk about the injustice of it, how graft and corruption is the norm and how it's wrong, but you also talk about this as a business opportunity, your first legal case. You had come up with a plan and it goes like this:

You could organize a truckers' collective, and in doing so you would have each trucker pay you what he would normally pay for the spurious fines the police would issue. That would be your legal fee, and then you would take their case to court for them, create a precedent against the kind of extortion the local authorities assumed with impunity. You had it all figured in your head. If you won the case, you would give half of the money the truckers gave you back to them, and if you lost the case you would pay the fine and clear the citation. They had nothing to lose and you had so much to gain, a first case, a first successful case, and the start of a career you hoped would flourish.

I like to think of you telling all of this to Avinash, your confidant now, and I like to think of her trusting you, even though it would be a risk, the implication that you would leave a steady job at The State to start something new.

And so on the day your exam results to become a lawyer arrived in the mail, it must have been maddening to Avinash that you insisted on finishing your lunch before you opened the envelope. Your wife and the rest of your family had gathered around as you sat on the floor, or so the story Raj told me goes, the envelope folded and wedged underneath your right leg. Everyone was so anxious except you. Between mouthfuls, you answered your family's pleading by saying, "What difference does it make if I open it now or after I eat? The results are what they are. I did my best, and now nothing can change it either way." This was how you were though, anxiety over what can't be changed wasn't worth it. What mattered was knowing that you had done your best and then doing what was in front of you, even if that meant something as simple as finishing lunch.

Not that you weren't pleased when you opened the envelope. Of course you were. You were a lawyer now. You quit your job that same day. The next day you win your first case for the trucker's collective and make in a day the same amount of money you would earn in a month at your old job. Not a bad way to start your own practice.

Your life is moving faster now, as if a dam has broken and the confluence of your efforts during these last few years suddenly begin to flow with real force, gathering momentum. Your first daughter, Rashmi, is born. She is delivered in that small 12x12 room with the help of a midwife. The labor is long and she is a big baby and you hold her in your arms—your daughter! little Nanhi you call her—and it isn't that she's your favorite, but she's your first and you bring her little treats every day you come home from work because it's all you can to do to contain the overwhelming feeling of wanting to give her the world.

It's 1952, and now that you have won the trucker's collective cases you have moved on to other cases and you are, somehow, despite having to work in such small quarters, building a name for yourself. The days of riding your bike to the state building are gone.

Now you ride your bike to various courthouses, sometimes, even, when you feel extravagant, taking rickshaws. You like your work, and you are making decent money, but what you like most of all is being in front of a jury and arguing a case and then afterward standing in the breezy halls of the courthouse and talking with the other lawyers. You are a terrific talker—a regaler with a true gift of gab—and your colleagues are quick to gather around and listen. Here you are in your element, holding forth, telling stories, disquisition on this or that subject. Always you hold a captive audience, and always you find something to laugh at, your joy echoing down the court halls and out into the street. "You could hear daddy's laugh a block away," Raj has told me, a deep baritone, unmistakable.

But you never forget what you're about. In a world where graft and corruption are commonplace, especially in your work where it's routine for prosecuting attorneys to make under the table deals with defense attorneys, where bribery is the norm, you stay honest—a straight shooter—going to work with a clean conscience and then always on the way home stopping at the open-air market for a treat you'd later give to Rashmi.

Do your duty.

Stay the course.

Honesty is paramount.

This is who you are. On those nights when Rashmi wakes up crying, when she can't sleep, sometimes you get up too and in a deep and mellifluous voice, you recite Persian poetry to her. You're a family man now.

You're also a community man, and you have broader loyalties. You had been living with this community of refugees since 1949, and though you are making enough money now for you and your family to move, find a place better suited to your needs, you don't. You stay because this is your community. You had been the vice president of the Cantonment Refugee Association, and then you became the president. You had already fought for this community and not just to get them into the Gun Factory in the first place, but to make sure that they could stay there when the government tried to have everyone evicted. You went to court for this community, showing that during the time that you all had lived in the Gun Factory that renovations had been made, the walls painted, wiring for electricity redone, ailing walls rebuilt, and because of this you were able to claim rightful ownership until further housing was ready.

And there *were* promises of housing. The local government had built a four-story apartment building in the heart of Lucknow—Bhopal House—but now that it's nearing completion, the Lucknow Municipality wants to rent it at a higher price to non-refugees who can pay more. In place of Bhopal House, the government has hired more contractors to build more housing, but you have heard that the construction is shoddy, cheap, and it is an insult not just to you but to your entire community. After what you all had been through, that the local government is willing to shuttle you from poor living conditions to poor living conditions feels like a slap in the face. You want something better for you and your family. Additionally, Avinash is pregnant again. Living in a tiny room isn't sustainable, not with your family growing, but nor is it sustainable to move into a cheaply built and poorly constructed building. You might as well be in another refugee camp.

So the temptation to strike out on your own, to find some place in Lucknow to rent is alluring, and you can feel the pressure to do so on behalf of your own family. And yet, you still don't abandon your community.

During those first years in the Gun Factory, you had become friends with a man named Fakeer Singh. He was a big man, sloping shoulders, these huge hands hanging from python arms, and he was active in the community. It's Singh who brings to your attention the housing that was built for the refugees, the bad construction, the cheap building materials. And one day he takes you to the building site, to assess it for yourself.

What you find is daylight between the floors and walls, wind blowing through the flimsy construction, and it's cramped, more cramped than where you were already living. I imagine you taking large strides across the room, estimating the square footage, and then pressing your weight against one of the walls. As the story goes, it's so flimsy you can feel it give way under the weight you apply. You have Singh press his own weight against it. Larger than you, more muscular, you ask him a quick question: "Do you think you could kick this wall down?"

He nods, certain.

You schedule a meeting with the Chief Minister, Govind Ballabh Pant. You've gotten to know this man. You know him through some of your own work as a lawyer but you've also dealt with him through advocating for your community and you know that he tends to be just and fair. When you talk with him in his office, you tell him you would like him, as well as the people responsible for building the new housing, to meet you at the construction site because you have some concerns to go over.

You organize the other refugees. You orchestrate it so that on that day of the meeting with Pant and the contractors, it isn't just you but everyone living in the Gun Factory. The time and date are set. It seems suitable to me that two weeks before the meeting, your first son, Babbu, baby Rajesh, is born. A marker to indicate a new chapter, the closing of an old one. He is a perfectly healthy baby, a few long streaks of white hair. You and Avinash say that a Sadhu, a holy person, had been reborn.

Then comes the day of the meeting. All the refugees stand in front of the new, half-built building. Maybe it's mid-morning, a normal day, nothing remarkable. When Pant arrives, he climbs out of a black car, his government vehicle, with official looking men behind him. The contractors are there, too. Pant is surprised to see so many people there and so are the contractors. In the crowd, your wife stands, watching you, nursing newborn Raj.

There is no speech or fanfare. You and Singh simply walk into the building, and at the decided upon sign, a quick nod of the head, a flick of a hand, Singh takes a few powerful strides, then raises his foot, kicks down an entire wall.

The disappointment is obvious on the faces of those who are watching, and equally so is the embarrassment on the faces of the contractors.

You are stern here, not threatening but stern. You walk up to Pant. "Is this where you expect us to live?"

He doesn't say anything.

You watch him. And then you say, "We are moving into Bhopal House."

This isn't a question. You aren't asking Pant, you are telling him, and when he doesn't respond you take it as his tacit approval.

That evening you and the other refugees bring to a close the lives you have lived in the Gun Factory, in your tiny barracks. You pack up belongings and then walk or take rickshaws or ride bikes. It's a minor exodus but significant, monumental even, for your life as a refugee has come to an end. You all stand in front of Bhopal House, a large building, nearly completed, that takes up almost an entire city block. There are 26 apartments on the second and third floors, and what will be shops on the ground floor and offices on the first. You slide open the catch of the front doors. You lead the way inside. Your family and your community follow behind.

It is 1953 and you are no longer a refugee.

Flat number 24 is your new home.

*"Small dreams
are the greatest crime."*

Three of Baij's children, left to right: Rashmi, Brij, Raj in 1958.

3

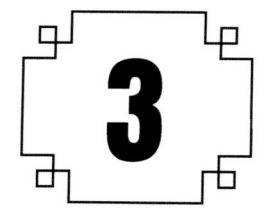

CONFLICTS AND DESIRE, CONFLICTING DESIRES

What is it about fall? Why the nostalgia? Why the feeling of soulful loss? Why the desire to retreat into one's own history, revise passions, dig up the dead?

It's October here, and I am telling your story, Baij. In doing so, I am digging up your dead, looking for ghosts, traces of past lives, but I am doing this with my own life, too, trying to understand how I got to where I am and where I want to go.

Your flat in Bhopal House is small. When you walk into the front door, there is a hallway, looking right into what will become your office. It has glass windows that open and close outward into the hallway, and a door on the right, as you turn left in the hallway. Further down the hall and to the left are the bathroom and the kitchen, and to the right is the great room, where you and your family sleep. Off the great room is a door that opens out onto the covered veranda. After you moved in you did what I am trying to do. You turned an empty space into a home, and then you built a future one day at a time. You lived so long with nothing, and now you are tasked with the slow accumulation of belongings. But there's joy in this, isn't there? The satisfaction of remaking your own world.

"Craft your life," is an expression Brij likes to use, and as you were doing that then, I am trying to do that now.

You and your family buy new dhurries, sheets, and charpais, roll them out in the great room at night and then roll them back up in the morning, stash them in the covered veranda. You hire a carpenter to affix the right wall of the great room with polished wood and a large mirror in the middle, and then five coat hooks on the right and five coat hooks on the left. You buy new clothes—you liked clothes and I like that you liked clothes. I can understand this small pleasure, the comforting feel of heavy fabric hanging from your shoulders. You buy a new sari for Avinash, and you buy white, pristine, muslin fabric for your father's Turban, a black wool winter coat for yourself. You get your own office ready for work. Wallace Stagner once made the observation that the scholar is never so happy as when he is unpacking his books. You didn't have books to unpack but you were readying your office for the accumulation of books, which must have been a close second. You purchase a heavy, dark-wood desk with a green leather top.

And then books accumulate—law, history, poetry, medicine—and you shelve them in rows behind the chair in which you sit. Across from you are the four chairs lining the walls on either side of your desk and then two directly in front, where your clients will sit. You hang a sign on the wall behind your chair. "Time is valuable, don't waste it." And another sign, "If you smoke, leave." You buy three porcelain monkeys, one with eyes covered, one with its mouth covered, and the third with its ears covered. You place these strategically, next to the sign. A reminder to your clients, yes, but also the dictum by which you have lived. You don't do this all at once, but that's part of the joy and care involved in rebuilding. You have to pace yourself, as I also have had to pace myself. In October I bought a bed frame, my own mattress off the floor now, and then I purchased a small rug to spread out beside it, eventually a couch, a modest painting of a crow to hang next to my desk.

But putting a life back together is more than the accumulation of things. There's routine, the motions of day-to-day life that allow us to fall into the dream of living. I think about the times other than this one in my own life when I've started over—a job in Alaska, graduate school, working for a newspaper in Maine—and it always surprised me how quickly the world snaps back into place, how quickly the unfamiliar becomes the given. "Your usual," a barista says. A first date becomes a second, a third, a fourth until you stop counting. The desultory walks through a new neighborhood become more precise, circumscribed. All the way up 43rd until Stone and then left on Bridge because that's the fastest route. Life on autopilot again.

You had your routines, and I am building my own. You started seeing clients in your home office—civil and criminal cases—and in the mornings, after you spend an eccentric amount of time on your dental hygiene, still tending to each tooth meticulously, you stand in front of the mirror in the great room and button your shirt for work.

While you do this, like clockwork, your father prepares his hookah for his first smoke, dumping the old water out, the astringent smell of used tobacco filling the house, and then he loads it anew, the dank scent of manure and

Lakhi's Hookah base.

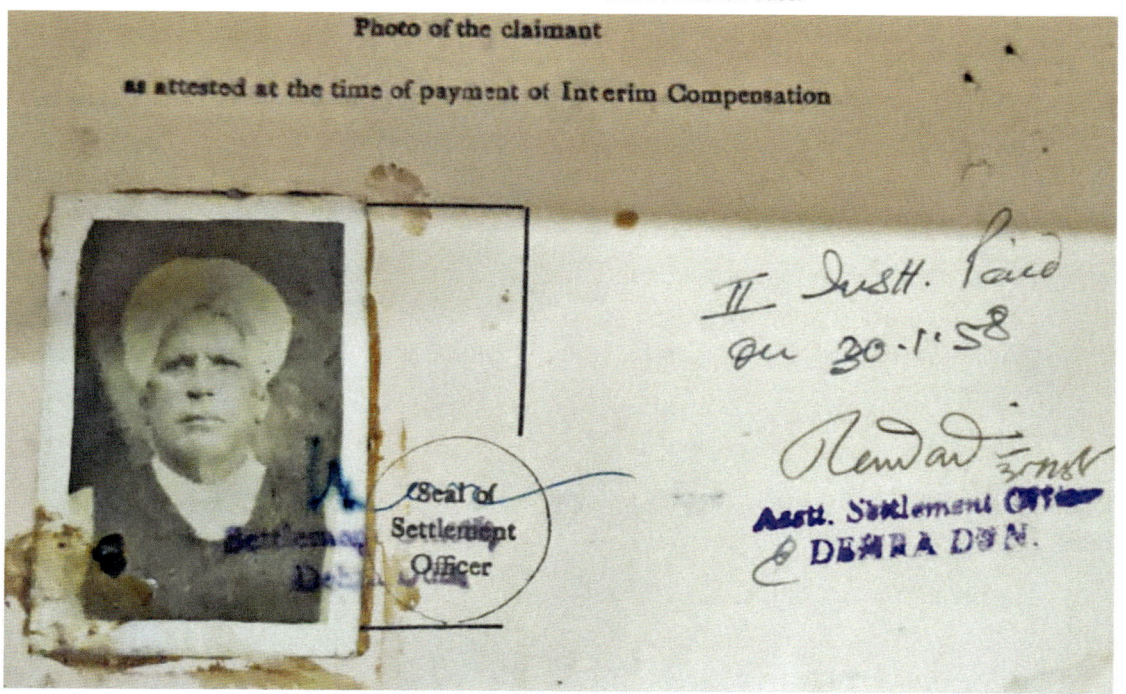

Lakhi, 1958.

LIKE A BANYAN TREE | 65

earth rising from his tobacco box. Avinash and your sister, Sarla, negotiate their own moments around your father's routine as the two of them cook. They stand in the kitchen, quietly joke as they prepare the day's meals. They have become close, Avinash and Sarla, but not just close like sisters-in-law. More like mother and daughter. Sarla only fifteen, still needing guidance, and Avinash, ever up-to-date, ever the reader of pop culture magazines, is quick to advise her on all manner of topics, particularly on becoming a woman.

You eat, and then go into your office, and if the wind is blowing in the right direction—or, rather, the wrong direction—the thick smoke from your dad's preparation of the chillum for his hookah blows in through the windows, and you pause over whatever you're doing, stand up briefly, yell the same words you yelled at him the day before and the same words you will yell at him the day following: "Shut the window. I have clients. I'm running a law practice." At some point you will hang a "No Smoking" sign in your office for your clients but I also wonder, too, if this sign was meant to exact some rule over your father, not that it ever stopped him.

And Gyan Devi, your mother, has her own routine. She has her own friends now. They are the older women she became close with at the Gun Factory, and who moved into Bhopal House as well. Her days are often spent with them, in their flats, drinking tea, filling the small apartments with gossip and afternoon games.

During the day when you aren't seeing clients, you're often at court, arguing cases, and then on your way home, you stop at the open-air market, indulge in street food, purchase bags of fruit to bring home—you loved fruit—as well as ingredients for Avinash's cooking, and a treat, as always—one for Avinash, and one for your quickly growing daughter. You talk to everybody, the shop keepers and food stall owners, the rickshawallas and policemen, the man with the tea shop whose family, for generations, has sold the best chai around. Four years in this city and practically everyone seems to know your name. "Anand Sahib," they yell and wave. "Namaste, Anand Sahib."

And then it's evening again and again you and your family roll out the charpais and the dhurries. You lay on your stomach and let Rashmi and Raj walk on your back, giggling as they do so, tiny feet on your spine, Avinash holding Raj by his arms. Barely ambulatory now, his steps tentative, but Rashmi, more confident, puts her arms out to the side and balances all the way up your back, your little masseuses, bursting with excitement to see you. They stay awake for your stories and tall-tales about your day-to-day adventures, but they never last too long.

Eventually they doze, their eyes fluttering to stay awake irresistibly close, and then it's quiet and still in your small flat. During these interludes of peace, Avinash rubs ghee into your hair to keep it thick and lustrous. She works her fingers intimately along your scalp, and these are tender moments, at least until your children are old enough to complain about the smell of the condensed fat. "It stinks!" they will yell. "It stinks!"

But that's still to come. For now it's just you and Avinash, talking quietly, the night air blowing in through the veranda window. And then sleep. And you always sleep. It's as if your life has seamlessly found its course again, the ghosts from your past either not there or haunting you so subtly you can't hear their voices.

Most nights I do not sleep, or at least not very well. My own routines start early in the mornings. I wake up at 6 a.m., and listen to classical music while I make coffee. And then I work on your story, Baij. I sit at my desk and try to write, but mostly I think about fathers and the timing of life's big events and how we make sense of them. I keep waiting for the leaves on the trees that line my street to change. And then one morning it happens, all at once as always seems to be the case with fall: a finale of burnt colors without preamble against an ever-darkening sky.

I do long-distance video interviews with your children and try to get as much background as possible on your life. Because of the time difference between Seattle and Lucknow, India, I talk to Ajesh, who at sixty-two is the youngest, early in the morning. I talk with Rashmi on the weekends, later in the night, 10 p.m. my time, 9:30 a.m. hers, all the way in Delhi. I talk to Brij and Raj, sometimes in the afternoon, sometimes early in the evening. I am getting to know your children, and through them I am getting to know you, and in some ways through me they are getting to know you all over again, their stories excavating your life, bringing a new presence to your absence.

I like this part of the work. I like being the go-between, relaying your stories between your children. Raj tells me a story that only he knows and one evening over a video call I retell it to Brij. It's a story about an incident that happened while you were still in the Gun Factory. You and Mohan Mehta were taking a walk outside of the barracks, walking the stone fence that runs the perimeter, when a slaughtered, skinned and cleaned goat carcass, as if falling from the sky, suddenly lands in front of you. I shared with Brij about how the mess cook was making a little extra money on the side, selling slaughtered goats the government had issued for the army recruits living in the barracks, of how he would toss them over the wall where they were then picked up by whoever was buying them, the cash stuffed into a crack of the mason work.

But on this day—as Raj tells it and then as I tell Brij—you and RTM Mehta are walking the perimeter and there's something so absurd and comical about a goat falling into the dirt in front of you with a hard thud that it made the two of you laugh, laugh and then rejoice because you had just been given a goat to cook, and cook it you did. Later that night, you and all the other men in the camp roast it over a massive fire like some Homeric sacrifice. It's such a lovely scene, the joy and strangeness of it, and when I tell Brij he says, "see, I'm learning from this too."

I often find myself reflecting on this process. The shared discovery, my own coinciding with your children's. But what I am most moved by is the way the discovery of your story is slowly becoming part of my own story. I can never know you, Baij, not really anyway, and yet, at the same time, I can't help but feel some connection and partnership in the latticework of how our stories have been brought together.

I am also cooking again. You loved to eat, loved the grounding presence of a meal prepared for family and friends, and I also like this. When I was sick, I quit cooking. I had lost the desire. But now, after I write or do interviews in the mornings, I walk down to the store and buy the necessary ingredients for the soup I plan to cook that evening, and then I come home and put on NPR, chop and peel vegetables, sauté garlic and spices in butter, put everything on to simmer, and the smell of split pea, or lentil, or African peanut soup fills my apartment. It's getting cold outside, and the first frost has broken, and I like these mornings and afternoons, the quiet contentment of working and the small pleasures of cooking.

It's in these moments that I can imagine a life for myself again. I like Seattle. I like living by the water. In the evenings when I go for walks, I can smell the

Puget Sound, the brine of mudflats and sometimes when there is a south wind, something sweeter, like hibiscus blowing in from the ocean. But I can still feel the cliff of anxiety, the pull of grief. I still feel that every day, and there are some days when it feels like I'm so close to it that if I take one wrong step, I will fall into it all over again and lose what little I am building. This anxiety makes me think of you, Baij, how you were somehow able to move through the present moment, even after the violence you had seen during Partition, even after all the uncertainty and loss, with real equanimity.

I'm also spending more and more time with E., and this, too, makes me think of you. We spend two nights together a week, but no more than that for now. We always stay at her place. I don't let her stay at my house because I'm embarrassed at how sparse my life still is, and while I enjoy our time together it still feels provisional, tentative. She wants to see how things feel but that doesn't mean that she wants to commit to anything beyond the present moment, beyond enjoying the time that we do spend together. It might turn into something long term. It might not.

My courtship with E. is so different than yours was with Avinash. I feel the gulf separating the individualism and personal autonomy that are paramount in my own culture from the importance of family and duty in yours—even in the way E. and I talk about the future. She wants to go slow. She wants to make sure that she remains self-contained, and because of this we have set clear boundaries. I respect the way she is going about the relationship, even admire it, and I feel her concerns. I, too, have always been afraid of losing myself in a relationship.

This would have been a nonsensical proposition for you. To not have family, to not have a wife and children, to be cut off from your own parents—that was to lose yourself. You lived in a world where relationships were a path to maintain the vitality of identity, and I live in a world where they are often seen as both something to be desired but also as a threat to autonomy.

This has always left me with a kind of cognitive dissonance. To want and not want a partner. It's a point of tension that afflicts so many people who share this contemporary, Western mindset. It also blurs that sense of duty you felt so strongly. Sometimes it feels like E. and I are trying to find a way to commit to each other without having to actually commit and our conflicts arise from dealing with the anxiety this provokes. I can imagine you shaking your head and laughing at these anxieties, this foreign uncertainty.

And yet, you did know something about losing yourself to others and the tenuous give and take of relationships. It's true that everyone who knew you saw how generous you were. You unflinchingly gave yourself to others, and I wonder if that was part of the reason you were able to move through Partition with such grace. You didn't dwell on yourself or your own suffering. You thought mostly of others: your sister when you went back into Pakistan, your own parents and siblings, the refugee you invited into your hotel room in Delhi, your community of refugees in the Gun Factory—you could have left but you didn't, you wouldn't leave them until you knew they would be provided for, too. In some ways, it's hard to even find you, your interior, your private worries and losses because so much of what I know about you is based on what you did for others. And yet, this was you. In the stories about what you have done for others I am finding you.

But it's also true that there was one relationship that stretched your capacity to give to a breaking point. There was one relationship where you gave so much you nearly disappeared in your own selflessness. I am thinking of your brother-in-law, S.L., this man who took so freely from you but to whom you also gave so freely.

You met him during your third year in the Gun Factory, when your sister, Toshi, married him. Like your own marriage, Toshi and S.L.'s was arranged through distant family connections. Your family had been looking for a husband for Toshi and word passed through cousins and uncles to S.L.'s family and then back to you and yours. They were married quickly and on their trip back to Lucknow as a married couple, you had your first misgivings.

S.L. was a handsome man. Alarmingly so. He looked like an Indian Sean Connery, his hazel eyes—cat eyes—were captivating the way ruthless things can be. During that first visit he does something that surprises you. When he gets off the train in Lucknow, instead of taking a rickshaw from the station to the Gun Factory, he takes the single taxi in all of Lucknow Railway Station, and the difference in price is exponential, egregious, a luxury for the very rich. When he meets you, the taxi still idling in the street. He pats his pockets, asks you to pay for it.

You look at him, confused. "Why didn't you take a rickshaw?" you ask him.

He shrugs. "It would have messed up the crease in my pants."

That was your first meeting with S.L., but he comes back into your life in 1954, shortly after you and your family settle into Bhopal House. He is in the military, though not very high up. He and Toshi live near the base in Delhi where he is stationed, and one day he is accused of stealing a gun from an officer.

Or at least this is what Toshi tells you.

She has rushed back to Lucknow, to Bhopal House. I imagine her standing in your office, fragile, scared, frantic. She tells you S.L. has been thrown in the brig, she tells you about what he has been charged with—about the gun and the officer—a charge, she tells you, that he vehemently denies. You tell her to slow down, you reassure her. This is your sister, and you will do whatever you need to do to help, and you tell her this, that you'll take care of it.

"Did they find the gun, do they have the evidence?"

Toshi tells you they did not.

You accompany Toshi back to Delhi, to the military base. You have your legal credentials now but not only that, you have experience. You've spent time in courtrooms, arguing, and you know when you have a case and when you don't. Later in your life you will become known for never taking a case that you know you might lose. With this particular case, you already know that without evidence, without actually showing S.L. has the gun he is accused of stealing, he can't be proven guilty.

It hardly takes you a day to free S.L. But there are still repercussions. He is discharged, and because he is discharged, he and your sister no longer have anywhere to live in Delhi, nor do they have any reason to be there.

You decide to take your sister and S.L. back to Lucknow. You can't leave her and her husband homeless in the city. S.L. is sulky, moody, a capricious man with a temper swayed by appetite rather than principle, and on the train he is sullen. You are suspicious of him, and you watch him. You were an excellent observer of people and so you must have observed him then, trying to read him, to weigh his innocence or guilt.

You wait for the right time, maybe when your sister has fallen asleep or leaves momentarily to use to the restroom, and then approach S.L.

"Where is the gun?" you ask him.

According to your children, you were one of the only people S.L. didn't respond to with defiance. Maybe because he knew that you would provide for him, maybe because he already saw that so long as he was your sister's husband, he could exploit your generosity? Or maybe there was something more primitive to it all. People always treated you with respect. You had that air of authority, and maybe for someone like S.L., that's indication enough of a natural pecking order, of something elemental that he understood.

But still he hesitates, a flicker of defiance.

"Where is it?" you say again.

"I have it," he says.

There is a story that Monkey Bridge in Lucknow is haunted by a daayan, a creature with backward pointing feet who sucks the life out of people through their mouth. It's hard not to think of this story when I think of you and S.L. standing there, on Monkey Bridge, overlooking the Gomti. He would take from you as the daayan takes. But right now there's only the dark brown water running swiftly below you, the banks of the Gomti swollen from the summer monsoons. Right now you can't know how much grief this man will bring you, how much conflict, the Janus-shaped obligations that will pull you in two directions at once. Cars and rickshaws pass. You and S.L. stand silently, waiting for a break in the traffic.

"Now," you tell S.L., and he pulls out the gun from his pocket and casts it into the river.

At night or during the afternoon or whenever you and Avinash can find private moments during those first few weeks that S.L. and your sister stay with you in Bhopal House, you discuss how to handle the situation. Avinash is suspicious, worries about the kind of trouble S.L. will bring if he and your sister stay in Lucknow, and she tells you so. "Give them some money, help set them up in another city, but nothing good can come of him being here. I don't trust him."

Neither do you, but at the same time Toshi is your sister, and this is what you tell Avinash, the reasoning paramount. You say to your wife, "She is family," and you say this in a tone that indicates it's already decided. If S.L. would prove impervious there were ways you were impervious too.

Avinash nods, acquiescent despite her reservations.

S.L. and Toshi take up residency with you and the rest of your family in the small flat. There are nine of you all sleeping in the great room: you and Avinash, your children Rashmi and Raj, your sister, Sarla, your own mother and father, and now S.L. and Toshi. During the day all manner of clients come and go: hardened criminals, petty thieves, people with financial disputes or suffering from minor injustices, and you give them all your undivided attention, somehow blocking out the periodic arguments that erupt between Toshi and S.L., ignoring the hookah smoke that blows in from the veranda window, setting aside the small family dramas of so many of you living in such a small space.

What to do with S.L.?

This is the question, and you puzzle over it, return to it, set it aside, return to it again. This is how you solve problems, ruminating and then clearing your mind, and then ruminating again and then letting your mind go clear, giving the problem space, until eventually a solution presents itself. And you needed a solution. S.L. and your sister are trying for children now and without work they won't be able to move from Bhopal House to another place. Your own wife is pregnant again too.

A solution does present itself.

You decide to financially back a rickshaw business that S.L. can run. Money is still tight—there's hardly enough to go around—but you figured this would be an investment, not just in the business itself but in your sister's future, and her own stability, and this mattered to you.

You purchase five or six rickshaws for S.L., rent out a small garage and office space where he can run his business. S.L. then recruits five or six rickshawallas who rent from him, who will then give S.L. a percentage of whatever they make each day. And at first it works. S.L. begins to make some money, not a great deal of money but enough so that he and Toshi can get their own place. He is still there, still a low-grade concern, but he fades into the background as life goes on.

*　*　*

And life does go on. Time passes and things happen.

In 1956 you and Avinash have a third child. Brijesh is born. It's an important birth, the first of your children to be born in a hospital. He has a full head of dark, curly hair. A real charmer from birth. He is a cute baby, almost obnoxiously so.

Your practice grows. You win more and more cases. What else? Sarla takes a job teaching primary school at Saint Mary's. She's nearly eighteen now. The monsoons come and go. Rashmi is old enough to start school and one morning,

Keshav (Avinash's brother) and Rashmi in 1955.

her first day when she is to accompany Sarla to school, Raj, devastated to see his sister leave without him, wraps his arms around her and pleads, "Don't go, don't go."

Raj's hoarse cries bring the whole family into the great room, where the boy is inconsolable, unwilling to let go of his sister. The two are pried apart. "Don't take my sister," Raj cries, and even his grandmother, Gyan Devi, who dotes on Raj—the first grandson!—can't console him.

During lunch, Avinash tries to feed him while you see clients in your office. She makes bhindi and daal, which Raj hates, an insult added to injury. He throws it on the floor, and Avinash, seeing this, slaps her son once, and then twice, the stress overwhelming her. Seeing her daughter-in-law slapping her own grandson, Gyan Devi raises her hand, delivers a slap of her own to Avinash's face. You rush out into the kitchen. Everyone is crying now, daal and bhindi scattered on the kitchen floor, everyone pointing fingers at each other, Raj still distraught. But you are becoming a master of family diplomacy and manage to calm everyone down. By evening everything is back to normal, order reestablished, and the next morning you are reciting Persian poetry in Urdu once again to your wife. "Tell me, Mr. Anand," you to say her, joking, as you button your shirt in front of the mirror. "What does the poem mean?"

Avinash smiles, swats this away. "I'm not a mister," she says.

You shrug. "She's not a mister, she says. She's not a mister."

Lakhi's hookah smoke pours in through the veranda windows.

Then winter gives way to another spring and the unbearable heat of summer descends upon Lucknow. After a sweltering day at court, you bring home ice cream for Avinash. "For the queen," you say.

And then later when outside the heat lifts, you and all the residents of Bhopal House—former refugees who moved in when you did as well as new tenants you are just getting to know—ascend onto the roof, and you all bring your dinners and bedding, the men hauling their dhurries over their shoulders, the boys dragging theirs, going thunk thunk thunk up the stairs. Someone hangs a large white sheet from a clothesline, and someone else gets the rickety old projector rolling, aims a scratchy movie onto the dirty screen, and for an hour or two everyone, except you, falls under the spell of actors pretending to live lives other than their own. When it's over and the women all return to their respective apartments, you and the other men and boys stay on the roof.

You roll out the dhurrie, the stars bright above you. How things have changed.

You adjust under the open sky and sleep like a baby.

The thing about S.L. wasn't just that he was handsome. He was charming. He charmed Toshi, certainly, but he also charmed your own mother. He saunters into your house, coming and going, singing songs, regaling your mom, complimenting her and then turning to compliment Toshi, who is always close behind. He divvies out little treats, talks with sweet cadences in a low voice. You had heard people tell him that he could have been a movie star, heard your own mom say this—broad shoulders, angular jaw, his thick, dark hair, and so so charming!—and he embodied this air of self-importance, believed that he deserved the world, and on the right day he could convince people, women in particular, to give him the world, or at least try.

But he could be violent, too, his temper capricious, extravagant in his readiness to take offense. He could charm, yes, but there were those other times when he was in the apartment, even during that period when he was living with you and on good behavior, when a small annoyance would push him into a rage. These moments come as quick flashes of aggression, startling in their extremes.

One evening, while still living in Bhopal House, S.L. can't find his just-washed pants and he asks your sister, Sarla, if she has seen them.

Sarla, already wary of him, invulnerable to his charisma, tells him to ask his own wife. She snaps, "I don't do your laundry."

"If you're so Westernized, why does your dad still wear a turban," S.L. snaps back at her.

But Sarla is quick, razor sharp, in many ways more like you than your sister Toshi. In the kitchen she turns on him, answers coolly, derisively: "And I've seen what your mom wears."

S.L. yells at her incoherently, punches a hole in the window, glass shattering all over, bloodying his fist.

Months later an argument erupts between Yash Pal, your sister Prakash's son, and S.L. Prakash had sent Yash Pal to live with you in Lucknow, hoping you would be a good influence on him. Though he was an adult and living on his own, Yash Pal often came over to your house for dinner, almost always covered in coal and soot from his job at the Lucknow train station.

On one of these evenings S.L. looks Yash Babu up and down, sneers and says to him, "If your dad is as rich as he is, why do you have one of the worst jobs in town, shoveling coal?"

"At least I work for my money," Yash Babu says, without missing a beat, hardly looking up from the dinner Avinash has served him. S.L. stands up, and tackles him and then starts smashing out the windows on the veranda door. He has absolutely no control over himself. How you would calm him during these moments is a mystery to me, but even a bigger mystery to me is how you don't lose your own temper.

One hot afternoon, Brij, four, maybe five, precocious, the little provocateur, is playing out in the hallway, just outside the door to the flat in which you all lived.

Above: Avinash with Raj and Rashmi, 1955.
Left: S.L. holding Raj with Rashmi in 1954.

LIKE A BANYAN TREE

Brij notices S.L. climbing the spiral staircase and makes a face at him, simply scrunches up his nose, teasing, as children do. S.L. charges up the stairs and grabs Brij by the legs, hangs him over the railing, dangling the boy three floors high. He holds him like that, torments him, threatening to drop him. Raj hears, runs up to S.L., begs him to let his little brother down, but S.L. drags it out, laughing, "That'll teach you, you little urchin," as Brij cries hysterically. S.L. finally relents, and you must have been furious when you found out, yet somehow you never lost your own temper on S.L.

After these eruptions, the incident with the rickshawalla couldn't have come as a surprise. The difference was that this was the first time that S.L.'s actions put pressure on your own moral compass.

Once you had decided to defend S.L. in court, you insisted that he give you each painful detail by painful detail. You can't defend someone who keeps the truth from you. You had to know everything. As a lawyer, this had always been your policy. It was good business practice, yes, but also honesty was paramount to you. You abhorred lying.

And S.L. does tell you everything, not that he has much of a choice, at least once he had been arrested. He tells you how one of the rickshawallas had been lying, reporting less than he was actually making, and consequently bringing S.L.'s cut of the money down. And he tells you how, once he found out this rickshawalla was stealing from him, he, S.L., beat this man senseless. S.L. tells you how he tied his feet together and then hung him upside down from the ceiling fan and left him there, would have left him there for who knows how long if it weren't for the rickshawalla's wife, who, late in the night, looking for her husband, went down to the garage and heard his muffled cries from inside. S.L. tells you this and it must have disgusted you, but you defended him, already the moral obligation to your sister pulling you away from what you knew was right. If you didn't come to S.L.'s defense, if you didn't help, and S.L. was convicted of attempted murder, your sister—a mother now—would have gone without a husband and your nieces without a father.

The competing demands in your life were beginning to take shape.

You get S.L. off, make a deal with the rickshawalla and his wife. It's not exactly a payoff, but it's not exactly not a payoff. Against your better judgment to defend S.L., you were obligated to do what you had to do.

After this, S.L. loses his rickshaw business. Once again, he and his wife, and their two daughters now are without a livelihood. And once again, you set your mind on how to find S.L. work, on a means to support his family, how to support your sister.

S.L. knows how to cook fish, and you come up with an idea. There is vacant shop space at the bottom of Bhopal House—the added advantage that you could keep a close eye on this next business venture must have been appealing—and you propose that S.L. rent this space, open a restaurant, with your financial backing, of course.

S.L. agrees, mulls over potential names, comes up with one: Frontier Fish Fry. He's from the frontier, after all, that contentious geographical space between Pakistan and Afghanistan that was, and still is, contested. Once everything is agreed upon, you pour your time and more of your limited resources into getting this restaurant started. At first the restaurant seems to do okay. On those mornings when you leave Bhopal House for court, and on those afternoons when you come home, you check on Frontier Fish Fry, check on S.L. and make sure all is well, no chaos, no outbursts of anger, no erupting tempers.

It's 1959 and then 1960. The months tick by. S.L. and Toshi have another daughter, and you and Avinash have another son, your fourth and last child, Ajesh, Baby Gugloo, you call him. You and Avinash have already decided that you wouldn't have any more than four children—a rare example of family planning given the time and culture—and so Ajesh is significant also for being the last. He is a skinny baby with a light complexion, but he is perfectly healthy.

S.L. and Toshi have yet another daughter, and then Toshi is pregnant again, and the rapid rate that their family continues to grow begins to worry you, most of all because Frontier Fish Fry isn't doing well. The problem isn't the business itself, but that S.L. is running it into the ground, always serving his friends, shady characters themselves, free food and drink. They loiter in the shop, drink, fight, provoke other customers, and quickly this becomes a liability. Nobody wants to eat their dinner or lunch while being antagonized by drunks. You try to stop this, sink more and more money into the venture, but it only gets worse, and eventually the restaurant becomes such a financial drain that you have no choice

Madan Mohan Sethi and Rambheji, one of the two of Baij's older sisters, in 1965.

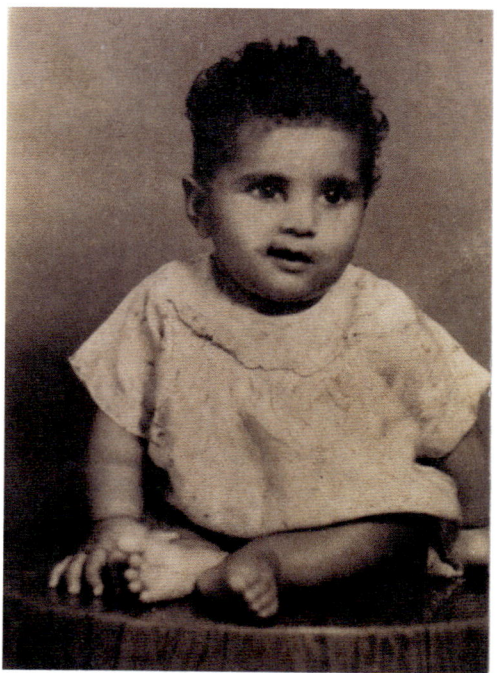

Brij in 1957.

Sarla and her daughter Anita in 1961.

Conflicts and Desire, Conflicting Desires

but to close it down, S.L. and Toshi once again reliant on you for money.

Next you invest in an ice cream factory, one that S.L. can own and run. The pattern is predictable now, the first few years go well, or at least seem to, and there comes that period just as it came in the past when S.L. occupies less space in your mind and life is normal, or normal enough to be punctuated by small events.

There is the weekend when S.L.'s son is playing with a BB gun that S.L. had given him, and he accidentally shoots Ajesh in the leg, the BB burrowing deep into the still soft baby fat of his thigh. At the hospital the doctor patches up Ajesh but because the BB is so deep, he leaves it where it is lodged. You were furious with S.L. for giving his son the gun, but you must have accepted, too, that when you bring children into the world you can't always protect them, not that it makes it any easier. "It's still in there," Ajesh recently told me during a conversation we had, referring to the BB, a strange marker of time that has stayed the same after all these years.

Then there's a lazy afternoon when Sarla, Rashmi and Raj are outside on the veranda, languid in the summer heat, and a monkey descends onto the balcony, harasses the three of them and then chases them inside.

You weren't there. You were in court. But later when they tell you about the incident, you laugh loud and openly at the telling. The image of Sarla, well into her teen years now, taking shit from nobody, especially a monkey, frantically hurling shoes through the barred window of the great room was irresistible. She threw one shoe after another, trying to scare the monkey away, while Raj and Rashmi ran back and forth from the shoe rack in the hall to the great room and back to the shoe rack again, replenishing her dwindling arsenal.

"Bandar Bhag," she yelled. "Monkey run!"

But then there were no more shoes.

"The wood pestle," Sarla commanded. "Get the pestle."

Raj and Rashmi ran out of the room and then came back with her request. Sarla took it from them, bravely gripped the pestle like a club, heavy and formidable in her hands, and then threw it at the monkey.

The wood caught the side of the monkey's face, bloodying his cheeks, and

Left: Ajesh, Yash, Baij, Rashmi, Brij, and Raj in 1966 at the Taj Mahal.

Below: Two photos of Raj and Rashmi with Gyan Devi, 1966.

82 | Conflicts and Desire, Conflicting Desires

the great room erupted with screams of joy at the hit. Stunned, the monkey stood there, dumbly abused. Then it came to and hurried off, defeated, climbing and swinging its way up one veranda after the other until vanishing.

But when your children tell you this story, they leave out, for some reason, the fact that the monkey nearly absconded with one of your beloved sandals, perhaps because they were so dear to you. And they *were* dear to you. You wore them almost every day, the back strap beneath your heel rather than behind it, pushing the leather irretrievably into the soles. You never noticed the teeth marks the monkey left behind, but you would have if you'd looked closely, an emblem of that contentious afternoon of children verses monkey.

Your own father continues to drive you crazy, but you love him nonetheless—the perennial dynamic between so many fathers and sons. Stubborn, like you, he thinks he knows best and you think you know even better. And sometimes you are both right. One afternoon, for instance, Raj breaks his arm when you are off at work, and your father, rather than taking Raj to the hospital, takes him to the town wrestler, who, familiar with broken bones—an occupational hazard in his line of work—takes Raj's small arm in his big hands and sets it in a swift jolt, the pain registering immediately on Raj's face. You are furious. "Why didn't you take him to the hospital," you demand, later rushing Raj out of the house for a proper X-ray. To your astonishment, after the examination, the doctor says this wrester did, in fact, set it. So sometimes your dad was right. But then the doctor points to two other fractures on the X-ray. "Though he also broke it again. Twice."

And of course, you read.

Three newspapers a day: The Hindustan Times, The National Herald (the local Lucknow paper), and one, from who knows where, published in Urdu. You continued to bring home copious amounts of fruit from the street vendors because you loved to share, but also because you were making enough money that you could help those in need and you knew that the street vendors were anything but well-off. To do your part, to help those in need, there were days when you would buy the entire stand, coming home with more bags of fruit than you could carry, mangoes spilling out on the stairs and in the hallways.

As your law practice grows, you knock out a wall in your office and expand your workspace out onto the veranda, building a little roof and an enclosed space for your steadily expanding library. And you tell stories, always when you come home from work or in the morning, you tell your children little narratives, some with a point and some of seemingly no consequence—a man wearing the strangest hat in the courtroom, for instance, or the skill and involved methods a street vendor uses to cook goat curry you so enjoyed—but all stories, as you knew, had consequences, because it's through stories that we understand the world. You understood this, I know you did, because when young Ajesh asks you why you tell such strange stories, you look at your son and answer his question with a question: "How else are you going to know the world?"

Summer. Winter. Summer again. You buy a car! A Hindustan Ambassador. You have Raj count the money before paying and he beams with self-importance. You hire a driver to get the Ambassador from the dealership back home. His name is Shammi Khan and he will remain your driver for years to come.

It had been nearly a decade since you had lived as a refugee. Your practice continues to gain momentum, but it has also occasioned one of the few conflicts between you and Avinash, a conflict that one evening comes to a breaking point. The fact that you practiced both civil law and criminal law had become a source of concern for Avinash. She had voiced this concern—nothing major, but concern nonetheless—about criminals coming and going in the same house in which the two of you were raising children. They would knock on the door at all times of the day, seeking your council, and they brought with them a certain presence that, despite Avinash's own openness and empathy, at times left her worried about the children and her own safety.

She expressed these concerns to you, and you set her anxiety at ease by explaining the simple truth that these men were there because they needed your help, and therefore what motivations could they possibly have to do any harm.

But there comes one case in particular that bothers Avinash. She finds it offensive. One of your clients, a man who claimed to be a priest, would marry young girls from small villages and then bring them into Lucknow and sell them into prostitution. After he had been caught he hired you as his defense attorney. This opened an ongoing discussion between you and Avinash about the difference between legal justice and moral justice, a distinction you often drew on to defend your work as a criminal defense attorney.

For you, legal justice was something different than moral justice. For the legal system to work, for there to be legal justice that was fair and impartial, even the worst criminal deserved a serious defense. But moral justice was something different, something that transcended legal justice, something that considered those more abstract qualities of human experience, considered the value of a human life outside of legal strictures, and I can't help but wonder if Avinash, sharp like you, used your own argument against you: It may be legally right to defend someone who sells girls into prostitution, but it was morally indefensible.

Even though this was a source of conflict for the two of you, I like to imagine your discussions about it with Avinash, mostly because I appreciate the respect for each other that you would have both brought to the conflict. I picture you leaning your head toward her, as the two of you walk through town, talking this over, listening carefully, and just as carefully formulating a response, and her doing the same for you. But in the end, at least on this case, you were intractable.

And then late one night there came a knock on the door, and Avinash, unsure of who it was but thinking it was likely important, opened it. Standing in the hallways was a man covered in blood, a man who had just committed murder and had come straight to you for legal advice, and this was the line for Avinash. No argument in favor of legal justice could convince her otherwise. You were raising a family and a murderer showing up at your door for legal advice wouldn't stand. You conceded the point. You stopped practicing criminal law.

* * *

Though this period of your life was free of serious conflict with S.L., he never entirely disappears. One afternoon Toshi comes to the house, blood trickling from her ear. S.L. has beaten her. She is shaking and crying, though also stunned, confused.

You bring up the possibility of divorce, despite the unlikelihood of it, despite the fact that you know what Toshi will say, which is that she loves S.L., wants to be with him, and even here, what could you have done? You weren't the type to threaten people, but even if you were, your empathy and loyalties were with your sister, so any threats you could have made to S.L. would have been empty.

Still, seeing your sister like this, bloodied and beaten, helpless in a way that had always elicited not just your sympathies but that deep loyalty, as if part of your obligation to her came from knowing that she did need you, must have made you want to protect her even more, especially because you knew there was so little you could do.

Then one evening comes a knock at the door. This was always how it went in your life, wasn't it? Normalcy punctuated by the knock on the door, the crisis. Always at night. Always the man standing in the doorway.

It's summer and hot, and you are in your office with your son Raj, who is hardly a little boy anymore. Old enough now to find his way into all manner of small troubles—flashing a mirror at a teacher to interrupt a lesson, or riding his bike past another teacher in the market and yelling obscenities—you are increasingly spending more time with Raj. You were a doting father, but you could be stern too, like the time Raj wasn't doing his homework, and you made him stay up all night, standing by your desk studying while you worked. Every time Raj nodded off you would admonish him, "If you keep nodding off I will tie your hair to the fan so you can't slump."

On this evening, Raj was watching you closely as you went over your work, discussing one case after another, when the superintendent of the ice cream factory S.L. owned came rushing towards you through the open door. You and Raj look up at him. His clothes are covered in blood. He starts talking fast, saying that S.L. had been attacked, that he was on the floor in the factory. "He looks dead," he says.

You get up from your desk and run down the three flights of stairs, Raj following close behind. Out on the street, the hot air hits you, and you don't stop running until you reach the ice cream factory, a crowd of people already gathered around the door. You push your way through the bodies, shouldering people out of the way until you reach the still opened door, the lights from the great room of the factory pooling around S.L.'s body, his blood dark against the concrete floor.

You bend down and feel for a pulse. It takes a minute to find, but when you do it's weak and fluttery to the touch. You turn to Raj. "Get a rickshaw," you say, and then turn back to S.L., lifting his body, slumping it over yours and carrying him outside. You meet Raj and the rickshaw in the street. The ride to the hospital is slow and bumpy. You cradle S.L.'s head in your lap. You know he is bleeding from his head and you feel around his scalp but there's too much blood to get a clear sense of his wounds.

When you arrive at the hospital you find that there is no doctor on duty, that he has been called for but has yet to arrive. Somehow you know to get an IV into S.L., to give him fluids and spoon powdered glucose into his mouth. You do this while Raj watches, in awe of his father's command of the situation.

"You saved his life," the doctor tells you when he arrives, checking S.L.'s pulse, and I imagine he looked at you with some wonderment, this lawyer who happened to know how to insert an IV, who happened to know what do in a crisis like this.

What had happened with S.L. wasn't entirely clear at first, but over time you learn the story, how S.L. had been having an affair with one of his neighbors and her husband, Alexander, had found out. How Alexander came to the ice cream factory to confront S.L. How Alexander's intentions weren't violent, but rather to confront S.L. about the affair, to tell him to stop seeing his wife. How S.L. became violent with Alexander, and then how Alexander left and came back later with five of his friends. They brought knives and chains. The doctor had counted 27 stab wounds.

That night after you and Raj return home, Toshi and S.L.'s kids are in the flat, hysterical, and again, as always, you calm her, tell her that S.L. will live—and he does, after months of recovery. You stand in your office, still covered in blood yourself, promising your sister that her husband, promising your nieces that their father, will be okay, and that you would be there for them until S.L. was out of the hospital.

The next day, you send Raj to take S.L.'s place running the ice cream factory. And it must have made you proud, the way Raj handled the situation. He not only runs the factory well, but creates new flavor combinations, and a system in which the ice cream hawkers were held accountable for wasted inventory by incentivizing a bonus for those who sold all of their ice cream by the end of the day. Even at a young age he was a little businessman, sharp and resourceful.

S.L. heals and he returns to work, running the Metro Ice Cream once again. What amazes me about this man is how impervious to change he is. When he gets out of the hospital, he's still arrogant, still temperamental, still charming,

63 Pandariba next to CB Gupta House in 2015.

63 Pandariba, Lucknow in 2023.

88 | *Conflicts and Desire, Conflicting Desires*

at least to some people. It sounds strange, but in some ways there's something admirable about a man like that, a man who is so undeniably who he is, so completely and fundamentally himself that even after being beaten nearly to death, he is still exactly who he is. And there's something about this, about S.L.'s stubbornness, the absolute fact of him and how unbending he is, that reminds me of you. You both could only ever be yourselves, and S.L. returned to exactly who he was in this drama, as did you, ready to help him and your sister. And they would need you again, in time. Of course they would. Neither you or S.L. could change your ways. He would go on to be selfish, and you would go on to be selfless, maybe even to a fault.

For a while things go quiet again with S.L., and you slip back into normal life. Your practice is now making enough money that you can afford a larger house, a home big enough for you and your wife, your parents, your four children, and whatever distant family might have been staying with you at the time—and it seems there was always someone.

In the summer of 1968 you and your family move to 63 Pandariba—a good house in a good neighborhood, close to the Lucknow train station, and the courts in which you work. The chief minister of the state, Chandra Bhanu Gupta, lives directly next door, and his house is the twin of your own. It is a huge house—two stories, a courtyard, the exterior exacting, clean lines, almost Art Deco. And because C.B. Gupta is your neighbor, you and your family grow accustomed to seeing serious people with political agendas coming and going. Indira Gandhi, politicians from the Congress Party, diplomats, film stars. By this time, you're nearly fifty years old. Rashmi is seventeen, Raj is fifteen, Brij twelve, and Ajesh, the baby, nine. The house is big enough for all of you, with room to spare for your law office on the first floor. Your father, for the first time, has his own room in the back of the house.

That first week you live there, something bothers you. On the front of the house, there's an arch with the last name of the family who previously owned the property carved into the stone. You spend days trying to find a mason to change it, to cover over the old name with cement and carve your last name in its place, but you can't find anyone.

To your surprise, one morning you step outside and turn around, and there's your name, Anand, freshly written in stone. You didn't know it, but when you couldn't find someone, Raj and your nephew, Yash Babu, who was living with you and your family now for a period, had taken on the work themselves. They built the scaffolding, knotted rope in the holes of narrow boards, and then mixed the cement. For an entire day in the summer heat, Raj hoisted buckets of water from the rooftop where his cousin stood on the wooden planking, spackling and carving, chisel against limestone. It took twelve hours, maybe more. But I like to imagine it, the surprise and joy, the sense of pride you must have felt when you saw it the next morning, shafts of sunlight cresting over the roof of your new home, "Anand" written in stone.

You've come a long way indeed.

Pakistan, Partition, refugee camp after refugee camp, Bhopal House, and now here, the last house you will live in.

It isn't a full house for long, at least not compared to what you must have been used to. Rashmi had started college in Lucknow. She was often gone during the day, studying. And somehow, someway, you had made what seemed like the impossible possible: You had sent Brij to The Doon School. He was gone when school was in session. So life was new and exciting in the big house on Pandariba, but in so many ways it was still the same life you had lived before, with the same markers of familiarity and routine.

Above: Ajesh and cousin Anita (Sarla's daughter), 1963.
Left: Rashmi in 1967.

Conflicts and Desire, Conflicting Desires

Lakhi smokes his hookah and plays chess with his friends all day, though there's space enough now so that the smoke doesn't blow in through the windows. You still read three newspapers a day, though now you also have a transistor radio, which you listen to in the evening for at least thirty minutes before going to bed. And always you are kind to Avinash, bringing her surprises from the market as you did in Bhopal House, reciting poetry, asking for her impressions and interpretations.

But S.L. Your life inevitably returns to this man. One afternoon when he is working, he attempts to repair the electrical compressor that runs the ice cream factory. Thinking he had turned the electrical current off, he grabs it, wrapping his hand around the wire cable. The shock nearly kills him. If he weren't strong enough to tear down the junction box as he tried to pull away, it would have. One of the ice cream hawkers finds him unconscious on the ground, the skin on his hand melted like cheap plastic.

The accident leaves S.L. disfigured, most of the flesh on his right hand gone, and what's left from one surgery after another is crooked and scarred, S.L.'s fingers curled into an ugly claw. He is in the hospital for months, and this time the ice cream factory goes under because Raj is now in school. Here you are again, the provider for your sister's family, and faced with finding S.L. yet another livelihood.

He begins to heal but a stench follows him. He comes in and out of your house with your sister and their children, and he always brings in the sunbaked smell of rotting fish oil, which the doctor has recommended he use on his disfigured hand. Because of this, his presence is overpowering. When they are home, your children avoid him, make private faces of disgust at his smell. But you are gracious and ignore it. You bring him into your office, offer him a chair on the other side of your desk, and the two of you sit down and discuss potential business opportunities, some new venture that can get him back on track, provide an income.

As you talk, S.L. massages fish oil into his hand. You offer up one possibility after another, and I imagine S.L., sullen, shrugging them off one at time, nothing quite suitable to this man who is both vain and opposed to working too hard. Weeks pass. He comes and goes out of your office, his fishy smell lingering in your home. Eventually the two of you arrive at an idea that seems suitable to S.L. You will finance a taxi business that he can run. You start with a small fleet of cars—two and then a third that S.L. drives.

As always, you pay the costs.

The cars, the gasoline, the maintenance, the garage space. You financially back the entire business in an effort to get S.L. back on his feet so that he can support his family.

Toshi comes into your office. The taxi business has been running for months, almost a year. She's distressed, talking fast. She tells you S.L. has been gone for three days, that she doesn't know where he is, and then she tells you that it's happened before, a night here and there, but never for this long.

"What if he doesn't come back?" she cries. "Where is he?"

You calm her, tell her you're sure he'll turn up, and I think at first you were sure that he would, the possibility that his disappearance was an affair very likely, obvious even. Wanting to protect her, I don't imagine that you say this to your sister, but you manage to calm her down, and this time you're right, S.L. does come back. He says that his car had broken down far outside of town, some distant village where he drove a customer. He couldn't find a mechanic, he says. He was stuck out there, with no way to get back until he found someone to fix his car. This is what he tells both you and his sister, and for the time being you let it rest, even though you must have had a feeling that he was lying.

It happens again, and then again, and then a month goes by, sometimes more, without incident, and then yet another disappearance. He'll be gone for a night, two, sometimes three, always your sister and her children showing up at your house, hysterical again—"Where is he?! Where is he?!"—and your own mom crying at her side, the two women this man has managed to charm and regale and deceive the most. You calm them down. You always do. And always he returns, his excuses over time running thin and then eventually I imagine him no longer giving excuses at all, doing what he pleases with impunity.

Do you confront S.L.? I don't know, but I want you to. The deeper your story gets with him the more I have to work to understand you, to understand that unlike most people in this situation, your duty to your sister and her family transcended the personal insult of being lied to, of being taken advantage of. I'd say you were being gamed by this man but you weren't. You understood exactly what he was doing and yet you stayed with him, time and time again. You hated lying and that must have bothered you the most, knowing that S.L.'s excuses were clearly deceitful, and yet you went along with it for your sister's sake, for her and her family.

His disappearances become more frequent still, longer now too, and Toshi becomes increasingly frantic. Hardly a month goes by where she isn't in your office at least once, imploring you to find him, and then comes one afternoon when she's crying and saying it's different this time.

"He's been gone for over a week. He isn't coming back."

You tell her the only thing you can tell her, the only thing you've been able to tell her this whole time. "He'll come back," you say. "He always does."

But this time he doesn't. A few more days pass. A week. Toshi is inconsolable, at your house every night, her daughters in tow, equally inconsolable. Your house is full of women crying. Another week passes. And then you get word, a phone call that S.L. is in jail in a tiny town a few hours from Lucknow, for smuggling drugs. You take a train to him, and you manage to get him out, and it must have been then that you learned the truth of his disappearances, that they were those periods when he was smuggling, filling his taxi with hash and driving to distant cities. You take him back to Lucknow.

This is the part of the story where I lose the thread. The pattern of this man in your life is so repetitive. You knew he would keep doing what he had always done. You knew that it was just a matter of time before he would disrupt your life again. I know you were doing all this for your sister, and I admire your generosity, your sense of duty. I do. But S.L. pushes far past the limits of what I would give, so your generosity also confuses me.

I'm reminded of that other story about you, of the time you had invited a thief into your house. I can't help but think about this thief when I think about you and S.L., not just because it happened while S.L. was in your life, but because this thief dramatizes something that is otherwise hard to articulate—draws out some metaphor that feels important—the way your willingness to give sometimes blurred into something beyond giving, somehow almost religious in your austerity, stubborn in your openness.

***

Stay with me as I track back in time to this other story that starts with your other sister, Sarla. You all are back to living in Bhopal House. Sarla is about to get married. It's a busy and chaotic time, and not just because of S.L. and Toshi and your work and your own family—everyone living under the same roof— but there's the attendant wedding preparations now, and planning that requires its own care. Meals must be arranged, the numerous moving parts of tradition considered, and venues and clothing, guests, and their dates of arrival, all need attention.

I imagine during this period there's not a quiet moment in the apartment. Always, it's crowded with people. Always it's full of smells: curries from Avinash's cooking, fried butter too, and there's that scent of burnt manure leftover from your father's hookah. But there's also the odor of people, of your clients, often crowded two or three at a time in your office—there's no privacy policy here—and because some of these clients are real criminals who lived precariously, because their lives were hanging in the balance, I also imagine the gamey smell of fear.

In between clients and one crisis after another with S.L., you are always on the run. You run to the open-air market. You dash to the courthouse, never late but sometimes cutting it close, maybe Avinash calling a reminder to stop at the tailor as you hastily slide into your coat. It's late winter when this story starts, the mild time of year in Lucknow, the hot season and the monsoons yet to come.

Then: enter thief.

You meet him in front of a juice stand. The day is unremarkable in its routine. The only deviation is that Raj, because he is at that age, nearly six now and getting into everything, is with you and has been all day, brought along at Avinash's urging. "He gets into trouble when he stays home."

It's sugar cane juice for the boy and orange juice for you. I imagine you, standing there in your coat, advocates tie parted neatly over your chest, and because you've always taken an interest in the world, ever curious about how things work, and because you want to foster this in your son, you draw his attention to the spectacle of Gulshan, the juicewala, feeding the thick stalks into the almost medieval contraption, the strange violence of two giant wheels cranked to pulverize fibrous shoots. "And then juice," you say, pointing to the cup under the nozzle as it fills with the milky liquid.

After you pay, after your son finishes his and you yours, after you stand there briefly in the mild winter sun, at ease as the day's work falls away, the thief approaches.

And how does this happen, exactly?

I think he asks you for money, gives you that almost universal phrase: "Anything will help." You look him in the eye, you always do, and then you say, "A young man like you should have a job." This isn't meant as an indictment to chastise him, but sincerely, to give him hope and encouragement.

He looks at you and you keep your eyes on him. There's something about this man that makes you pause.

How much can fit in a pause between two strangers? Is it long enough for you to consider the game you play with your children? "Who is that person?" you say to them when they are with you, walking down the street or driving with you to one of your appointments. "Who is that person and where are they from? What do they do? What's their education? Do they have children, a family?"

It's a deceptively simple game, the object always to get as close to the truth as you can by simply observing. You have this uncanny talent for finding those same people, say, that same afternoon, or a few days later—it's a relatively small city, after all—and in your amicable way people trust you, they just do, and they want to talk to you—you'll simply ask them: "So what *do* you do? Where *are* you from? Do you have children?"

And once you find out, later you'll tell your children they were right about that man with the hat, but wrong about the man on the bicycle and then you would ask them why they thought what they thought. It's an exercise in rhetoric, and in ethics, meant to get your children to think about why they make the judgments that they do.

Is this pause long enough to run through this game in your own head, to formulate the kinds of judgments you ask of you own children?

Observe everything, you always say.

Observe and watch, watch and observe.

This is how you get to know another man, and you do have this remarkable ability to hit the mark so often, to pin another man, to know his character in a glance. But not this time, not this man, with his open face and honest appeal.

"Anything at all," he says, and how could you not see in his desperation the same desperation you've seen countless times, a reminder of your previous life as a refugee, of that same desperation in those voices of worried family members for whom you translated or wrote letters. And I wonder, too, if you even recognized in this man's plea an echo of your own voice from those same days, after you'd interpret another note, transcribe another letter, and then ask for compensation—"anything at all"—knowing that most everybody had no more than you.

So in a pause, a flash of recognition, you appraise this man, form a judgment. You don't give him money but what you can offer is work, and you do. You give him your address and a time to come by.

On your way home you talk to Raj about human suffering. Never waste an opportunity that could be used as a teaching moment, never waste a lesson. But lessons are as slippery as stories, open to interpretation, wily things, sometimes conveying the opposite of what's meant. Your point is nonetheless well-intended, one that you've given so much thought to. There's a tension in this world between character and circumstance. Character is how a person responds to circumstance but circumstance shapes that very character. This is why you must always place a person in context before you can judge them. This is how you understand another's humaneness. Not that anyone's perfect. We all misjudge character sometimes and we misjudge circumstances, too. Including our own.

Later that evening at the intended time, the thief knocks on the door. You've already explained to your family how you met this man, how you want to help, but mostly you've discussed this with Avinash. And considering this discussion makes me think about how she's different than you. While you share a similar kindness toward others, where you tend toward the garrulous and tend to hold court, she harbors quieter currents—her deliberateness in speech, her serious demeanor—a difference you noticed those first weeks together in the Gun Factory and a difference that remains a point of distinction. In this way she balances you. And it would have been hard not to notice earlier that evening when you told her about this man whom you offered to help that, even though Avinash agreed, she agreed with a certain reserve, a very subtle caution, perhaps already alert to the ways your generosity toward S.L. was increasingly becoming a subtle source of tension.

But in the end, she did agree. He can come every day and help with errands, which is much needed, for it's a busy time in your house these days, almost chaotic, what with your sister's wedding fast approaching. So when you open the door and introduce him, nobody is surprised. He will start tomorrow.

And he does. Punctual, not unpleasant at all, wearing the same brown pants, visibly lighter in patches where he clearly attempted to spot clean dirt and stains, he stands in the hallway, waiting instruction on what he can do to help.

And he *is* helpful. He runs to the open air market when your wife realizes she's missing an essential ingredient for her mutton curry or eggs bhurji; he dashes off to the tailor when you need an article of clothing hemmed or altered; he jokes, however quietly, with your sister, while fixing the water faucet; and he takes your son, always on the precipice of trouble these days, to the corner store for a small piece of candy, a treat he hides in his hand and then opens under Raj's eyes, a magician's trick.

Spring arrives. You begin to trust this man who comes into your home day in and day out. But it isn't just trust; you begin to think of him as part of the family. I know this because Raj has told me, and how could you not, the way familiarity leads to intimacy, and with you especially, your curiosity toward others, your openness. "Where *are* you from? Tell me about your family." You undoubtedly ask him these questions and more, and he tells you, surely he does, maybe in the evening, after the day's work is done, the two of you sharing a brief chai or juice together, or perhaps more casually, a passing comment while handing him a grocery list and money: "You like mangoes. Get extra for yourself." And isn't this, after all, how we become human to each other? The slow process of filling in what is otherwise just an outline made of preferences and personal histories until that outline becomes something more embodied, richer, more complex. You were always quick to see the complexities.

You hardly notice the small privacies this man sees. You don't notice, for instance, the way he has watched you take your jacket off when you come home, and then put your wallet into the inside pocket while it hangs on the coat hook by the large mirror. Nor do you notice the way this man begins to pay attention to Avinash, how she leaves the big Godrej lockbox in the great room, the one with your sister's dowry—all four sets of jewelry—unlocked for part of each day, the keys tucked into her saree at the waist as she tends to chores.

Top to bottom:

Bhopal House, close-up.

Bhopal House in late fifties.

Sharma Chai House, Lucknow.

98 | Conflicts and Desire, Conflicting Desires

In late spring it happens. There's a traveling circus in town, and its ranks swell the street below your apartment building. From your office in the hallway, you can hear the commotion, the jugglers and fire throwers eliciting excitement from the crowded streets, and you can hear your own children standing on the veranda applaud and call out as the acts pass below. In the kitchen, Avinash is making lunch.

You recline in your chair, a brief moment without clients, and it's nice to sit here with your law and history books in view, breathing the comforting smell of your wife's cooking, the dusty smell of the open pages on your desk. You listen as she moves about in the kitchen, into the great room and then back into the kitchen, and it's moments like these, the quiet familiarity of a domestic life predictable in its routine that leaves you with a deep feeling of contentment, especially after everything you had seen.

Avinash calls out to you.

At first it's no different than the countless other times she has called for you. Thinking it can wait, you call back that you'll come in a minute.

"Right now," she responds, the urgency in her voice unmistakable. "Come right now."

You find her standing in the great room, in front of the Godrej lockbox. It's empty, your sister's dowry gone, all four sets of jewelry, gone. You go for your jacket hanging on the coat rack and check your own pockets. Your wallet is gone as well as your watch. Back at the lockbox you lift up the folded blankets that hide your family's backup cash. Gone.

After the initial shock, the initial panic, the questions and realizations, your response to the loss is, almost incredibly, your characteristic optimism. "We'll have a bigger wedding," you say that night. "With a bigger dowry. The festivities will be grander." It would almost be hubris, this undeterred optimism, your self-assurance at times bordering on magical thinking, except for the fact that you always did have a way of solving problems, even the most intractable ones.

"The wedding will be much, much bigger," you say again, one final time, almost as if to reassure yourself as much as your family. What you don't say, however, what you keep to yourself is that during the next few weeks you will have to borrow money. You will have to ask old friends, acquaintances, and even former colleagues, and this won't be easy, but you do it because your sister Sarla's disappointment would devastate you, especially when your other sister Toshi's livelihood is always in the balance these days. And I wonder about this, the nuances of carrying this secret, but also of this role reversal. You are so accustomed to helping others it must have been difficult to be the one doing the asking. There is nothing more vulnerable than having to ask for what we want or need, but especially for you, and the way others would always come to you for help.

But ask for help you do, and life goes on. The rainy season comes, the wedding is a success, and while no doubt this violation of trust, this betrayal still needles you, the thief and what he stole slowly recedes from the footlights to backstage, and eventually begins to take up residence in the storehouse of memory.

Then one day, months later, you and your son, Raj, are in a rickshaw going to the open-air market. Your son sees him first, riding a rickshaw coming in the opposite direction towards you, and points at him. You would have hardly recognized him otherwise, his expensive grey coat, the shine of his leather shoes, and the neat part of his hair as unfamiliar as a complete stranger. For a second you doubt yourself, doubt your son. Then you see your watch on this man's wrist, and as it catches a reflection of the afternoon sun the flash of recognition is undeniable.

He looks at you and you look at him. You call out for the rickshaw driver to stop. When the rickshaw draws to a halt, you drop down onto the street, and then the thief does as well, nearly falling out in a panic. Strangely, instead of running in the opposite direction, he runs toward you, and then past you, which throws you for a second, his odd strategy, but you regain yourself, and chase him, Raj close by your side.

The thief is younger and faster. Quickly winded, you tell Raj to run for the police constable across the street, standing at patrol. The police know you, your work in the courts, your work with criminals, and the officer who your son goes to runs after the man you point to, already a few blocks down the street, and he's quick to apprehend him. The whole scene takes no more than 10 minutes.

Later that day in your apartment with Avinash and the rest of your family, there's real relief that the thief has been caught. Your wife is especially grateful. Why wouldn't she be? This man has wronged you and your family. But this is no longer about retrieving what has been stolen. You quickly discovered that afternoon that the jewelry had been sold, the money spent, and with the exception of your watch and your wife's purse, emptied and discarded in a ditch months ago, muddied and weather beaten, worth nothing now, there's no compensation or real gain from this development, so whatever satisfaction your wife felt was only about ideas—the *idea* of justice, the *idea* of righting a wrong.

Not to say that ideas don't have their power. In so many ways they are more seductive than anything tangible, anything material, but I don't think this was true for you, Baij. Your sense of legal justice was always so pragmatic, always about balancing and rectifying wrongs in tangible ways. So maybe you were already having your doubts, already feeling that conflict you talked about so much between the polarities of legal justice and moral justice? Was your mind already made up that afternoon before you went back to the police station with Raj to confirm your witness statement, to identify this thief and press charges and set all the official—and relentless, you must have known—wheels of justice in motion? I don't know.

But what I do know is that later that evening when the police brought the thief into the waiting room for you and your son to identify, he no longer looked anything like the dapper man you saw hours ago enjoying a ride in a rickshaw. His clothes were ripped, and he stood there, hardly conscious, bleeding from his nose and mouth, one of his eyes bruised shut, skin split along the eyebrow, looking like a piece of ruptured, overripe fruit. Half conscious, he swayed in the constable's arms. He had been beaten into confession.

When he saw you, he managed to break free of the constable's arms. He threw himself at you, begged for forgiveness and for you not to press charges. And there's something so elemental about this moment. Repentance, the father, the crime. It's a scenario as old as humanity.

You forgive him. You don't even think about it. You refuse to press charges and the thief walks free.

That night, you have a rare argument with Avinash. There was a pattern to your life—your generosity toward S.L., yes, but with strangers, too, as well as your clients, not to mention more distant family members, minor relations who would at times show up randomly, looking for a handout—and it would have been hard not to read this thief, who you invited into your house, trusted, and forgave when he betrayed you, as an acute example of that pattern.

It's not that Avinash's kindness isn't also extensive. She was always willing to help her own family and yours, always willing to see how need and want drives us to do things we wouldn't normally do. Like you she understood what it meant to go without.

But that night her frustration boils over. I imagine her putting her hands on Nanhi's shoulders and looking at you, her voice quiet but red hot: "Why don't you ever learn from your past experiences? How can you just let that man go without punishment?"

And how did you respond? Surely by saying something about human suffering, about circumstances, perhaps, but more than anything, in the end, how it simply wasn't worth it, this man's suffering, prison, for something so trivial as stolen material possessions.

But it was the principle, I think this was the case Avinash was trying to make, that you can't just let people take from you, from your family.

I see her point. I also see yours.

*　*　*

"One foot in the world and one foot out of the world." This is how Brij describes your disposition. I see this in the way your duty tethered you to the practical and concrete while your generosity left you floating above it. Your doors were wide open, figuratively, and literally, and yet you fiercely guarded your family and your community. If there was one conflict that ran through your life, it was in the contradictions that arose from these two sensibilities, those times when your generosity interfered with your sense of duty.

There's a very human dilemma here. Part of coming to terms with living in this world is learning how to balance generosity and self-interest. On one extreme is absolute vulnerability. The other is life lived on the defensive, always on guard and closed off to others. To find that balance between these extremes is to learn to make judgments, small and large wagers on when to open our doors to others and when to close them. "I'm generous with people who are deserving," is how Raj has put it to me. He doesn't invite just anyone into his life, doesn't give without first knowing the person is worthy of giving to. He learned this by watching you, Baij. From a young age he saw your generosity exploited, and because of this, he is watchful and mindful of the thief. It's a lesson one way or another we all must learn.

But why didn't *you* ever learn? In the heat of the moment, I see the relevance of Avinash's question. But in the cool appraisal of your life as you lived, I think you did know. I think you did learn. I think you always had known. I say this because you weren't a poor judge of character. If anything, you were the opposite, discerning, perceptive. You knew S.L. would keep being S.L., and you must have known what you were courting when you invited a stranger into your house. For me, this changes the question from why don't you ever learn to why didn't you act differently.

Your answer? With S.L., in part, your answer was your sister. Your loyalties were with family and she was family. This meant dealing with S.L. Do your duty. Period.

But I think there was another answer, too, and I think it goes like this: You understood that life is a thief. A generous thief, but a thief nonetheless. A thief that gives you love and family and health. A thief that gives the very thing it exacts: life. For someone who was so pragmatic and operated within the concrete realities of duty and responsibility, I think you also understood and acted with the knowledge ever-present that life takes what it gives. That's what it is to live with one foot in the world and one foot out of the world, isn't it? To fully grasp what it means to be here is to fully grasp that you can't take any of this with you when you leave.

There's something liberating in this, isn't there? Go ahead, take it. You can have it all. It's not mine to keep anyway. I have nothing to hide and I will walk through this world with hands open—not to better take what's mine but to give what will be taken from me anyway. I'm not sure if this was what you felt, but I can say that when I think of your life, I feel the pull of this point of view. It's not complacency. It's the acceptance of impermanence. I also feel the inverse of power in this position. If I have nothing to defend then I have nothing to fear, and the less I must guard the sturdier I become. Did you feel this too?

I've been trying to put this into practice, mostly with my relationship with E. At times I feel myself giving up the desire to control the outcome of what I hope will happen with the two of us. This is difficult. The pull of desire coupled with uncertainty has always been a deeply unsettling combination for me, and during those moments when I feel the trust E. and I are building run headlong into hesitation on her part, my inclination is to seek reassurance. But there are other occasions: When I have exhausted myself writing about you and your life and I'm too tired to analyze my last interaction with E., I sometimes feel myself letting go.

Whatever happens, happens. I can't change how E. feels about me. Giving myself over to these truths isn't just vitalizing, it's affirming, the way forfeiting the desire for control is a reclamation of control. It's a reminder that control is within and not out there. It's in these moments of ceding ground to larger forces that I feel myself reestablish my own ground. I think I am learning this from you, but where I struggle most is in not letting acceptance curdle into something darker, like nihilism. The seductive draw of acceptance either threatens to carry me away or I'm rip-corded back to earth by desire.

"Balance," I hear you say. "Balance."

One foot right here in this world and the other out there, above it. If this was your dance, as your relationship with S.L. went on, he would become your most difficult partner. As he pulled you one way and then another, his presence continued to threaten that delicate balance you were otherwise so good with.

S.L.'s last disappearance starts just like the others. At first he's gone for a couple of days and then days turn into weeks, and then, for the first time, a week turns into a month. Toshi has reached a new low. Complete despair turns into something darker as one month turns into two. Again you try to comfort her, to offer reassurance, but at this point you have your own doubts, and this in itself is difficult. Because you are a man of such certainty, doubt is a foreign state to you. You had this faith in yourself, in your ability, and you had a larger faith in the individual against the world. That people are capable of overcoming whatever obstacle presented itself felt like a universal truth to you. You had this belief in yourself and humanity and yet, perhaps for the first time in your life, as two months turn into three, you must have had to reckon with the difficult fact. This might be a problem you can't solve.

Still, you try. You begin asking questions, looking for answers. You've lived and worked in this city for well over two decades now, and your contacts are extensive: the police, criminals, shop keepers, Muslims, Hindus, Sikhs. You know everyone and you ask everyone the same questions. If they have seen S.L., if they have heard anything, anything at all.

Much of what you are told is one variation or another of what you already know: that S.L. was using his taxi company to smuggle drugs. The police were aware of this and were watching him, keeping tabs on him, until he disappeared. It stops there. That's all they know. Months turn into half a year, and your sister and her daughters are now entirely your responsibility. But it's more than this, too. The ambiguity of S.L.'s disappearance is a burden of its own for Toshi, and she carries with her an atmosphere of grief. You know, in part, this is because she has no answers, no closure.

Between court cases and your work, between your obligations to your own family—taking care of your parents, being there for your own children—you are now increasingly torn away by this other task, following tips and clues, talking to people on the streets: a stranger who you hear from another stranger who may or may not know something, or a wayward police officer, corrupt, perhaps also smuggling drugs. They offer cryptic clues that fold back on themselves, circuitously trailing back to where you started. I imagine you following strange men into dark alleys, calling after them, only to have them shrug off your questions. Avinash begins to worry. How could she not? You are also disappearing, there but not there, preoccupied as you have never been. "If S.L. owed money," she says to you, one night, "and whoever else is looking for him finds out that you're connected to him, that you have money…"

As you have tried to calm your sister you try to calm your wife. Nothing can happen to us, you say to her. Nothing *will* happen to us.

* * *

In so many ways you were vulnerable during Partition and when you lived as a refugee. You were vulnerable to illness, to violence, to starvation. You were vulnerable to a political context that you had so little control over. But there's something about this period in your life that cracks open a different kind of vulnerability in you, the vulnerability that comes with trying to protect your sister who you care about and love, as well as the vulnerability that comes with being torn away from other people you care about and love—your own children and Avinash. The more you give looking for S.L., the less you are able to give to your own family, and this is the vulnerability of being torn in two directions at once.

Rashmi is quickly becoming of marriageable age, and this requires preparations and arrangements from you that you now aren't always able to meet because of S.L. Additionally, Brij is home from The Doon School, having graduated, and you are worried about him. Against all odds, you were able to send him to that most elite and selective school. Up until this point, this is an accomplishment unparalleled in your life. As a refugee when you had nothing, to tell yourself that you wanted to send one of your children to a school that was prohibitively affluent and selective, and then years later to make this happen, is astounding. But now you are worried about Brij, and it's true that Brij needs you. He needs your guidance and he needs your attention and I think you knew this.

Out of all your children, it's Brij that you have the most tension with, perhaps, in part, because he is most like you in his social precociousness and cha-

A stock photo of a Hindustan Ambassador.

risma. The way he holds court like you do, the way he can talk his way in and out of any situation. This worries you. You are aware of the liabilities and seductions social fluency pose, the temptations of power it creates, and already this is creating problems for Brij, small conflicts, nothing major, but you notice it and it worries you.

Brij wants to move to Delhi, where many people his age are moving, where there seems to be more opportunities and adventure, but because you are worried about him you want him close by. You want him to live with you so you can keep an eye on him, so you can try to shape him, teach him, develop his character where you think it is lacking, give him the moral instructiveness that you feel he needs. But your time is so limited, so strained in your increasingly demanding efforts to find S.L.

You have Brij run the taxi company S.L. left behind, but even this, the logistics of it, are overwhelming for the seventeen-year-old Brij. Eventually all he can do is sell the cars, yet another one of S.L.'s businesses, with your financial backing, irreversibly sunk.

So you are pulled in one direction after another, one moral obligation tearing you away from another. You get a tip that S.L. was spotted in a small town, near the Nepalese border. The next day you go there, taking the train, and you spend the day in this middle of nowhere village, standing out on dusty streets, talking to strangers, showing them your single photo of S.L., describing him as people shake their heads that they've never seen him. It begins to feel like another dead end, until right before your train home you ask one last person, going through the script passively, describing S.L.'s car and then S.L.—"handsome, hazel eyes, about this tall"—when he tells you, yes, he's seen the car, at the end of a road, way up in the foothills of the mountains. You ask more questions: When? Where, exactly? What road? You keep pumping this man for information, excited, and he keeps telling you what he's already told you as you write it down in your small, pocket-sized notebook.

You miss your train home. You get in late, two, three in the morning. Rather than wake your family, you wait out the night in the Lucknow train station, and I imagine you there, alone, those darkest hours of night, eager to follow this new tip, but it also must have felt ominous, knowing that S.L.'s car was abandoned on some forgotten road. I imagine you pacing on the train platform, waiting for the first sign of daybreak.

When you get home, Avinash is boiling over with concern, anger too. "Where were you? You didn't come home! I was worried!"

Her words echo Toshi's except instead of S.L. that didn't come home, it's you.

You try to explain that you didn't want to wake her, you try to explain that you were safe, that you are all safe.

"Next time I'm coming with you," Avinash says.

This isn't something you can argue with.

Chote Lal, your new driver, is at the wheel of the Hindustan Ambassador, you are in the front seat, and Avinash sits behind you. It's hot and because of the heat the windows are down. The sound of the Ambassador cuts through the silence of deep jungle, the undercarriage occasionally bottoming out on a rut, a rogue pothole. Mottled sunlight twists across the road, shadows crawl up and over the hood as Chote Lal slowly navigates, and there's the smell, the overpowering smell of decay, of soil and tree rot heavy in the summer heat.

The dirt road you are on is more desolate than what you could have imagined and the whole car must have been full of doubt, your own, certainly—why would S.L.'s car be hidden on some jungle road? Why would S.L. have been out on some hidden jungle road at all?—but also Avinash and Chote Lal, their tense uncertainty. How far will you follow this road? In the car the three of you are silent.

You drive all afternoon, at times Chote Lal stopping the car, the two of you getting out to clear fallen branches, pushing aside a toppled tree, the ticking engine swallowed up by silence. Finally, the road narrows. It's nearly sunset now. And then there's S.L.'s car, ransacked, doors still open.

It makes you feel crazy, finding S.L.'s car like that, knowing that you were close to offering Toshi something, even if only closure. You and Avinash go back, Chote Lal driving. You search the car again, this time in the daylight. You comb through the glove box. You pull up seat cushions. You tear up floor panels, your fingers worn raw. When you find nothing, you turn to the jungle—that dense, green-black tangle of relentless vegetation and insect noise. You rip through the undergrowth while sun sifts through the impossible canopy above you. Still you find nothing. Chote Lal drives you and Avinash back again. And then again and again you come back to S.L.'s car. Your driver and your wife wait in the Hindustan Ambassador while you hack new paths deeper and deeper into the jungle, sweating and starved for more clues.

When you return you are lacerated by the thick foliage, sucked and bruised by leeches, empty-handed. You hear from someone, somewhere, that somebody had seen a body in a river near S.L.'s car. You find the river and follow it, patrolling downstream and then back up like some old tribesman alert to every noise and change in the wind. Still nothing. You go back, and each time you do you are pulled further away from your own family obligations, your daughter, Rashmi, having finished college now, the meeting of potential husbands postponed one after another, and Brij, increasingly distant, moody. You are a man split in two, further halved by competing obligations, and all of your children have told me, this is the thing that almost broke you, that almost brought you down.

What is character? This is the question I used to always ask my students. If stories are ultimately about characters and conflict and change, how do you identify that elusive bundle of attributes that makes someone who they are, that makes them tick and act and fight for what they want and believe in? You find out what they are most afraid of. And then you make them face whatever that thing is. This is how you understand someone's character.

Since I was young, I had always been afraid of losing my mind, of losing my cognitive abilities and control of my own interior space. Since I was young, I had always been afraid of physical suffering. But when I became sick, I realized that what drove my grief, perhaps more than all of that, was the feeling that I had become a failure, the shame of having worked so hard to be the person I badly wanted to be only to find that person gone in a matter of months. This is what scared me the most, and I fought against this. People turned away from me, yes, but I also pushed them away because I didn't know how to deal with having built my sense of self around these markers of success—publishing, teaching, intellectual superiority—only to find them untenable. What I learned from being sick is how bound up my own fears were with my ego, with my sense of identity, but even more significantly, how fragile that sense of identity was.

If I were a character in a story—and I am; I'm a character in my story—I would mark that period of illness in my own life as that which didn't almost break me, but did, in fact, break me. I would mark it as the period where I had to face the thing that I am most afraid of and learned something about my character that I didn't like—that so much of my suffering was ego driven. I've always known about fear, and I came to think of my own experience with illness as an object lesson in narrative theory.

But with you it was different, Baij, and this is the important thing that I'm trying to get at, that I'm trying to make sense of and understand. If you were a character in a story—and you are! You're a character in this story that I am telling!—your search for S.L. would say something about your character because it's the period in your life that does almost break you. It's the period in your life that pushes you up against your biggest fears, even more so than Partition, which amazes me. But your fears were different than mine. Your fears weren't about *you*, as mine have been about *me*. Your fears were about others, being able to care for your family and provide for them while also being able to look after your sister and be there for her and protect her.

And I keep wondering about all of this in relation to the writing itself of your story, in relation to me telling your story. I think there is something in telling your story that can allow me to enact what I admire about your selflessness. So much of how I've thought about telling your story has involved *my* abilities to tell your story. So much of my anxieties around telling your story have been about *my* capacity to do so. I keep wondering if *I'm* the same writer I was before I got sick. I keep wondering if *I'm* going to be able to tell your story the way *I* want to tell it. But I also realize that these fears are the same kinds that I had to let go of when I was sick. They're about my ego. About me and mine. But if I relate to you and simply try to understand your story for its own sake, I'm moving closer to who I want to be.

This is both the irony and a truth about your life I'm trying to articulate. In living for others, I think you did live for yourself. In being there for others, I think in some very real ways you were there for yourself. It was how you located *your* integrity. Trying to relate to your story for its own sake and not because it will indicate my success or failure is, in a way, to locate my own story and retell it through yours.

So you never did find S.L. You look for him for two years, and you were never able to give your sister what you had hoped to give her: closure.

But there must have come a breaking point for you, maybe in the middle of one of those twelve-hour days baking under a snarl of vines and afternoon sun, your hands calloused, your neck welted red and raised where mosquitoes stuck you, your feet soaked and raw in the muck of your own sweat mixed with dirt, maybe in a moment of utter depletion you stopped just long enough to hear the echo of your panting, looked up through the tent of leaves at a barely visible sky, and thought, "What am I doing? When will this stop?" And then realized. It won't stop. Not until you do.

Or maybe it was something simpler, even more obvious. Maybe it was just that after two years of searching, one day you came home, exhausted, and seeing that your life was right there, in 63 Pandariba, where your dad smoked his hookah incessantly, where your wife warmly joked with you in the kitchen, where your kids—even moody Brij—still needed you. Maybe one day you come home and the pure weight of this hits you like the most obvious thing there was. S.L.'s disappearance was leading to your own.

But here's the thing: S.L. only thought about himself and in some ways his selfishness is what led to his disappearance. His obligations to his own children and his wife, your sister, didn't stop him from squandering opportunity after opportunity. But unlike S.L., you couldn't disappear because you just had to be there for others. You had family who needed you. You had children and a wife who needed you. You had clients who needed you. But I think you needed them too. You needed them so that you could be there *for* them. And there's vulnerability in this.

"Where is your character most vulnerable?" This is another question I would ask my students. "If you know where your character is vulnerable, if you know what they care about, if you know what *matters* to them, then you know what kind of character they have." Your family mattered to you, and I think they mattered so much and in such a way that when you went back to them you went back to yourself.

I keep thinking about this paradox of living for others and finding yourself in doing so. I keep thinking about it and the vulnerability in it because when I was sick I, too, almost disappeared, and now I am trying to return to myself, to find myself again. But the more I fixate on what I lost the further I sometimes feel from finding the new life I want, a new way to live, a new self to be in the world with again. But now I have this work, this writing. This is the other point I'm trying to articulate. Now I have your story to tell, and if I were a character in it, the one I am writing right now—and I am! I'm the narrator!—this is where I would be most vulnerable, because I think in a strange way, I need you and your story, and I need your family to need me to tell it. How else am I going to pull myself out of my own jungle?

> *"Smile at obstacles,*
> *welcome them,*
> *overcome them."*

Brij, 1982.

4

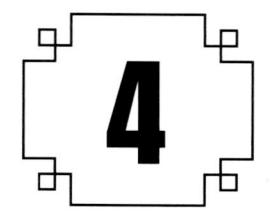

STORIES, FATHERS, AND LABYRINTHS

But not everyone makes it out of the jungles in which they find themselves. When I think about how you were stuck in your search for S.L., it calls to mind those places in my life when I've been stuck, but it also makes me think of my own dad, his affair with my mom, the situation he created for himself. "They were both caught in the same karmic circle," is how Raj put it when I brought this up with him. My dad with his wife, Donna, how he fell deeper and deeper into a maze of circumstances he had created and to which he then had to respond. You with S.L., how you kept responding to him and in turn created more situations you had to manage, more conflicts that required your attention.

"It's almost like being in a labyrinth," Raj had said, and that's how I've come to think of it: Your life and my own dad's running parallel—not necessarily in terms of moral content, but in the way both of you found yourselves in situations where your decisions created the labyrinth with which you had to contend. The difference is that you were able to find a way out of yours, to disengage with your search for S.L. before you lost yourself in it entirely. I don't think this was true of my own dad.

In the same way that I have stories about you in your labyrinth, how and when it started with S.L., what those first choices were like, I also have stories about my own father, and the choices he made that brought him into his own labyrinth.

Since I was young, my mom had told me the story of how they first met: She was in college, a student working at the restaurant my dad owned. He was married to his second wife, Donna. Donna was the woman he had an affair with during his first marriage. My dad had a history of affairs, and I know that his dad, too, was something of a playboy. Friends with Hugh Hefner, my grandfather spent time in the Playboy Mansion, and when my dad was younger, hardly even a teenager, my grandfather would sometimes take him along. My mom always speculated about how this affected Chuck, if it forever colored his relationship with women.

The restaurant my dad owned was called, "The Sprouted Seed." My mom was twenty-two years old, and my dad hired her on the spot. "He had this draw for me," my mom had told me, and I knew what this draw was. Chuck was a Lutheran. He was a Sunday School teacher. But he also had this sort of JFK quality, and for my mom, the draw of attraction to Chuck was that he felt a little like both of her own fathers.

You see, my mother was also a product of an affair. My grandmother was married to a man named Silas and having an affair with a man named Bill when she became pregnant with my mom. Even though my grandmother knew that Bill was the father, she told everyone that it was Silas. Eventually, my grandmother left Silas and married Bill, yet she continued to hide the history of their affair, lying to my mom and Silas, promising that he was the father. She lied for twelve years, and for twelve years, Silas helped raise my mom as his daughter, sharing custody.

My mom didn't like Bill; and she thought of him as her stepdad, but then on her thirteenth birthday, my grandma told my mom that Bill was her real father. It devastated my mom, left her confused, but Silas remained in her life, and continued to treat her like his own daughter.

They were completely different men. My mom's fathers—my grandfathers. On the one hand, Silas was literary, a political science major from Berkeley, and when I was younger, he would record himself reading books to me and then send me the tapes. "Your time with grandpa," is how he would start the recordings.

I can imagine you doing something like this for your grandchildren. While my own dad's conflicts with women had the same labyrinthine quality as your conflicts with S.L., it's my mom's dad, Silas, who I think was most like you. His sense of duty and obligation toward my mom, his insistence that he continue to raise her as a daughter, even after my grandmother revealed the truth about her affair, strikes me as the kind of choice you would also make—though I'm not sure choice is the right word. The sense of duty that Silas felt toward my mom and the sense of duty that you felt toward your family transcended choice. It was just what you did.

Bill, on the other hand, was a used car salesmen. He was a Lutheran, and had the puritanical and moody disposition that came with it. When he had an affair with my grandmother, he was also married and already had children. Once Bill and my grandmother married, he left his other family behind, and that he left them is the perfect example of what you wouldn't do. To this day I know almost nothing about them. Many of the stories that my mom told me about my dad had always seemed to ricochet around these two men, her two fathers, and the way Chuck, my dad, felt familiar in relation to them.

When my mom first met my dad, from the minute she saw him walk through the swinging doors of The Sprouted Seed while she waited at a table with her resume in hand, she felt the familiarity of her two fathers draw her in, and it felt like fate, that draw, that pull. "There was something about those doors swinging open," my mom had always told me. "And your dad walking out with his white apron around his waist. It almost felt like time slowed down. The doors of fate."

And I can almost hear the restaurant noise, the way the sun shone through the south facing windows. I know that restaurant well. Though it had changed owners and names throughout my childhood, after my dad left, moved back to Southern California with his wife, it stayed a restaurant. The high school that I briefly went to was right down the street. I've walked past and driven past that restaurant hundreds of times, I've eaten breakfast in there more times than I can count, and I know that light, the way the Northern California sun breaks through the fog by mid-morning, casts everything in a watery warmth.

So I know the place and I know what my mom felt when she saw my dad, a feeling of destiny, of fate, the familiarity of her own broken relationship with two fathers circling back, maybe a sense that my dad could fix old wounds.

But there's another thread to it: A few months before my mom got her job at The Sprouted Seed, she had come up to Northern California. Arcata is a small town pushed up against the Oregon border and the Pacific, and she moved there to go to school, but also because her brother, Jeff, was already living in Arcata, already a student at Humboldt State University.

When my mom makes the move, transferring from Sonoma State, what she feels more than anything is a sigh a relief. She is out of the Bay Area, away from her parents, away from her childhood, so fraught as it was with half-truths, the lies about her fathers, and an underlying feeling that she simply didn't belong. One of four children, two from my grandma's first marriage and two from her second, with Bill, my mom always felt like the black sheep. One of her first childhood memories is a moment when she was looking out the front room window, at the cars going by, and feeling homesick even though she was at home. I've seen the photos of the house where my mom grew up, and she's told me about the tension, the stain on the kitchen wall that never completely came out from when Bill threw a casserole dish mid-screaming match with my grandma.

My mom desperately wanted to leave all that behind, and so now finding herself six hours away, tucked behind the redwood curtain, under the cover of that Northern California fog, she felt, for once, at home, like she belonged.

One night during those first couple of weeks in Arcata, my mom goes to a party. Her brother, my uncle, and his band—Jeffery B and the Hot Nuts—are playing. This is the early eighties, a house party, in a liberal college town. There's surely a crowd gathered on the front porch, trading cigarettes, sharing bottles of beer, and inside the front room is hot, fogged with weed smoke and the low lighting of cheap lamps, and the humid musk of bodies dancing to a band that, admittedly, while fun, probably isn't very good.

But it *is* fun, and my mom is enjoying herself. She loves to dance and that it's her brother's band playing at this small house party makes her feel especially welcomed, the little sister hanging with the older brother's cool friends, and when she laughs—tipsy now and dancing—she throws her head back, her dark hair shoulder length and wavy. How free and vibrant she looks, her olive skin tan and especially so in the party's half-light.

This is when my dad first sees her. He's ten years older than my mom, and what he's doing at a college house party when he's got a fiancé, Donna, at home, I can't say. But there he is, watching my mom.

This is months before my mom will walk into The Sprouted Seed, resume in hand, months before the affair starts. But one night, when the two of them are alone together in the restaurant, closing, he'll mention this night. Maybe he still has his apron on, maybe he's standing at the till, counting money, and maybe he gives her one of his tentative, dramatic looks before he says it: "I probably shouldn't mention this," he'll say. "It might not be appropriate, but I watched you dance one night at a party."

This will catch my mom off guard, but more than anything what she'll remember is how he describes looking for her later that night, how shortly after she left the party, he got into his Volvo and spent hours driving around town, looping block after block, windows down, early fall night air blowing in, searching. "I knew I shouldn't be getting married then," he'll tell my mom that night in the restaurant. "I wanted to find you."

But that night he won't find her.

He won't see her again until she walks into his restaurant. And when he walks through those swinging doors and sees her, it must have felt a little like fate to him, too. The girl he saw and searched for late one night, come back to him.

Whenever I've imagined my dad in this scene, I've always thought of him as selfish. From the beginning, I see him acting on what he wants despite the consequences. From the beginning, I see him as careless. But maybe, in some ways, he couldn't have known exactly how much one choice would change his life. Maybe, in some ways, he was like you when you brought S.L. back to Lucknow. Two choices—his, yours—and neither one of you could have seen the full outcome and trajectory of those choices when you made them. That's the nature of life, isn't it? We know not what we do. Except of course for those times when we know exactly what we do and we do it anyway. Where my dad's choice lands on these two extremes I can't quite say.

Shortly after my mom started working at The Sprouted Seed, Chuck enlists her to babysit for him and Donna. They have a son, Chaz, who will soon be my half-brother. In those early months, my mom goes to Chuck's house to watch Chaz so that he and Donna can go out. My mom has shown me the house where my dad and Donna lived, where she babysat, a one-story craftsman on the corner of 11th and K, with a red door and a small porch. I've imagined my mom in that house, putting Chaz down for a nap. Though their affair hadn't started yet, she must have wondered what it would be like if the baby were hers, if she were in Donna's place.

But if she does wonder this she forgets it quickly, or pushes it aside. She likes her job at The Sprouted Seed. Her life is good. She likes her classes. She takes Russian Lit, discovers Tolstoy, is captivated by Anna Karenina, Anna's affair with Vronsky erotic and poetic. She meets friends, a guy named Cedar in her History class who wears Birkenstocks and smokes weed constantly but somehow remains articulate and engaging, somehow is able to remember the order and anfractuous deviations of the Tutor succession, the important dates leading up the Russian Revolution.

As you knew as well as anyone, there's excitement in building a new life, in starting over, even when new beginnings are borne of hardship or upheaval. Just as I have pictured a kind of happiness and contentment for you during those early days in Bhopal House, I think of this period in my mom's life the same way. She was leaving behind her past and finding her feet in a new world.

She meets Cherise, who will become one of her lifelong friends, in a psychology class, and they move in with each other, a small, two-bedroom apartment in a cul-de-sac of slumping apartments where I will grow up. On the weekends they go to The Alibi and listen to live music and come home late smelling of smoke and sweat. I think what my mom must have felt more than anything was a sense of freedom and possibility and the sense that she had finally outrun her childhood.

And then it starts.

I imagine my dad one impulsive night. He tells Donna that he has to go back to work, maybe clean or take care of a kitchen repair before the start of the next day's breakfast shift. I imagine him conflicted, driving around town, somehow knowing at this point where my mom lives, but not yet letting himself drive by her house. I imagine him in his Volvo, tense, vibrating with desire, but also somehow knowing what he would do, that he didn't even really have to think about it. He simply found himself driving closer and closer to my mom's apartment, and then, just like that, he's there, parked out front.

He turns the car off, sits there for a minute, the excitement and romance of knowing he was about to make a mess of his marriage and my mom's life—the freedom in chaos. He is unable to stop himself, or simply doesn't want to. And yet, he is making a choice here, I have to remind myself that, though it may have not felt like it. He takes the first step into his own maze.

It must have been late, after midnight. He gets out of his car. My dad was tall and muscular, and there was something about him that was always a little unhinged, my mom has told me, so I imagine his shadowy figure, bulky and determined, head bent forward, slightly frightening, a little mad. He inches up to my mom's window, presses against the glass, listens to see if my mom is awake. When he doesn't hear anything, he raps on the window, at first quietly and then when she doesn't wake up, a little louder.

And so it begins.

There's something cliché about all affairs. The desire masquerading as need, as necessity, and the language around this equally trite.

My mom opens the window and there he is, a little crazed, the Sunday School teacher who can't exorcise his own demons, her boss, that strange feeling of destiny, something familiar in it all.

"What are you doing here?" my mom says.

"I had to see you," he says. "I just had to."

I keep wondering what role the stories we tell ourselves play in the choices we make. Do we get lost in our stories or do we get lost in our circumstances, our choices? Is there a difference?

You had a story you told yourself, and I keep thinking about how it related to your relationship with S.L. At times you told this story seriously, and at other times I think you told it as a joke. Not that jokes aren't serious. Nothing is more serious than a joke.

You told this story to your family—your children and your wife, and you told it to the people who were close to you. In this story you were four years old, at least according to one telling, and you're at your mom's side, walking with her out into an open field. It's mid-afternoon and in that field is a peepal tree—the lineaments of its trunk braided, the limbs outstretched, offering shade—and under this tree is a holy man, meditating.

You and your mom are there to pay respects. There's the exchange of food, something as simple as bread, passed from your mother's hands to the holy man's, that almost chalky feel of flour loosening onto the fingers. There's a brief silence. And there's an easy breeze coiling the leaves overhead, ticking as they brush together. You catch the holy man's attention. There's something about you. Something about your presence. "This boy is blessed," the holy man says. "He will have many close encounters with death, though death will not take him. And his life will be like a banyan tree. Many creatures will enjoy his shade, but he will be in the sun."

You told this story, or some variation of it, again and again. That night you forgave the thief and Avinash, frustrated, asked if you'd ever learn, you threw your hands up in the air, as if bowing to fate, as if acquiescing to what's already been written. You said, "What can I say, I'm like a banyan tree." You said the same thing when Raj, older, an adult now, asked you the same question, the specifics different but the pattern the same. Your generosity overflowing and someone taking advantage of it, mostly likely, in this case, S.L.

"When will you learn?" your son asked you.

"What can I say," you answered. "I'm like a banyan tree."

You would also draw on that other thread of the holy man's prophecy, that you'd encounter death many times, but death wouldn't take you. You would reassure others with this story, and maybe even yourself, when you needed to feel safe. You told it to your wife and children while you were all living in the big house on 63 Pandariba to reassure them that the latest round of threats over the eviction case you had been working on would come to nothing, even though you still took precautions. You had at least two bodyguards, formidable and serious men, with you at all times, careful always to take new and creative routes to work.

"Nothing can happen to me," you'd say, and you'd say this same thing to Avinash during those dark years when you searched for S.L.'s body: "Nothing will happen to me." I wonder, too, if on that train ride, back into Pakistan while you

The Lucknow Lawyers' Association, 1963-64. Photograph taken on the annual general meeting, held on May 2nd, 1964. Baij is in the third row, second from right.

A lawyer protest in the sixties, Baij front right.

held your Sikh companion's hands as he slept, if you told yourself, "I'll be safe. Nothing can happen to me."

But the thing is, the holy man's words were true of so much of your life. There was the time, for instance, with the cobra, your first dance with death. There was a time at the river. Still a boy, you were pissing off the bank of the Chenab, and the image of what happened is almost funny, like a Norman Rockwell from another time, another country—"dunked while peeing"—until it wasn't funny at all. The river was swift and powerful, the way only deep water can be, and just as you slipped in, just as you were sucked out into depths still black against the dawning day, somehow, someway, an eddy, a passing current that felt almost willful, at least in hindsight, gave you a stern shove, almost a reprimand—"you don't belong here"—and pushed you up on the shore again.

And similarly, there were all those ways you were so giving, so generous, the way people in need would find you and the way you would always offer them shelter. You were like a banyan tree. But was the evidence there because you were told a story that trained your eye on what to look for, because you were told a story that guided your actions? Or was this who you would always be anyway, the holy man's story prophetic and with evidence to prove it?

You asked this question yourself. When Raj was in his early twenties, and working, he happened to get some papers delivered to one of the holy men in Lucknow. In passing, the holy man had commented that Raj would travel overseas, that his fortune was in another country. And later, when Raj told you about this, your response was strange, ambivalent even: "You never know if what holy men say is true or influences you for it to become true." It's hard not to think of this as a comment on your own relationship with the stories you were told by your holy man.

A literature professor of mine once told me that when a holy man appears in a story, pay attention. I think he said this because prophecies highlight the ways stories work on us, how they guide us toward certain perceptions and actions, and how this can feel like fate. Maybe it is fate. Maybe it isn't. The point is that stories have a certain binding quality. You can become stuck in stories, lose your agency to them. They have a certain gravity that can pull us in even when we don't want them to.

When you decided to help S.L., when you decided to take him into your life in Lucknow, I wonder if you drew on the holy man's prophecy that you would be like a banyan tree to explain this choice to your family, but I also wonder if you drew on this story to understand yourself?

This is what we do with stories. S.L. had created competing demands for you. You were stretched to a breaking point, torn between being there for your sister, Toshi, and your own family. That you were like a banyan tree would have been a narrative to help make sense of these two demands. At the same time, that you thought of yourself as a banyan tree might have also helped precipitate the choices that created these demands. It's a cycle that has me thinking of karmic circles overlaid with narrative circles.

In other words, as your choices to help S.L. bound the two of you closer together, I wonder if those same choices also brought you closer to the story you told about yourself. Each time you helped S.L. you *were* becoming more and more like a banyan tree. And when you finally turned your back on S.L. when you finally gave up on looking for his body and giving your sister the closure you hoped to provide, did you also have to give up a story you were telling about yourself?

*   *   *

Unlike your children, Baij, I don't know exactly what kinds of stories my dad told about himself. All I have is guesswork, clues, scattered insights my mom has given me.

But my sense is that my dad needed women to validate the stories he told about himself. My mom used to tell me that, "he couldn't handle his own charisma." I think what she meant was that his charisma drew women to him, and he couldn't resist how intoxicating that was. When I think of him, I think of a man whose identity depended on women desiring him. In the same way that I wonder if your relationship with S.L. drew you closer to the story you told about yourself, I wonder if, for my dad, the more women desired him, the more his sense of identity depended on that desire.

And so, perhaps, like you with S.L., the more my dad became entwined with my mom, he created a labyrinth of circumstances, but he also created a narrative circle he couldn't step out of. There's something in this that feels true to me. When I look at my own life and the labyrinth's I've found myself in, they feel equally constructed out of the choices I've made as well as the stories I've told about myself.

When I was twenty-three years old I wrote my first essay about my dad. As your own children have used stories about you, Baij, to understand themselves, I have tried to understand myself through writing stories about my dad. I wrote this first essay about Chuck when I was just becoming interested in writing. It was a time when I thought what it meant to be a writer was to be unsparing and brutal with everyone in my life, especially myself. It's a short piece, just under ten pages, and it reads quickly, the sentences short, the jumps in time big. When I wrote it, I was clearly still under the influence of Raymond Carver, and the unsparing prose of Richard Ford, masculine writers whom I admired and with whom I wanted to feel a strong affinity, but who sometimes left me feeling cold.

It's still the first two sentences in the essay I'm most drawn to because of their symmetry: "Chuck Horn, that's his name. I met my dad last spring when I was twenty-two, living in Bellingham, Washington, and having an affair with a thirty-one-year-old married woman with two kids." It's this echo of affairs I find myself retracing. First my grandma when she was married with two kids, than my dad when he was married with two kids, and then me with A., also married and with two kids. The possibility that A. told her husband the same lies that my dad told his wife and his children is an irony that's never been lost on me. Still when I think about my own story I feel that pull toward symmetry, that desire to understand myself in relation to the themes and dramas of my own parents.

It's also a point of connection for me between me and my dad. My own recklessness with A. aligned so well with how I had always imagined Chuck's recklessness. There was that line my mom had told me that had become like a mantra when I thought about my dad: "He couldn't handle his own charisma." Over time I began to wonder if this was also true of me, if I needed the same kind of affirmation from women that my dad needed, and because of this if my own story would always run parallel to his.

Like my mom and dad, A. and I met in a bakery. I still think about how she put her hands on mine, showing me how to braid rosemary twists. I felt so at home in the satisfaction of knowing this woman was willing to risk her marriage for me, and I think this is when I learned to associate my dad's desire with a kind of negative of my own, the power and thrill of knowing my mom would follow him through whatever chaos he made of his own life replicated in the intoxicating feeling of my own affair.

If there was a story I told about a connection my father and I shared, this was it. What was dark and violent and selfish in myself was the dark and violent and selfish thing in him that he gave to me. It was a story that had its own element of fate, its own biblical calling: The sins of our fathers will be visited upon the sons. This was what I told myself to understand my affair with A., what I told myself to justify my own recklessness. Like my dad with my mom, each decision I made that brought A. and I closer, the story I told about my dad became closer and closer to the story I told about myself.

And it was a story that couldn't have been more different than the one you told about yourself. But the point still stands. We need our stories, and despite the differences in ours, they illustrate the same need. Without our respective narratives we wouldn't be able to understand our actions and who we are.

It's strange, to be in a place where I am rethinking who I want to be while also writing about two fathers, my own, and you, Baij. It has me thinking about fate and choice. Maybe it's true that the sins of our fathers will be visited upon the sons, but maybe only if the sons use their father's sins to justify their own? Maybe only if the sons tell the same stories their fathers did. I feel the pull of fate but also the draw toward choice when I think about this. They are the two contradictory sides of meaning-making.

Your life had contradictions and tensions just as every life does. As I have come to think of the conflicts that arose for you between generosity and duty playing out within the larger metaphor of having one foot in the world and one foot out of it, I have come to understand the tension in your life between fate and choice traversing this same metaphorical ground.

When I think of you having one foot out of the world, I think of you deferring to fate, of letting go and placing faith in the belief that there is some larger force guiding events and placing them into a context that is so much bigger than what we can know in the here and now. And when I think of you having that other foot in the world, I think of the actions and choices we make—that you made—that do influence the outcome of our lives, as well as the lives of others. It makes me think of the possibility of change.

One foot here. One foot there. It's just a metaphor, but isn't that the point? Through stories we make our lives legible. And what are stories if not complex metaphors? I think that to learn from stories means to understand the metaphors that operate within them, as I am trying to do with yours.

I can never know, exactly, what it was that made my dad unable to stop his affair with my mom, and I'm glad he didn't. It's the reason I'm here. But I also know that it caused so much suffering. His indecision was a source of so much agony for my mom and his wife, Donna. The affair with my mom turned into three years of a protracted back and forth, my dad promising Donna that he would leave my mom and then my dad promising my mom that he would leave Donna. These are painful scenes. How at an airport my mom chases my dad to his gate, begging him to stay; or how after my dad decides to stay with Donna and moves to Southern California with her, he drives the nearly 16 hours back to Northern California, knocks on my mom's door and begs her to take him back. Once she does take him back, the next morning he goes cold, says he can't stay, that he can't leave Donna and his other children. He leaves as quickly as he came.

I can't know exactly what was going through his mind during these points in the affair, but what I do know, what I can say, is what's obvious. He couldn't disengage. He couldn't make different choices, and I can't help but think this was, in part, because he couldn't tell himself a story that offered an alternative. Perhaps one way to understand my own dad is like this: while you had that balance between one foot in the world and one foot out, he couldn't find that balance. His actions were either completely out of his hands, fatalistic, or the opposite—all choice with no concern for anything bigger than himself, with no perspective beyond his own desires.

*　*　*

Stories are in the details, and to reconsider a story is to reconsider the details. I keep going back to a conversation I had with Ajesh in September. He told me how when you were just a boy, maybe four or five years old, and still living in

Chokkar Kalan, an unspecified illness swept through the village leaving many dead. He told me how one day during this season of sickness, you and your older brother were out playing in the streets, "moving around here and there," the aimless games of kids on a summer afternoon. It was hot, and when I think of this story I think of a stillness too, the kind of heat that slows down time, the kind of heat that swells and rises in waves from the brick-and-mortar houses clustered tightly next to each other. There's an almost fable-like quality to the story: Two thirsty brothers stumble upon an unattended jug of water.

It's hard to know how to stage what happens.

Do you see the body first, only a short distance away from the water, or does your brother? Or maybe you both see it at the same time, recognizing the uncanny here-but-not-here quality of someone who has just died, both you and your brother familiar enough with death to know its presence. And it's remarkable, in a way, your reasoning, at such a young age. As your brother goes for the jug of water, you try to stop him. "Don't drink that," you tell him, recognizing that if that man was sick and drank from the jug it could be contaminated. "You'll get sick," you say. Quick, declarative, certain. This is how I hear you, even as a boy.

But your older brother doesn't listen. What older brother would?

He drinks and, a few days later, dies.

This is Ajesh's telling.

I talked to Raj the next day and he told me the same story about you. But this time it's different, however slightly. Raj was talking to me from his office in Hampton, Georgia, and it was the same scenario: You and your brother, thirsty, the aimless play of young boys in the afternoon heat. But a minor change in detail somehow jolts the picture and erases my previous impressions. Instead of a bottle, Raj told me it's a well—the water just as tempting, the scenario equally ominous, and the dead body only a few yards off. But it's strange how much this one change throws the whole situation into high relief. Instead of a narrow street tucked in somewhere near the center of this village, I imagine you and your brother now at the edge of town.

The image is more myth than fable: Two boys at a precipice, civilization here, wilderness and the unknown there, a dichotomy drawn out by the juxtaposition of youth and death. Why a well rather than a jug of water should bring this out I can't say; maybe there's something more ancient about wells, the associations more elemental. From here the stories merge. You warn your brother not to drink from the half empty water container, the same reasoning remarkable in its foresight, given your age.

But, cavalier as ever, your brother drinks. A few days later he dies.

The point isn't who misremembered what. That's incidental. The point is how slippery stories are, how they can move on their own accord, and how one minute we have control over our stories and the next they have control over us.

But stories are also in who is telling them. You were a father, Baij, but the way I imagine you as a father depends on which of your children I am talking to. Those early months in September and October, when I would talk to Rashmi, your first child, the picture I got of you was of a doting father. She was your first, yes, and so you couldn't help but love her extra for that, but she was also your only daughter and I think she was special to you for that reason, too. You loved to surprise her with treats, as you loved to do with Avinash. As all your children do when I talk to them, Rashmi always mentioned the key values you held, always stressing the importance you placed on education, how honesty was paramount, how generosity and kindness were essential. You didn't deviate from these core values, but there is something about the stories Rashmi tells me that give you an almost mystical quality, a quality that is also echoed in the stories Ajesh tells me about you.

There's the one about how when you were in your early twenties, before Partition and living in Gujranwala, you healed a close friend who had contracted tuberculosis. He owned a small auto-repair shop and when he became sick, it seemed certain that he would die. As his condition worsened, his business began to fail and his family suffered. But you had all this weird medical knowledge, recondite cures that you had read about in dusty books at the medical college in the town over from where you did your undergraduate work. In your time off from your studies, you'd take the train to this other campus and sink into the library there, reading copiously, sometimes attending lectures, simply because you were curious.

During this period of extracurricular study, you had come across a theory about tuberculosis that one could dig a hole for the sick and then bury the patient up to his or her neck. The patient was to spend days like this, weeks even, being tended to and fed while convalescing, the weight of dirt and soil hard packed and regulating each breath. I have no idea why or how this would have worked, but you tried it, digging a large pit for your friend, and then burying him. You held spoonfuls of soup to his mouth when he was hungry, lifted a cup of water up to his lips when he was thirsty, and when you weren't caring for him, you helped his family run his business. And it worked. Somehow this cured him, and by the time his health was restored, you had grown his business, made it more prosperous.

There were other stories like this, too, stories where providence almost seemed to intervene. One morning you give money to someone in need, more money than your budget would allow. You had food to buy and bills due that very evening. You needed that money, but you gave it freely with disregard to your own needs. You did this all the time, but on this particular day, the day Ajesh recalls, he asked you, mystified, how you planned to pay for what you owed later that day, and you answered cryptically like some old sage. "It will come," you said, and sure enough, that afternoon, an old client, someone you defended who owed you money but you hadn't heard from in years, knocks on the door with a glut of cash.

It isn't that Raj and Brij haven't also told me stories that hit this same tenor. They have. But they've also told me stories that depict a side of you that Ajesh and Rashmi's stories leave out. You were also a practical and sometimes stern father, more focused on instruction than indulgence.

Raj told me how when he was a young boy, he found some change on the bus. He pocketed it, as any boy would, and when he came home, excited about his new find, your response is stern, austere. You told Raj that he didn't work for that money, that it isn't his, that money you don't work for isn't money that you can claim as your own, period, end of discussion. It's nearly ten at night, but still you tell him to put the money back on the bus immediately, and so Raj does. Disappointed, he goes out into the night, finds a bus, and throws the change into the open door as it idles at a stop, surely to be picked up by another stranger. But Raj has carried this lesson with him. When recalling this experience, he told me, "To this day, I'm suspicious of windfalls. I don't like it when a business opportunity yields more money than I've worked for."

You were intent on teaching Raj a similar lesson a few years later. A teenager now, he and his cousin, Yash Babu, found a wallet at a park with 200 rupees in

"Use your intellect to do what is right and win."

Brij and Ajesh with Baij in 1966.

130 | Stories, Fathers, and Labyrinths

it. Yash Babu wanted to keep the find a secret because he knew you wouldn't let them keep the money. He and Raj had plans. They would buy a cricket set with the money. But you found out that evening, and your response was predictable. You told them to turn it in to the police station. Yash Babu argued with you. He was one of the few people who could.

"Why the police station?" he said. "Nobody is going to go to the police station to look for their wallet. And besides, the police will just take the money anyway."

This was true. You knew this was true. You worked with the police and knew how corrupt they were. You conceded the point, and then came up with an alternative. You had Raj and Yash Babu make posters advertising the found wallet with your phone number listed, should the rightful owner need to contact you. Then you had them leave the posters all over the park. You were more lenient this time, making them wait two weeks, and when nobody contacted you about the money, you let them spend it. You and Raj didn't know this, but the truth was that after Raj had hung the posters throughout the park, Yash Babu went back and took them all down, as admitted by Yash Babu to Raj many decades later. Nonetheless, your point was the same. Don't take money that doesn't belong to you. Only spend what you have worked for. You are the father as instructor here, the father as moral arbiter.

As the instructor, you were never rigid. The lessons you imparted to your children could be creative, unorthodox. In primary school, Raj's handwriting was sloppy, loopy letters trailing down the page. He was unable to write in a straight line. What you did was hire an art teacher to come to your house and to teach Raj how to draw. "Why are you hiring an art teacher?" Avinash had asked you. "He needs help with his handwriting." After a few months, Raj's writing had improved drastically, his attention to line improved, his hand steadier, one of the benefits of having practiced drawing pictures.

So with Raj, you were the teacher, the instructor, and you imparted one valuable lesson after another. But that isn't all you were. You were also supportive, quick to come to his aid. There's an incident Raj told me about that leaves me envious because you gave him something that I never had from a father.

Raj was away at school, at The Indian Institute of Technology (IIT) in Delhi. He was sixteen and living in the dorms, sharing a room with an Iranian. There was a language barrier between Raj and his roommate, whose native language was Farsi and who spoke only passable English. But still, Raj and his roommate got along fine, good even, sharing brief moments of comradery over their studies as students will.

It was sometime during the second semester that Raj's roommate's transistor radio was stolen. And shortly after that, Prithpal Singh, a professor at IIT Delhi as well as the warden of dorms that Raj lived in, called Raj into his office. Singh sat Raj down and told him, point blank, that he suspected Raj was the thief. Raj was confused, said he had no idea who took the transistor radio but it wasn't him. Pushy and threatening, Professor Singh kept at him, and over the course of the next few days, continued to call him into his office, said he knew Raj had taken it. "Just admit," he said. "Nothing will happen to you if you admit it, but if you don't, you'll get kicked out of school."

Nearly a week passed, and Singh kept at Raj, enlisting other faculty to apply more pressure in a concerted campaign of coercion. Singh would call Raj into his office each day, and sometimes there'd be other students there, senior students—the general secretary of the dorms, student affairs council members—all insisting in a strange, Kafkaesque scene that Raj admit what he had done. "We know that you did it," they'd say. "Admit it."

Raj doubled down, refusing. But he was scared, especially once Singh referred Raj to the Dean of Students, who flatly told Raj that the school would simply expel him if he didn't confess. This was the breaking point for Raj. He skipped his afternoon classes. He called you, crying. He explained the situation, and you listened intently. "Don't worry," you said when Raj finished. "I'll be there in the morning."

That night you took the 9:30 p.m. train, the 29UP, straight to Delhi. You had brought a change of clothes, sharp clothes, like you might wear to court. Having hardly slept, when you got off the train you changed in the station bathroom, combed your hair, washed your face. You were capable of presenting an intimidating presence, and I imagine you that morning, there to defend your son, as intimidating as you could be.

You had instructed Raj not to go to his morning classes, to wait for you in his dorm, and that's what he did. You picked him up at 9 a.m., and then together the two of you walked over to Professors Singh's house on campus. You knocked on his door. Singh answered. You told him who you were, that you were a lawyer and Raj's father.

"Why are you pressuring my son to admit to something he hasn't done?" you asked. "This is coercion and it's illegal, and I want to meet with the Dean of Students and you, today, before noon."

An hour later you and Raj were standing in the office of Mr. Swani, the dean, and you stated the legal facts once again, pointing out that it was a crime to pressure and coerce someone to admit to something they haven't done.

"If you don't apologize right now, I am going to file a case against the university, and you personally." And you took it one step further. You spoke Farsi, as Raj's roommate did, and once you made your case, you asked them to bring Raj's roommate into the office. In Farsi, you asked him if he thought Raj had taken his radio. Raj's roommate shook his head adamantly, saying no, not at all, Raj was his friend and he never imagined Raj doing something like that.

When you were finished, Mr. Swani and Mr. Singh suddenly became very different men than they had been all week with Raj. They apologized profusely. But it's Raj I am thinking about here. "I was so proud of my dad," he told me after he related this story, and that's a wonderful thing to have given a son, the feeling of pride in his own father.

You were proud of him, too. You were proud of him for standing up for himself, for having the integrity to not back down when pressured to admit to something he didn't do. That day before you left, you took him aside and told him this, how proud you were of him. That he did the right thing. I'd be lying if I said I didn't wish I also had a moment like that with a father I was equally proud of.

With Brij you are the sternest, the disciplinarian. You were harsher with him than you were with your other children, and I have wondered about this. You and Brij were so much alike. You knew everyone, talked with everyone, socialized with people who drank and smoked, who were womanizers and criminals, who couldn't care less about education, about culture, art, morals. Though these people couldn't be more different than you, you not only socialized with them, but you welcomed these people into your life. I think you sincerely appreciated their perspective because you were curious about different ways of being in the world. But it was your charisma that drew all of these people with myriad backgrounds to you.

Brij is the same way. Almost every time I talk to him he tells me some new story about a random person who is or who was in his life: His dog walker who is transitioning from male to female, a former girlfriend he had in Alaska who read the bible every morning while Brij laid in bed and smoked copious amounts of marijuana. He has friends who are diplomats and bartenders, friends who are CEOs and weed dealers. This is even evident in the fact that he sought me out, a stranger whom he invited into your family's life to write your story. What Brij has is the kind of social fluency you had and that allows him to move with ease in all these social situations. He also has the charisma you had.

Even in the ways that he isn't like you he still reminds me of you. During one of our interviews when Brij told me that you had no vices, he lit a cigarette himself for dramatic effect. As he inhaled deeply, I couldn't help but note a certain irony. Here's the son enacting one of the ways he is least like you, his own father, and yet in the enactment itself, the way Brij brandished his cigarette as a prop, he indicated the impulses of a natural storyteller. This made me think of how he is like you, his enjoyment of narrative, of a dramatic moment, of taking pleasure in the playfulness of conversation calling to mind how much you also loved to tell a story.

I think you saw all this in Brij, and you understood early on that he was a mirror for yourself. But I think this worried you, too. To rely on charisma rather than integrity, on charm rather than character, could easily become an evasion of responsibility. There was another factor, too. All your children are smart and wildly capable. I know because I've talked to them and have been impressed by each of them. But I think you understood something about charisma and charm combined with intelligence. It has the potential for something very big, and if Brij had this rare combination of attributes, you wanted something big for him. To not realize his potential felt to you like a waste.

It's true that you were quite successful, but beyond caring for your family and making sure that they had everything they needed, you didn't have big ambitions for yourself. You wanted to live comfortably. You wanted your family to live comfortably. But you didn't have serious personal motivations beyond your sense of duty and obligations to your family.

Countless times you would be nominated for judgeships in the High Court of Uttar Pradesh, and just as many times you would turn them down because you could better support your family as a lawyer. There was even a point when you were still living in the Gun Factory and attending Lucknow University Law School, when a visiting professor from Yale offered you a scholarship to go to the United States and study there. But this hardly interested you, not least of all because you wouldn't leave your family or your fellow refugees. You cared far more about your duty to loved ones than you did about conventional markers of success, even though you could have gone far, very far. But you must have known that Brij could go farther, and you wanted this for him, maybe even wanted to live vicariously through him.

You sent Brij to The Doon School in part because you hoped its environment would shape his character, would set him on the path you wanted him to pursue. But Brij wasn't a very motivated student and you were hard on him for this. During his time at The Doon School, he wrote letters to you. You demanded this. You wanted him to keep you updated, tell you what he was learning. When you received his letters, you read them closely. They were poorly written, riddled with grammatical errors and misspellings, loosely constructed sentences.

As lawyers do, you wrote all the time. You understood the power of a well put together sentence, of cadence and clearly formulated ideas. You expected this from your children, but Brij was attending what The Wall Street Journal a half a century later would call the most selective boarding school in the world. To see firsthand, in the letters your son sent you, how feckless such an ostensibly prized education was made you furious.

More maddening though was your suspicion that Brij simply wasn't trying. This was borne out by his report cards. They all said that he was highly intelligent, but he didn't apply his gifts. You would rant to Avinash about this. It would have been perfectly acceptable to you if the report cards said Brij was not blessed as Raj was. We all have our limits and you understood this. But to not apply and realize his potential was unacceptable. So you had to correct the course.

You sat down with a red pencil and marked each letter, correcting mistakes, writing in the margins. Your editorial remarks were incisive and cutting, and then you wrote your own letter, this time to the headmaster, demanding to know how this was possible. How could it be that such an elite institution of serious learning abided such poor writing? Then you stuffed Brij's letters with your editorial remarks as well as your own letter in an envelope addressed to the headmaster at The Doon School and posted it.

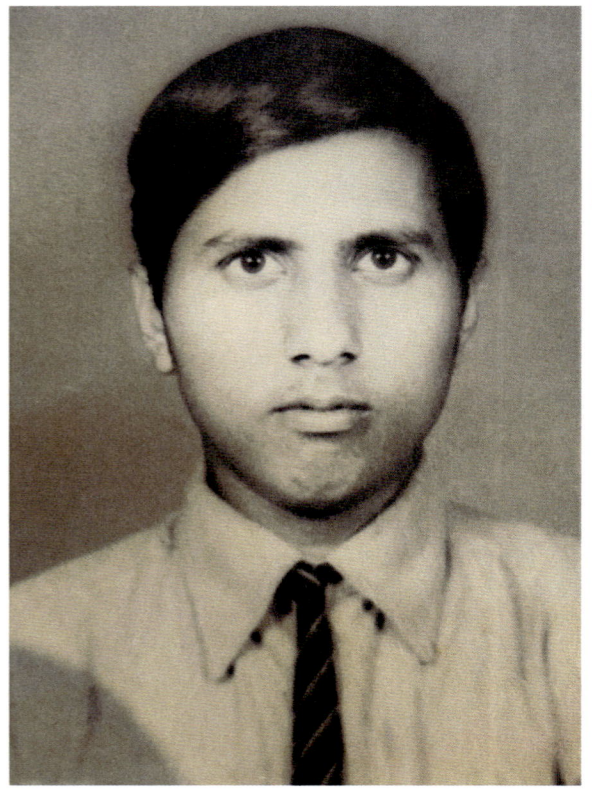

Above Left: Raj in 1975.

Above: Raj, IIT, 1969.

Left: Brij, Doon School, 1968.

When the headmaster received this, he called Brij into his office. He had embarrassed the school, Brij had, and thereafter the headmaster would keep a close eye on him, making his time there difficult.

Not that your letters helped. Out of 80 students, Brij graduated 68th in his class and this stoked your anger even more. He should have done better. He could have done better. When he came home from The Doon School, he was hardly any more cultivated as a student than he was when he started. Increasingly, he was spending time with shifty characters, and you worried that if Brij didn't get on track he would grow up to become a criminal.

He wanted to move to Delhi, but you wouldn't let him. You had him stay home with you, made him live in the big house on Pandariba, and shadow you at work, thinking that you could get him to become a lawyer. During this period Brij attended The University of Lucknow, where you had attended law school. He was seventeen. One evening he came into your office, nervous. He started to explain how earlier that day, after his history class when he was still on campus, talking with a friend, a guy named Shukla came up to them and tried to insinuate his way into their conversation.

You knew who Shukla was. He was an associate of Bakshi, one of the most serious thugs in Lucknow, a criminal with a brutal reputation. Like Bakshi, Shukla was also a criminal. You knew Bakshi because his father was one of the Sikhs who you helped start the trucker's union, your first court case. And because Bakshi had become a trucker like his father and was now part of that same trucker's union, he had great respect for you. He was forever indebted to you because of all that you had done for the truckers in Lucknow.

And now, standing across from you in your office, Brij was asking you to collect on this debt. You listened as Brij explained what had happened, how when Shukla, Bakshi's associate, had come up to Brij and his friend, Brij had made a derisive face. Shukla was fat and funny looking. He was bulky and carried his weight awkwardly. And though it took Shukla a while to realize that Brij was making fun of him, later that day, he came back to campus, looking for Brij, patrolling the open grounds and walkways between buildings with a bat. Brij's friend had called Brij later that day and told him, "You can't come back to school tomorrow. Shukla is going to beat the shit out of you. He's looking for you."

When Brij finished explaining what had happened, you leaned back in your chair and looked at your son. You could tell he was scared. Like this Bakshi, Shukla was known to be violent. These weren't schoolyard bullies. "Can you call Bakshi," Brij asked, hoping that you could bring the whole issue to a close. And you could have. All you had to do was call Bakshi and ask that his associate lay off and he would have done it in a second. This man, Bakshi, when he would see you, would touch your feet in reverence. He would bow to you. That's the kind of respect he had for you because of what you had done for the truckers in Lucknow, for his own father. He was one of the most hardened thugs in Uttar Pradesh and he would defer to you in a minute.

But you didn't ask people for favors. You hardly ever asked anyone for anything. So much so that after you moved into Pandariba and had been living next to the Chief Minister for months, you never once reached out and asked anything from him, this man who was in such a position of power and could have easily offered you all kinds of favors. One morning he knocked on your door and when you opened it the Chief Minister looked at you and said: "The world comes and stands in line to meet me, and you are my neighbor and I have to come here to meet you." You smiled, put your hands together and offered a slight bow. "Gupta Ji," you said. "That's because the world wants something from you."

So you weren't about to call Bakshi to intervene on your son's behalf. But this wasn't just because you didn't ask people for favors. There was something else going on here. You were trying to teach Brij a lesson. I imagine you leaning forward now in your chair, studying your son. "Why should I get involved in this?" you said.

"Because this guy is going to beat me up," Brij said.

"Well you created this problem," you said. "You need to solve it. I'm not going to go to Bakshi and escalate this problem. You need to go and find a way to apologize to Shukla." Maybe you knew Brij would be able to get out of the situation, maybe you trusted that he would be fine in part because he was like you, because he did have a certain social fluency and grace, and with that often comes the ability to maneuver out of difficult conflicts. But still, it was a bit of a gamble. He could have beaten up Brij. After a pause you offered some advice. You knew that one of Brij's friends associated with people like Shukla. "Ask him to set up a meeting," you told him.

That's what Brij did. He had one of his friends who knew Shukla set up a meeting, and Brij apologized profusely, and he was able to diffuse the situation. But it was a stern lesson from a father to a son, and I wonder if you would have been as stern with your other children, not that your other children would have gotten into the same mess in the first place, and maybe that was your point. You were trying to teach Brij something that Brij, specifically, needed to learn. Actions do have consequences and the task is to take responsibility for those consequences, to solve the problems you're confronted with.

When Brij told me this story, he told me he was grateful you didn't help him, told me that he did learn from it, and I couldn't help but feel that flash of envy I had felt from those other stories your children have told me, where you are affirming and supportive. You were harsh with Brij, so much so that there was a period in his childhood when Raj and Rashmi would often try to protect him from you, and it isn't that I would want that in a father, the harshness, the strictness. I think I would struggle with that, rebel against it, but I see the underlying tenor of what you were doing, that it came from a place of concern, of love, and that is something I missed out on in a father, something I didn't have. That I wish I did.

With Ajesh, your youngest child, there is yet another side of you. You were always a storyteller but with him I think of you telling stories the most. It's Ajesh who took over your law practice and carried on your work, and during those days when he would accompany you to work—after Brij and Raj were in the US, and Rashmi was married, and living in Delhi—you talked about your childhood, your life before Partition. I could be wrong, but there's a reflective mood to these stories, to this time, perhaps because your major accomplishments were behind you. With Ajesh, I see you as more relaxed, your relentless drive and bottomless capacity to work mellowing. You're the meditative father in these scenes, imparting, perhaps, a different kind of knowledge than the practical skills you were so eager to give to all your children.

You also became slightly disillusioned in the human capacity to do good as you aged, and to me, this deepens you, rounds out your optimism. Some people take and take and take. This is what you would tell Ajesh on those slow afternoons, driving back from the courthouse.

"That's some people's character," you'd say. "It's who they will always be." This was different from those days with S.L., with the thief, with the homeless man in front of your hotel room asking for shelter whom you welcomed and who took from you. Then you were open to the world, and you still were—you were still generous and always would be—but you saw it differently now. Your past belief in the individual to do good given the right circumstances was now imbued with a harder realism. It wasn't bitterness. You were never bitter. But there was a shift and it didn't come until later, and you shared this realism with Ajesh during those afternoons working together.

Of course, you were all of these fathers. That's what makes you complex, a human. All these stories were true. They all contain aspects of who you were. I think part of finding room in our stories for change is understanding and learning to live with the fact that we already contain multiple versions of ourselves: there is no one single story that captures everything about who we are. I can't know for sure, but I think you might have understood this.

* * *

Baij, 1988.

I watched video footage of you sometime in November, and in the footage you told part of your story yourself. I confess that I was reluctant to watch it. You were starting to become complex, a real human being. I saw you as generous and kind, sure, but I was also beginning to see you as stubborn and difficult. Not authoritarian, but certain of how the world should be and who your children should be in that world. I often thought about your frustration with Brij. I thought about that time Raj had fallen behind on his studies, his reading for History, and you made him stay up all night, splashing water on his face every time he drifted off. You were a strict father, and I realized that as I started to fill out the picture I had of you I was becoming protective of who I thought you were, of how I saw you.

In part, I realized, I was having a hard time telling a story about you because the story I had of you in my mind was becoming more solid, and when I tried to write it, I kept losing something in translation. Details kept shifting, creating what I didn't entirely intend. I worried the video footage would present yet another story that conflicted with the one I had been building, yet another set of details that would alter my picture.

But then again, the difficulties that varying details in your stories posed started to feel like an important detail itself. How many competing stories can a single story contain without becoming incoherent? And is there something good in an abstract moral way in making room for as many stories as possible in one larger story? I think there is, and I think you might have thought this too.

The footage was from 1994. I watched it over a video chat with Raj, who had filmed you. The first shot opens with a view of the big house on 63 Pandariba, a street view. The picture is gravelly, the poor quality a function of the days of camcorders. A couple cyclists pass in front of the camera. There's the sound of traffic. The sky above is hazy but otherwise clear.

At first there's something monochrome in these early shots, browns and tans mostly, even the greens of trees in the front yard somehow less green than in real life, gritty. Raj pans right, then left. There's a flash of a cow on the sidewalk, the sound of a diesel engine firing unpredictably as traffic passes in front of the camera. Then we're back on the house, this time the front view, and it's clearer now, the whole image, the way the light shifts so that the sky blooms from brown to blues, shafts of morning sun forking over the roof. Trees come into focus, become green. Living here seems plausible.

It's the first time that I've seen the house, and it's not quite what I've imagined in my writing. The house and its twin, the Chief Minister's, are each two stories, wide and sturdy, and they both have a modernist look, combined with something austere, almost cold. Over the video call, Raj explains that as a boy living next to the Chief Minister of the state was a big deal, the close proximity to power ever fascinating. And I try to imagine Raj then, riding his Java Motorcycle around Lucknow, smoking cigarettes, the teenager dabbing his cheeks with gasoline from the tank to cover up the smell of tobacco, a habit you would never stand for. But I also try to imagine him at the time of filming, when he's no longer the eager adolescent.

In 1994, Raj was the manager of Business Development at Siemens Energy & Automation and worked at the headquarters in Alpharetta, Georgia, and he has returned home for a brief visit. He has a daughter of his own now, Shelly. She is eight years old and in third grade at Woodward Academy North Campus, a private school in the Atlanta area. He has a wife. Her name is Vandana and she is doing her residency in Psychiatry at Morehouse School of Medicine. They live in a nice 4-bedroom house. Life is busy and hectic as both Vandana and Raj live far away from any family to help out in child rearing. It was hard for you when he left India, but now you must have been proud of him, your first son, come home at the start of his own success.

Raj and Vandana at their wedding, with Rashmi and Arun, 1982.

Stories, Fathers, and Labyrinths

Baij and Avinash bless newlyweds Raj and Vandana, 1982.

Raj and Vandana Wedding, 1982. Raj and Vandana with Gyan Devi, and Baij's sisters – Prakash, sitting, Toshi, Sarla and Rambheji standing.

LIKE A BANYAN TREE | 143

And then it hit me.

As Raj starts and stops the footage again, camera zoomed in on the mason work on the rooftop arch, the place where Raj and his cousin changed the previous family name to yours—Anand—that this particular moment of watching the footage is overflowing with complicated ways in which numerous points in time and details hang together. I'm watching video footage from 1994 in November of 2021, and in this footage you will relate your own childhood from the 1920s, interspersed with moments when Raj recalls his own childhood from the 60s. And then I will freeze all of this when I write it down, sometime in 2022.

Stories are strange, layered things, architectonic, always half frozen and half fluid. But it isn't just time that is layered in this footage. It's language, too. Part of what Raj will do is translate your Punjabi into English for me. And somewhere in all of this I will then translate what Raj tells me into this narrative, the story that I will tell.

Raj starts the footage again, and then we're on the grounds, the property, the driveway. The house gives a strange sense of both openness and closedness, something hermitic about the narrow windows, the clean lines, that modern sensibility combined with an occasional softness, a rounded corner here, an openness under an awning there. Then we're in the downstairs—kitchen, dining room, bathroom—all laid out around an open courtyard, which gives the place a communal effect I like, a sense of shared space.

Raj enters further into the house, and there are voices: Ajesh, still a young man, and his wife, Jyoti, their newborn baby, Anuj, all living with you. From somewhere a dog barks. Raj moves into the kitchen now where Avinash cooks, and it's the first time I've seen her on film. Your wife wears an off-white salwar-kameez, hair pulled back into a tight bun, and she stands at the kitchen counter glancing once at the camera, a subtle smile, maybe a slight glance back toward the man behind the camera, Raj, her son—your son—the familiar Ice Cream Boy gone off to become an American Man and now returned to document the daily comings and goings of a family an ocean apart. She knows him and she knows what kind of advice to give him and when he needs it.

Later, in years to come, after Raj takes over Southern States she will tell him very simply, "Paying workers promptly and well is the most important part of running a business," and it's so simple and straightforward that it's easy to overlook. But it makes me think of the kind of advice she must have given you from time to time, the even and balanced way she must have weighed in when you asked her about her thoughts on a poem, a court case you were working on, what to do about S.L. There's a dignity in this precise advice she will give to Raj, an integrity, and it feels true to how I've imagined her. Now she looks back to the counter, rests her hands there and trains her eyes on the work in front of her, and I can see what her children have all told me. The deliberateness, the quiet thoughtfulness. "I never once heard her say anything stupid in my life," Brij once said.

The camera whips around and I adjust myself on my couch. Raj explains that part of the room where the kitchen used to be is now used for a shrine, and as the camera hovers over the alter with the depictions of Hindu gods, Raj says that "every home in India has a shrine," and I liked that, thinking about all those shrines, each personalized to suit the specifics of family and region but all recognizable under a broader and shared sense of spirituality—little stories inside of larger ones, like Russian dolls.

Then the video cuts abruptly. We're still in the house, but now it's a close-up of a framed photo of Lakhi, Raj's grandfather, your own dad, the man with the hookah who couldn't have been more unlike you, but who, at the same time, was like you, stubborn and sure of himself, just as you were. Raj pauses the video, says that the photo was taken for Lakhi's refugee card. He's handsome, not what I imagined. And for some reason it's hard to match his endless distaste of work, his sole occupation of smoking the hookah, with the face in front of me, chin upturned slightly, proud. He has a very symmetrical face, angular jaw, and his eyes are deep set, contemplative, shadowed under his heavy brow. It's a photo that throws into question my ability to imagine the people I'm trying to write about, and it makes me think about those places where I have failed to do so.

While the camera lingers on the grandfather, there's a voice in the background from some distant room in the house, and it's you, the first time I hear what you sound like. It's true, what your children have said. You had a deep baritone. But we don't get to you yet.

There are two more photos, and the camera jumps to one and then to the other. First, your mother: an old black and white photo. Her head is covered by a dupatta, a loose fabric, but I can see her white hair parted down the middle and tucked behind her ears. She also has deep-set eyes, her face wrinkled by time but not without grace. And then it's a photo of you, your graduating class from

Lucknow University Law School. The camera scans the rows of faces, zooms in on yours. It's hard to make out, exactly, but even in the grainy photo I think I can see a slight smile. You always had a smile, your children have told me, and I think I can see it.

The footage cuts out, cuts in, focuses.

It's this very slight smile that I notice again as the footage places you front and center behind your desk. Here you are. The man who's story I'm trying to tell. It's the first time I've seen you on film, seen your movements and mannerisms.

In the video, Raj asks you something in Punjabi, and then translates the question to me in English: "Please tell me what year you were born."

These first shots move fast, without preamble, but before you answer Raj, you reach up to your collar, adjust it subtly, and then there's the smile again, almost imperceptible.

There are other things to notice, too: Like your father, you're handsome. You have prominent features. Glasses, and your white, receding hair is combed back. You are well-dressed: gray suit-jacket, white collared shirt under a sweater, no tie. I think of something Brij once said: "He liked clothes." And your movements, the way you sit in your chair behind the desk—there's something comfortable in how you move, something distinctly self-possessed. You sit there with the camera on you as if very much at home here, not just in your house and being filmed, but in this world. This is where you belong.

The thing about Raj's question is that there are different answers to it. Your documents, passports, and IDs say 1921, but Raj has told me before that you could have been born as early as 1917. Why the discrepancy? The uncertainty? Raj doesn't know, but when you answer, you say 1917. And then there's that smile, and I can't help a half-hidden smile myself, finding our attempt to translate layers of ambiguity into the specifics necessary for coherence feels almost comical. An uncertain origin story told by a father in Punjabi and then translated into English by a son, only to later be written down and re-imagined by an American stranger, someone who couldn't be more foreign to you yourself, an American boy who doesn't even know the story of his own father. And yet, here we are, moving forward detail by detail.

So you tell your origin story, most of it I already know. Your childhood, education, the snake in the courtyard. The Glass House. The big, open fields of the Punjab of your youth stitched together by deep rivers, wide and winding, in which you would swim.

And then you come to the story of the holy man, the prophecies. As I expected, the story you tell on the footage is different than the stories your children have told me. This catches my attention right away. The way you tell it this time goes like this: instead of going to see the holy man with your mom, it's your grandfather, Radha Kishan, who goes to see the holy man, and it's shortly after you're born. He has your astrological chart drawn up, and then the holy man makes his prophecies. The prophecies are more or less the same but with a few added details: You will have four encounters with death but death won't take you; you will receive a very good education; and you will be like the banyan tree. It was said that you would make a very good living but you won't be able to hang on to the money that you make, and this will be, according to what the holy man told your grandfather, indicated by a birthmark on your right palm, just below where your fingers close when you make a fist. And here you hold up your right hand, point to the birthmark on your lower palm, and make a fist to show that the mark is just out of reach when you clench it.

You go on to say that when you were still a boy, but old enough to check the written records kept by the town priests, you verified that what your grandfather had told you was true.

I know stories change, and I know that each time we tell a story it often changes with the telling, but the story you tell in the footage and the story your children have told me is different enough that it gives me pause. There was also the technical problem it presented, which was that I had already drafted one telling of the holy man, and if I was going to tell it accurately, or at least in some way that was true to your experience, which telling should I use?

I stopped Raj mid-footage, and told him this, that the scene I recently wrote about you and the holy man is different from the one you just told.

Raj thought about this for a minute and there was something in his contemplativeness that reminded me of how I imagine you. "Sometimes he would tell the story about the holy man as he had just told it," Raj says. "And maybe other times he would tell it differently."

I tried to explain something to Raj then, something that I still wonder if you thought about. You used to tell stories, in part, because you thought that they were instructive, because you wanted to teach your children something. And it occurred to me that maybe there was something instructive in the fact that the details of your stories would change depending on the telling, that there was some kind of larger lesson here. I told this to Raj, wondering if maybe he had a sense of what that lesson might be, of what you might have been trying to communicate with the fluidity of the stories themselves.

Again, Raj is quiet, thoughtful, and I had a feeling that I sometimes get when talking to him, that I can't quite read him, can't quite get a sense of how he is thinking about something, and because of this I sometimes worry that I might overstep, insert too much of my own thinking into your story, and I'm not sure if this is welcomed or not. But then your son nods.

"I think the point is," Raj says, "that the stories he told might change a little depending on his audience, but the essence didn't change." Raj pauses again, and then goes on to say that he and his siblings would often question the various tellings of your stories. "We were always struggling with what was true or not true, but every time we probed it…there was enough truth in there to make it interesting. It was not a total fabrication. Nothing was a total fabrication. But it was embellished in his own way."

* * *

Over the months, I've tried to piece all of this together. I keep coming back to this last point Raj made about how you told stories—the way you made room for variations while staying true to the larger story itself, what's essential. Again, it reminds me of how I've come to think of you during those last days searching for S.L. Maybe giving up on S.L. meant you had to accept a variation in your own story, that you couldn't help your sister as you wanted to, that you couldn't always be the banyan tree. And this highlights my own father, as a counter to this, how he couldn't choose for himself, couldn't craft anew his own story.

And yet, there's something unsatisfying in all of this for me, something tenuous, more grounded in theory than in what it means, practically, to be caught in making difficult moral decisions. In crafting our own stories.

I recently talked to Raj about all this one afternoon, how I had come to understand your conflict with S.L., the role of stories, and how making difficult moral choices means contending with how we think about ourselves. It was a warm day and I squinted through the glare at my computer screen while I talked with Raj. I went on about how in some ways it seemed like my dad's inability to make a choice indicated a larger inability to change how he thought of himself, and how perhaps your ability to finally disengage with S.L. signified a larger choice for you, a choice to find space to change your own story.

As usual, your son listened quietly as I worked through this. Over the months, Raj had come to remind me of a former professor from undergrad who would listen intently while I exhausted myself working through an idea, and then offer one piece of incisive insight or feedback that reoriented my thinking.

Raj took a breath.

"I don't know if I would agree with what you're saying," he said, and I could feel that incisive point coming, something I'd overlooked that would help me fill in what was otherwise starting to feel unsatisfying. "After two years of searching, my dad had to sit down and say, it's impossible, I'm never going to find S.L.'s body," Raj said. "He came to that conclusion. But he had the support of people around him. Like my mom, who said, 'you need to get out of this.' That support system is what allowed him to step out of the labyrinth. In your dad's case, it was the opposite. The people around him were not supporting him to accept the fact that he had another child. It was going the opposite direction. Donna was encouraging him to deny the reality, and deny his responsibility. It seems to me that your dad wanted to make the right choice, but he didn't have the support system around him."

This is such a simple point that it catches me off guard for a minute. It reminds me of the last time I had talked to my mom about my dad, months earlier. There were all these letters my dad had written my mom when she was pregnant with me. My mom had always told me how well composed they were, how in some ways he was a deep thinker, a sensitive man with a great deal of feeling. I had always assumed that these letters were about my mom, that most of the content consisted of the typical clichés of an affair like physical desire, passion, but as my mom recalled these letters the last time we spoke about my dad, she said they were often about me. "He couldn't stand the idea of not being a father to you," my mom said. "I think it really hurt him to think about that." She started to cry as she said these things. "Sorry," she stopped herself. "I promised that I wouldn't get emotional. I think he really did care. I think it really did hurt him that he couldn't be a father to you."

To simply summarize my dad's conflict as his inability to choose for himself misses the complexity of what it really means to be lost in confusion of moral conflict. It misses circumstances, the real and lived experience of what it's like to want to do the right thing but to have everything work against you. To truly acknowledge the complexity of the stories we tell ourselves is also to recognize how circumstances can work against are ability to change, to find new variations of who we want to be. We don't just tell ourselves stories. We react and live with the people who inform the stories we tell.

It's not just that you were able to change, Baij. In a way, you were also lucky. You had people pushing you in the right direction. In this sense, I think Raj is right. My dad isn't just a counter example to your ability to change. He was also unlucky in his circumstances. They were working against him.

Raj leaned back in his chair and put his hands together.

"It goes back to dharma," he said. "Dharma is basically pushing you toward thinking and doing the right thing. But you don't just need your own mental capacity to think what's right. You also must act on it. But if you're being prevented from acting on it, you must go into another labyrinth." Raj paused, and then went on to say that as he saw it, there was no choice my dad could have made that would have been the right choice. Either way he would have been estranged from one of his children. Either choice would open the door into another labyrinth. "He was tied down," Raj said. "Like Gulliver by the Lilliputians."

The reference made me smile, the thought of circumstances being tiny little people slowly wrapping their ties around us. It's a strange image, but it feels true. There's something fitting about it.

And then Raj said something that struck me. "Your dad was tied down," he said. "But I still see goodness in him. His intentions were in the right place."

This, to me, seems to reach toward the larger point I've been trying to make but haven't quite been able to articulate.

What does it really mean to make room in one's story?

I can never change what is essential to my own story. I don't have a dad and no amount of shifting details can change that. But there are complexities and details within that story that matter. Which details and complexities I acknowledge is where I have some choice. Making an effort to see where my dad was stuck, where his circumstances resisted his good intentions, where he wanted to do the right thing but couldn't—this is where I have a choice. It's in my choice to see his story informed by larger circumstances that I feel room in my own story to open up. In this empathy for my dad, given his circumstances, it feels a little easier to empathize with myself.

But here's the thing: To miss the role of my own circumstances in all of this would be to miss the point I'm trying to make. In a strange way, Baij, you have become part of my circumstances. Your past, your conflicts with S.L., your life, is the occasion for rethinking my own dad's life, his conflicts with Donna and my mom, and the larger significance of his circumstances.

Would it be too much to say that your story has become a part of my own support system that has allowed me to make certain choices in my own thinking? I don't think it would be.

This is the power of connecting with other people's stories.

Your story is part of my circumstances. But I'm also making a choice to find support in your story. Here, my own action and circumstances come together. And it feels right. It feels like good intentions under the right circumstances. It feels a little like fate. But it also feels a lot like agency. It feels a little like having one foot in this world and one foot out.

I'm not totally sure, but I think, in a way, it might be what Raj calls Dharma.

"Don't owe anything to others."

Avinash, 1984.

Stories, Fathers, and Labyrinths

5

AVINASH AND LOVE, REALITY AND FANTASY

It's true that Avinash was your support system. She was there for you more than anyone else during that difficult period in your life when you searched for S.L.'s body, as she was there for you throughout your entire marriage. But in a way, your marriage to Avinash was an accident, a direct result of the contingencies of history. "If it weren't for Partition," Avinash used to tell Brij. "None of you children would be here." This may sound harsh, but what she meant was simply that before Partition, you and Avinash existed on different socio-economic plains. That was just a fact. Not that you didn't have your own privileges: your own lineage of relative wealth and opportunities had been on your family's side for centuries.

But Avinash's family had real wealth. Substantial wealth. She had affluence beyond what you had ever known. Because of this, at least from a material perspective, Avinash had lost more than you did during Partition. During those first few weeks that Avinash and her family lived in a refugee camp, she nearly starved. "I couldn't hold my hand out to receive food," she had once recalled to Raj. With their great wealth, her family had always been in the position of giving, of being the ones who offered their generosity. After Partition, it seemed like an impossible reality for Avinash to be on the receiving end of charity. It seemed like an impossible reality for her to hold her own hands outstretched in front of her, in need of food.

But she didn't starve. Like you, she was quick to adjust to her circumstances, and she was able to do so with dignity and humility. Despite the vast difference between the marriage she likely imagined for herself before Partition—the marriage her family imagined for her—and her married life in a refugee camp, she adjusted with grace. And you must have noticed this right away. Before she married you, Avinash had never cooked in her life. She never had to. She never did the dishes for the same reason. Her family had servants to take care of all those kinds of household tasks, and now she was confronted with not just the work of maintaining a household, but of doing this work in a refugee camp. And she took all this on without ever complaining once. She never lamented her circumstances.

"She had such class," is how Brij put it, and I see what he means. It's hard to imagine having lived a life in which meals were prepared, household chores tended to—a life of real opulence—and then suddenly living in a single 12x12 room with five other people. It's hard to imagine adjusting to the numerous discomforts, physical, yes, but also the psychological and emotional alienation that must have arisen from such a precipitous transition. Given all this, it's harder still to imagine never once complaining, never once slipping into self-pity, never personalizing the difficult circumstances Partition had created. It makes me think of my own experience with illness. And even then it had been so hard not to slip into that trite platitude—"Why me?"—when in some ways, the real question is, Why not me? Why not anyone? To make suffering personal—even though it feels personal—is to make the universe revolve around you.

You and Avinash were also similar in your shared resistance to this kind of thinking. Neither one of you ever personalized the hardship brought on by Partition. Both of you adjusted, moved forward, and directed your efforts toward the life you hoped to build.

Avinash's family history isn't as detailed as your own. You and your family had a longstanding interest in lineage, and you were lucky that this was passed on to you, and that you were then able to carry this tradition forward, detailing your own past to your children.

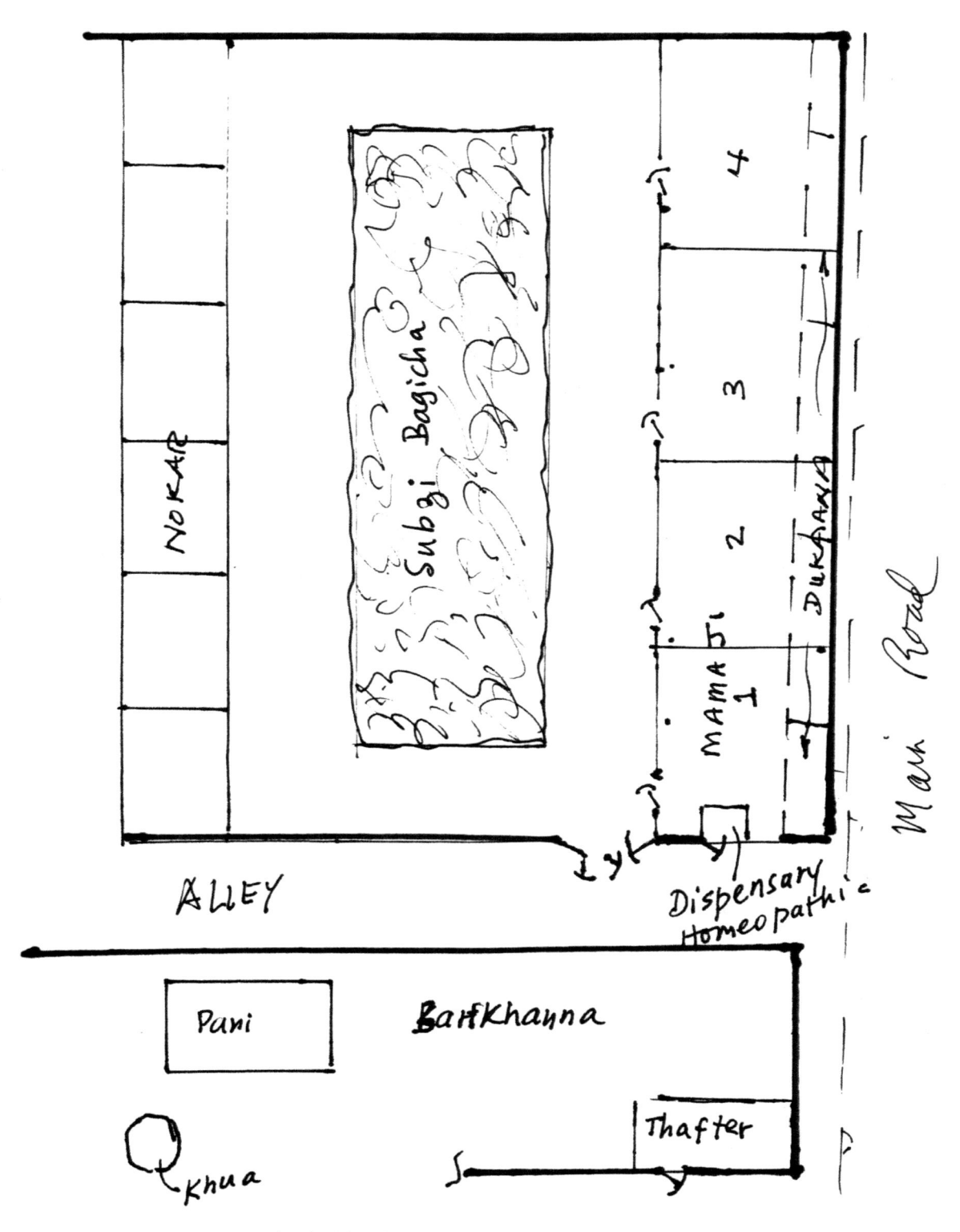

*A sketch of the Chadha Ice Factory in Lahore, India circa 1946.
Sketched by Davinder Anand (Avinash's cousin).*

LIKE A BANYAN TREE | 155

Avinash, 2010.

Avinash, 2013.

Ann and Avinash, Lucknow, 2011.

156 | *Avinash and Love, Reality and Fantasy*

It was different for Avinash. As with so many families on both sides of the India/Pakistan border, her parents were forced to leave behind so many of their possessions. Partition was a period of monumental upheaval and displacement, and this was first and foremost physical—the actual movement of people from one side of the border to the other—but it also resulted in displaced personal history. So much of what was lost during Partition was a connection to the past and to family lineage. The few remaining relatives and contacts from Avinash's life that I was able to talk to all mentioned this. Her family didn't just lose their home, their belongings, and their livelihood, but they also likely lost some of their own story as a result of Partition, and this is, perhaps, part of the reason why your wife's history is more limited than yours.

What is known is that her grandparents were from Ichhara, a small suburb of Lahore. Bhim Sen Chadha, Avinash's grandfather, was a wealthy landowner. It seems a good deal of Avinash's family's wealth—if not the origins—can be traced to this man. His wealth was substantial. He owned seven villages, and a small railway station was named after him. Bhim Sen also started the ice factory and the cold storage company that would become a source of further income. He and his wife, Avinash's grandmother, had six sons, and three daughters. Two of their sons died very young, and of the four living brothers, Khushal Chand Chadha, Avinash's father, was the middle.

Bhim Sen also died young. But the wealth he had accrued only grew under his sons' purview. After his death, Khushal and his brothers took over the ice factory and cold storage business and expanded it. Already a success, the business only became more profitable under Khushal and his brother's ownership. From there, Khushal and his siblings also started a ceiling fan company—Laxmi Fans—and eventually opened a bank: Laxmi Bank. By the time Avinash was born, Khushal and his brothers were one of the more affluent families in their community.

When Avinash started primary school, her family's wealth was such that every day she would go to school in a horse-drawn buggy. That fall morning when she was delivered to her first day of class in carriage-like opulence couldn't have been more different than your own first day of primary school, as your grandfather walked you to the humble schoolhouse across the street. And while your parents also owned property, the extent and category of property Avinash's father and brother's owned was of a different category.

LIKE A BANYAN TREE | 157

Khushal and his brother's lived in a series of row houses, each two stories and luxurious. Combined, the four row houses spanned the length of an entire block, and the brothers lived in these houses youngest to eldest, in ascending order, positioning the house of Avinash's childhood in the middle. The front doors of each house opened out onto the main road, and the back doors opened onto the land the family owned. Here there were crops—wheat and maze—and tended gardens of herbs and flowers. On the other side of the property were the servants' quarters.

The Ice Factory the brother's owned bookended and ran parallel along one side of the property and was separated by a narrow alley. In this alley and off the one row house that abutted it, there was also a small homeopathic dispensary, where the herbs from the garden were sold. Khushal and his brothers also owned houses in Lahore that British officers rented. That the British rented property from Avinash's family is a detail worth considering, particularly in early twentieth-century India, when often property ownership cut the other way. This was the world that Avinash was born into and because of Partition this was the world she lost.

She was a smart child and excelled in mathematics. She was also one of the few daughters in her family. Because of this she was often surrounded by boys—her uncles already had sons—and during her early childhood she played boy games with her cousins. She flew kites out in the open garden behind their row houses, and she rode her bicycle along with her cousins, weaving through narrow alleys and brushing by street vendors in the market. By the time she started school, she had a mischievous side, once getting in trouble for sneaking up on her teacher and batting the teacher's long ponytail back and forth.

But Khushal doted on Avinash. He couldn't help but be lenient with her. His first daughter had died shortly after birth, so Avinash was special to him. When she would fake a stomachache on those early mornings when she didn't want to go to school, he would stand at her bedside, his hand placed on his daughter's head, checking for a fever. Feeling that her forehead was cool to the touch, he would bend down close to her. "Is this a real stomachache or a stomachache because you don't want to go to school?"

Because Avinash couldn't lie to her own father, she would shyly confess that it was a stomachache because she didn't want to go to school, and Khushal would nod and let his daughter stay home. She would play in the garden or in the ice

Avinash with Akshay, 1991.

Avinash with Jyoti, Ajesh, Akshay and Anuj, 1997.

LIKE A BANYAN TREE

factory across the alley, sucking on ice chips when the afternoons got hot, giggling in the shadows with her cousins. Life was good for young Avinash, idyllic even. Hers was a childhood surrounded by beauty and elegance, and surely what must have felt like great security.

But the events of that August in 1947 changed everything.

Shortly before Partition, Khushal recognized that tensions were heading in an ominous direction, and he sent the women in his family to Shimla, a small mountain village to the east of Lahore. Once Partition happened and Khushal and his brothers fled Pakistan, they signed over a great deal of the family wealth and property to a trusted deputy in the family, a Muslim man who served the functions of what would now be a secretary or a business manager. Because of this man's loyalty, they were able to get a portion of their wealth back, which in turn, in the years following Partition, would allow the family to recoup some of their losses and start another Ice Factory in Allahabad.

But during those years directly following 1947, Avinash's family, her father, Khushal, and mother, Vidyawati Chadha, as well as Avinash's two sisters, Updesh and Subash, and her brothers, Kailash, Santosh and Keshav, lived in Allahabad as so many refugees did. They had lost everything.

And yet, even during such a monumental loss, life goes on, and for Khushal that meant he still had a daughter, Avinash, of marriageable age. Part of what it meant to take care of her, even in these uncertain times, was to find her a husband. Where once he had imagined Avinash marrying into a family of similar economic status, Khushal was now faced with the fact that post-Partition India meant that so many families of means had been reduced to refugees. Given the circumstances, Khushal wanted for his daughter someone who worked hard, was educated, had a good character, and would have a good chance at building a life in a world where so much was uncertain.

There would forever be subtle class differences that would come up between you and Avinash. Even after the two of you were married and had children, these differences would sometimes arise in strange ways. One of the most salient examples I have of this is a story that Raj told me. When he was still very young, he and Rashmi had always used the Punjabi words for "mom" and "dad"—"Bebe" and "Pahya Ji"—but once when Avinash's sisters came to visit, they insisted that your children switch to what was thought of as the more proper, upper-class

English usage of "mummy" and "daddy." As Raj put it, this indicated one of the big class differences between your family and Avinash's—"country, village folk versus affluent Lahore."

But that evening when you first met Khushal and he found you doing the dishes, humbly working hard but not without dignity, he recognized something in you that transcended some of these class differences. You also had that certain magnetism that people were attracted to right away, and surely Khushal felt that and was drawn in by it. Though quieter, and in ways perhaps more subtle, Avinash also had her own magnetism, and you must have noticed it, as Khushal did yours, when you first met your wife on your wedding day.

There are stories about how the children at your wedding fell in love with Avinash. They were so enamored with her that after the long celebration the children attending the wedding wept at her departure. Children are perceptive. They have that uncanny ability to see people for who they are. They are quick to notice grace and beauty. And just as they are quick to notice sinister intent or dubious character, they also notice that gentle magnetism that only some people have.

Your wife had this.

But your wife could also be startlingly serious. In one of the photos Raj had sent me, she stands holding her granddaughter, Raj's daughter, Shelly. You are standing on her left, and Raj directly behind her, touches her right shoulder. You were the jokester. You were light and optimistic, and in this photo your slight smile is the perfect contrast to the way Avinash has been described to me. Her brow is slightly furrowed, and her mouth is closed. She isn't frowning, but there is something distant in her look, thoughtfully occupied with some concern not otherwise present in the photo. Her hair is mostly gray at the sides. She looks stately, elegant, but also steely. She isn't looking directly at the camera. Instead, she is looking just over it, into the distance. And it's this look, preoccupied with something in the middle-distance, that informs so much of how I imagine her as a young mother: I think of her as always considering some problem just out of sight—a kind of ambient concern that never quite went away.

Verifying Brij's comment, Raj had told me that it was true, he also never heard his mom say a stupid thing. But Raj added something that struck me as insightful. "People who don't joke don't say stupid things." And it's true, judging from the photo alone, the woman with the elegant yet steely face looks to me like someone who has never said and never would say anything stupid in her life. But she also doesn't strike me as someone inclined to make a joke, especially standing next to you, poised, or so you appear, to laugh.

Partition had different effects on different people. Your children have speculated, sometimes obliquely and other times more overtly, that because Avinash's losses—the distance between her former life in Lahore and her life after—were so drastic, the trauma of 1947 may have left a different mark on her personality than it left on yours. This makes sense to me. If the mark of trauma is the degree to which an event is incommensurate with what seems possible, Partition itself may have felt like a larger break from reality for Avinash than it did for you. I think it's important to remember that, and yet, I also think there's a risk to reducing someone's character to one, single event. People aren't reducible just to circumstances. You understood this as well as anyone, and your wife had her own complicated set of sensibilities that may or may not have been exaggerated by Partition.

Perhaps, even before Partition, before you knew and married her, she already had a serious predisposition. Though if this were true, it's easy to see how Partition could have heightened that, further drawn out what was already serious and thoughtful in her.

"Serious." "Dignified." "Classy." These are all words that have come up when your children have talked about Avinash, but her loyalty and love for you has also not gone without comment. She stood by your side in so many ways. That time when you had quit your job working for The State, for instance, Avinash's father was alarmed by the prospect of you and your family going without a steady income. He had taken the train all the way up from Delhi to offer you 2500 rupees, which was equivalent to six months of your salary. But you were proud. You insisted that you would be able to provide, that it wouldn't be long before you were making enough money as a lawyer to provide for your family.

So you refused his offer. A slight shake of the head, a firm "no"—I picture the two of you standing somewhere private, perhaps just on the other side of the barrack walls. You refuse his offer once and he still pressed you to take it.

"To build your library then," Khushal implored you, and he had a point. You would need law books. But, resolutely, you shook your head no again.

At a loss, Khushal went to Avinash behind your back. He tried to get her to take the money, to keep it, just in case. But she also refused his offer, and it's in moments like these where I see her unswerving loyalty to you. She understood that to take her father's money, even if it were just to be on the safe side, would be a kind of betrayal to you. She treated this very seriously.

She showed this same loyalty to you during those years when she would accompany you on your search for S.L.'s body. But there were other, quieter efforts she also made, efforts you may have not even noticed, to support you and advocate on your behalf. Avinash understood that your generosity, as virtuous as it was, was also something that could be exploited, and easily taken advantage of by others. She worked to prevent this, sometimes without you knowing, standing in the way of too many people coming to you and asking for favors or money.

And even those times when your generosity was taken advantage of, like the occasion when you invited the thief into your home and he had stolen Sarla's dowry. Avinash was still there for you, even though she may have been frustrated with you for naively inviting a stranger into your home. She helped replenish your sister's dowry with what was left from her own. It wasn't just that Avinash stood by you and supported you. When she married you she also took on the responsibility of caring for your family as if they were her own. She never wavered from this.

Avinash could also be stern and severe, too, in ways not entirely dissimilar to you: When Rashmi was attending the Loreto Convent School, there was a school fair. You had given your daughter 20 rupees to purchase something from the fair. She came home with a rosary that one of the sisters—sister Cyril—had sold her, and when Avinash saw what Rashmi bought, she made her daughter take it back. She didn't like the idea of Christianity, The West, a foreign religion having an overwhelming influence on her family. You were this same way: When Raj and his siblings were attending a private school, which was Christian, and they had to read the Bible, you had a Hindu priest come to Bhopal House in the afternoon to tutor your children in Hinduism.

Both you and Avinash valued education, understanding and a broad perspective, but you also both understood something about cultural erasure, how the West, Christianity, wasn't a substitute for you own cultural backgrounds, and you both guarded this, protected your children from an outside Western influence.

But when I think of Avinash, what I think most about are those ways that she was different from you. Avinash was a reader of novels, and while I don't want to make too much of this, I do think it points to a larger distinction in personality. The modern novel is so often about characters who are caught in emotional conflicts, who struggle against their own contradictions. You didn't read novels, but you also weren't someone who struggled with internal contradictions. Your worldview and your place in it couldn't have been clearer to you. This was that side of you, despite your openness and your acceptance of others, that could sometimes be dogmatic. You had your idea of how the world should be and nothing would change that. You also weren't one to entertain emotional strife, and your reading habits reflected this. You read law books and books on history and medicine. The poetry you did read was poetry with philosophical or moral import. What it was not was the poetry of anguish to which so much modernism spoke. Avinash, however, did relate to literary genres that dealt with the kind of internal turmoil that was foreign to you.

Brij had once mentioned to me that his mom, at times, could be depressed. I wonder if this had something to do with Partition, a loss that never quite fully went away. Whatever the reason, depression was also a foreign state to you. Depression itself was categorically opposed to your sensibility. You were so external, and your belief and faith in your own ability to manifest your will through your actions made depression itself always beside the point. But for Avinash, there was something different, a heaviness that was internal, ruminative.

This isn't to overlook the nuances of who she was. Along with the introspection, Avinash could be as practical as you were. Brij has told me about his time living in Alaska when he was reading anything he could get his hands on to make sense of life—the Russian masters, the existentialists, the Sufis, philosophers and writers who wrote directly about life—he felt particularly drawn to Herman Hesse's Siddhartha, a book that traces the story of the Buddha and the spiritual journey of relinquishment, the path of non-attachment toward enlightenment.

Avinash responded to Brij's enthusiasm about these ideas and writers with practical criticism. "You'll have enough time in life to ruminate and now isn't it. As a young man you should be immersed *in* life." Of course, this wasn't quite your blistering critique of Buddha, that he was a coward for leaving his wife and son and neglecting his duty, but your wife's orientation toward the concrete realities of life is unmistakable here. Avinash may have ruminated more than you did, but she also saw the pitfalls of it. Live now, in short. Dwell later. Like you, she understood something about balance.

I think one of the hardest challenges is to find balance between these two states—the internal and the external. I know, for myself, I have tended far too much toward the former. If I were to pinpoint the one thing that has stood most in my own way, it'd be myself and my feelings. You didn't have this problem. Part of the reason you were able to accomplish so much was because your obstacles were out there in the world. They were movable. To battle yourself can feel Sisyphean, impossible. There is no greater obstacle than contending with your own will.

Above: Raj in Portland, OR, 1977.
Right: Raj (holding a friend's baby) with Vandana and Brij 1982.

LIKE A BANYAN TREE

You contended with the world. That's where your fight was. Because of this, I'm not sure that you understood how formidable internal conflict could be. I know your children could come to you with practical concerns, and I know that you offered them a rich intellectual life, full of immaterial insights, but I'm not sure they could come to you in emotional turmoil and find understanding or real comfort.

Avinash was different. Like you, she was practical and like you, in so many ways, she was a pragmatist. But when I think of her reading novels, her seriousness, her occasional dips into depression, I see something that I recognize in myself, and it's the seriousness of introspection. Where your children couldn't go to you for emotional conflict, I think they could go to Avinash.

Out of your four children, Rashmi was closest to Avinash. She recently said something about her mother that seemed telling to me. In some ways, your own sisters were closer to Avinash than to your mom, especially Sarla. She would come to Avinash whenever she had relationship questions, questions about marriage, matters of the heart, or conflict in her own relationships.

"She was a very balanced person," Rashmi said, regarding Avinash's role as confidant. Sarla would come to your wife instead of her mom because Gyano was prone to extremes, prone to acting from a place of emotion rather than reason. Rashmi's point was that Avinash had an even hand when it came to offering advice about family conflicts, about love and matters of the heart. And while Rashmi's point does indicate Avinash's balance, her ability to be reasonable when emotions were high, I also see it as a sign that Avinash *understood* emotion. I think Sarla could come to Avinash not just because she was balanced, but because your wife could relate to emotional conflict, could appreciate the nuances this kind of struggle presented.

Rashmi's acknowledgment that her mom was rational when others could be emotional and impulsive indicates, to me, not a lack of emotion but, perhaps, an emotional intelligence, a depth of feeling that made her an ideal confidant for your Sarla because she recognized how emotions threatened to derail reason.

This isn't to say that you didn't also have your own emotional side. You did. Your compassion for others, while often part of a larger sense of duty to do good, did have an emotional side for you. You often helped others without thinking and on those occasions you must have felt compelled to do so not intellectually but emotionally. There was the time, shortly after you purchased your first car—the Hindustan Ambassador—when you were driving and saw a man sprinting alongside traffic.

Behind him, you noticed, was another man wielding a knife, giving chase. Without a second thought, you slowed and pulled up next to the man who was being chased.

There's something slapstick about the situation, you reaching across the passenger seat, one hand still on the wheel, swerving slightly as you open the door. You waved your arms at the running man. "Get in! Get in!" And then he dove into your car, legs still hanging out of the open door as you swerved back into traffic. You didn't know this man and you had no reason to help him, but it's these kinds of situations that seem to me driven by an immediate emotional response, an impulse to help.

So, too, was another situation around this same time. Again driving in your Hindustan Ambassador, you saw a man on the side of the road, bloodied and lifeless, perhaps hit by car. In India, in your world and during your time, people didn't just help one another if there had been an accident. There were too many potential legal ramifications, weird tangles of liabilities, as Rashmi explained it to me, which could potentially accompany bringing a stranger to a hospital. But you did it anyway, again acting without thought, again acting on that impulse to help. You pulled over to the side of the road and lifted this bloody and unconscious stranger into the backseat of your new car, and then drove him to the hospital.

You saved his life.

Six months later, a man you didn't recognize walked into your office. He stood there, expectantly.

"Can I help you," you asked him, thinking he was a potential client, someone coming to you in need of legal counsel.

He bowed his head slightly. "I wanted to meet the god who gave me a second life," he said. It was the man you had saved, he had come to thank you. It wasn't just that you had saved this man's life, it was also that acts of this sort of benevolence were so unusual in those times.

But for you, helping others like this wasn't unusual.

"My dad was very emotional," Rashmi had told me, when we discussed what compelled you to be so helpful. You couldn't stand to see people suffering, and when you took action to stop the suffering of others, it did come from an emotional place. But this still wasn't an emotional orientation toward your own psychology. It was emotions directed toward the external world, with practical implications.

You wanted to help, to make something better in a concrete way, and I think this was true of how you expressed love generally. Your love was always grounded in material and practical concerns. You loved as you lived, as a realist and a pragmatist.

Avinash also loved this way, but I think there was more romanticism woven into her sensibilities.

The last time I talked with my mom about my dad, she said something that articulated what I have always struggled with in love and relationships, and it strikes me now as the opposite of how you related to the people you loved. I asked my mom if her relationship with Chuck was one of the defining relationships in her life. She was silent for a moment, and then she sighed: "I want to give you information about Chuck," she said. "But I don't have much information about Chuck. I have a fantasy, and when I was young I called that fantasy love." It seems to me that your relationship with Avinash couldn't have been more different.

I'm not saying there wasn't any element of fantasy between you and Avinash. Maybe there was. I'm not sure that anyone could ever stand to be with another person for long without there being some element of fantasy, of illusion. And I don't think this is a bad thing. Illusion, art, fantasy, romance—they all make life palatable. "We have art," as Nietzsche said. "So we don't die of the truth." The problem for both my mom and dad—and I think this has also been true of my own life—is that we've often completely mistaken a fantasy about another person for reality, those times when we've lost sight of the real person who is front of us and instead seen an illusion. As my mom and dad were, I think I've been a romanticist to a fault.

You didn't have this problem. If anything, at times, you may have erred on the opposite side. This isn't to say that you didn't have your moments, small gestures of care that conveyed something romantic. I like to think, for instance, about those improbable times when you found a way to get Avinash ice cream, late at night, when most other husbands would brush aside the request. You found real pleasure in this simple task, and it had significance too, not just because Avinash liked ice cream, though she did love it. It has significance because her parents owned an ice factory and ice cream reminded her of her childhood. When you did this for your wife, you were offering a deeper comfort here. Each time you got her ice cream during those late summer nights, in a way, you were bringing her a small piece of her childhood. That is romantic, and it's also an overture of love.

In other ways, your capacity for romance left something to be desired. There's a comical story that took place around the time your practice became more secure, and you had enough to provide for you and your family. Leisure, taking time to enjoy smaller indulgences, suddenly became possible, and one afternoon, Avinash asked you to take her to a movie, just the two of you.

This would have been a rare treat, an indulgence, and the prospect for Avinash must have been exciting. Knowing how she related to novels and popular magazines, I imagine movies held more appeal for her than they did for you. Maybe she had to talk you into this, asking once, and then when you were hesitant, asking again, insisting even.

But you agreed, and later that afternoon, the two of you walked down the street together, not holding hands, but side by side. You walked past the juice-wala, the chai shop, the small markets, the food vendors with all their smells of curry and fried food, and then, or so I like to think, down along the river, where the canopy of peepal trees offered shade, a brief respite from the heat.

At the theatre, you pay. I'm not sure what movie you saw, though I know you didn't approve of most Bollywood films, the morality in those movies something you always found reprehensible. There was one summer when Raj and Rashmi—hardly ten years old, both of them—had to sneak out of the apartment and up to the roof of the Bhopal House to see a screening of *Sahib Bibi aur Gulam*. This was a movie that you found particularly distasteful, and it makes sense that you would.

The drama of the film circulates around a deteriorating marriage between Zamindar and Chhoti Bahu. Zamindar is a drunk and a lech, and he likes to spend his time intoxicated and watching prostitutes dance. Chhoti Bahu, his wife, tries to keep him home, tries to save him from his vices. To do so she starts drinking with him. This was the only way she could get him to stay. She figures at least this way, even if she becomes a drunk too, she can at least keep an eye on her husband and can at least share time with him. So together they drink, and together they spiral into unhappiness, bankruptcy, and alcoholism. The depiction of the drinking and the prostitution itself bothered you, but I think what bothered you more was the way Bahu's attempt to save Zamindar from his vices turns into a vice for her. She ruins herself for him, and I think this kind of self-debasement upset you.

Your aversion to this kind of narrative further illustrates your orientation toward romance itself. Romance informed by the kind of desire that leads to self-destruction indicated, for you, a lack of integrity, of character bankrupt of self-respect. It couldn't be more antithetical to your pragmatism of caring. But so much romantic poetry has circulated around this kind of love, and I confess that it's always had a certain purchase on my own imagination. There's an erotic thrill to desire that leads to self-annihilation, but this wasn't part of your vocabulary of desire. There was something of the purist in you, and this was evident in the way you didn't drink or smoke, but as I see you, it's most evident in your relationship to desire.

So it makes sense that when you found out that Raj and Rashmi had snuck out of the house to watch *Sahib Bibi aur Gulam*, you were furious. You stormed upstairs, onto the rooftop, and to your children's embarrassment, dragged them back down to the apartment.

Surely, whatever movie you and Avinash had gone to see, it wasn't one of the classic Bollywood depictions of failed romance, of vice and passion, of illusions colliding in an explosion of desire and destruction.

After you pay for the tickets, you lead Avinash into the dark and open space of the theatre. There's the big screen, the rows of seats, and the dank smells of so many theatres, of enclosed spaces crowded with bodies, and of those delightful moments of a collective acquiescence to fall into the dream of another narrative, another world, the suspense of watching a story unfold. The two of you sit down, the first scratchy shots light up the screen, and the old chairs creak beneath you.

At some point, you get up, telling your wife that you need to use the restroom. You make your way toward the door, back down the rows of seats in the hushed theatre, conscious not to make too much noise and distract others. Five minutes, ten, fifteen minutes, and still you don't come back to her. After you use the restroom, you leave the theatre, make your way back to your office and pick up your work where you left off. An hour or so passes, and you return to the theatre and find Avinash, looking confused, passing in front of the marquee.

"Where did you go?" she asks you. "I've been looking for you."

Casually you say, "I had some work to do," as if this couldn't be more normal.

She gives you a strange look, still confused. She tells you that you were supposed to take her to the movies.

And you give her an equally strange look, equally confused. "I did take you to the movies," you say. "Now I'm picking you up."

And so that was that. Avinash doesn't ask you to take her to the movies again.

It's a funny story, the peculiarity of it, your almost eccentric naivety—or seeming naivety—toward Avinash's bid for a date. Your practical nature overrides Avinash's attempt for a more subtle kind of romance. And yet, at the same time, it wasn't that you were insensitive to Avinash or to her feelings. In other ways you showed great sensitivity toward her. I am thinking of those times you had female clients—widows or divorcées—and those occasions when you would need to go to their homes to discuss their cases.

You weren't a womanizer. You didn't have affairs. I'm not even sure that your own desires or passions ever troubled you, even privately. I don't think they did. Avinash must have known this about you. She knew who you were, and she knew you weren't deceitful. But whenever you would go to see a woman client, you made a point of bringing Avinash with you, and you would do this just to make sure that she never had even the slightest doubt that you were loyal.

I find this very moving, the consideration and thoughtfulness in the gesture. But again, it's the opposite of the kind of romance my parents shared, and the opposite of the kind of romance I have often been drawn to myself. Where you were trying to dispel the possibility of any illusions, of how things may have *seemed* to Avinash, my own dad was always busy making things seem different than they *were*. Always he was trying to get my mom to believe that he would leave his wife, and I think at the same time he was simultaneously trying to get his wife to believe that he would never abandon his marriage. His was a romance of illusion, and my mom's was too. She was attracted to something about my dad that seemed like it could heal her own fraught relationship with her own father.

But eventually illusions collapse, they always do, leaving the ruins of reality in their place.

From an early age, I learned to think of love as something that was inherently antagonistic, implied conflict, a kind of power struggle that was never resolved. Of course, each broken promise in my mom and dad's affair articulates this antagonism, but it's also true of my grandparents too, my grandmother's affair with Bill and the lies she told to Silas, her ex-husband. Knowing the stories of these relationships always gave me the sense that love was a secretive, destructive thing, and that what was good in love—those moments of connection, however brief, or those periods of gratified passion—were even more poetic for the doomed future that was around the corner.

I also witnessed this antagonism play out again and again growing up. As my mom dated various men, I watched her go back and forth, always reenacting an attachment pattern that would retread the same push and pull of her earlier affair—my mom sought commitment from the men who pulled away and resented the men who were committed and available for the demands they made on her time.

Though to a lesser degree, this was also true of my own relationship with my mom. During those periods when she would fall into a depression over another failed relationship, I could feel my own demands as a child become a source of resentment for her, and then those other times when she was affectionate, when she was overwhelmingly present, I would withdraw, suspicious of when her mood would drop again.

I think part of the reason A. and our affair felt so familiar was because our relationship followed this same path. When she would pull away and return to her own family, I wanted her more than ever. And when she would offer me her attention and affection, I was suspicious, distant, which would cause her to need me more, at least until she went back to her own husband again. It's this kind of push and pull, this constant conflict between connection and rejection that has always been conducive to romance for me, in part because it creates illusions. What you can't have is easiest to idealize, and the kind of love that I was most familiar with growing up and throughout my twenties was the kind that was unavailable and as a result easily idealized.

The more I learn of your relationship with Avinash, the more I realize it was the complete opposite of this. Where you would bring Avinash with you when you saw a woman client to show her that she had no reason to be suspicious, I could easily see myself leaving the same situation vague, not out of anything spiteful or with the intention of hurting whoever I was with, but because I would feel that intuitive pull to create mystery. I always thought this kind of mystery created desire, an idealized image of myself in the other, and this was just as seductive to me: knowing that I was idealized as much as I was idealizing. I found nothing more seductive than two false mirrors reflecting each other's false image.

* * *

This is going to sound strange, but E. reminds me of you, Baij. The first six months of my relationship with her were difficult, as I think opening up often is. Some of the hardest points arose for us because of her suspicion around romance, around me idealizing her and then, once the illusion and mystery passed, leaving her. I, too, had grown suspicious of this dynamic. After being sick for four years, it was hard for me to imagine idealizing anything or anyone, but I hadn't yet found a new way to be and to exist in a relationship. There were times, especially in the beginning, when I mistook the way E. expressed that she cared for me as disinterest because I was looking at it from a skewed perspective.

During those first six months, we didn't fight, exactly, but we did have a lot of miscommunications. Your story had been underway for months now, and paycheck by paycheck, chapter by chapter, I was gaining confidence in myself again. The act of writing about your life had become scaffolding for my own. Every day that I sat down to put words on the page, I engaged with the kind of work I feared I would never get back to when I was sick. And the content of your life had become it's kind of mirror as well. As I wrote, I thought about my struggles in relation to yours. What you had been through and what you had accomplished gave substance to my own sense of what was possible. But I was having a hard time transferring these feelings over to E. There was something about the relationship that still left me uneasy.

I remember the first time it became clear to me that I had misunderstood something important about E. It was November, and E. and I were walking on the beach in Port Townsend, a small town up near the Strait of Juan de Fuca, where the Puget Sound empties into the Pacific Ocean. She reached for my hand, and as we walked we scanned the gravel beds for agates. It was a cold day. The Cascades were already snowcapped, and the Olympics, rising up in the distance before us, reflected back the icy glow of the winter sun.

E. fell quiet, and we walked along in silence for some time. Then she told me that she felt very comfortable around me. She said, "It's nice. I feel like I can just be myself." And there was something so straightforward and honest in the way E. said it that it made me think of you. I don't think there was ever a trace of dishonesty in your relationship with Avinash and I think in part this was because you always were yourself around her. You never pretended. I think E. possesses this quality, too.

Yet, it was this very quality that at times left me uneasy around E. because I had misunderstood it for disregard. She seemed never to agonize as I did over our miscommunications. Like you, she isn't like that. But I would agonize over her lack of agony. Why wasn't she obsessing, I would ask myself, as I am obsessing? For as long as I could remember, since my childhood, obsession always seemed like an indication of interest, of burgeoning love. And so these moments of unrequited agony, to me, seemed indicative of what might potentially become unrequited love. If E. really cared about me, she would worry over our miscommunications, over the mystery of what I was thinking about her, over an idealized vision of me. This was romance.

As E. and I walked along the beach I thought about these things. There was the steady rhythm of the waves pushing and pulling at the gravel shoreline, and the clouds above were a gray-blue, soon to lose rain. The air was still. She squeezed my hand and I looked at her and she smiled. I felt myself relax. "It's nice," she said again.

And that's when I realized that her barometer of wanting to be in a relationship with me was actually the opposite of what I was used to. What made her feel like our relationship was something that had real potential was the fact that she *could* feel like herself, and this meant that she didn't have to obsess over arguments or miscommunications, she could trust that they would resolve themselves because she could trust that I saw her as she was. She could let things go, and that was a good thing. That was an indication that she didn't have to project a false self. In short, I realized that it was a mistake to misread her comfort for ambivalence, because it was, in fact, the opposite. It was interest.

You never projected a false self, especially with Avinash. I think this came naturally to you, as I think in some ways it comes naturally to E. There is something grounded in how you both care for others. It's different with me. I'm having to learn to trust that romance doesn't necessarily mean idealization and projection, that it doesn't require a false self. Learning to accept this sometimes leaves me feeling unsettled and vulnerable.

Not that you didn't have your own vulnerabilities in your relationships, and not that you didn't have your own idealizations. They're subtle and I've had to look closely for them, but they are there. I think they are particularly evident in your relationship with Brij. When he was younger, in his twenties, after he had moved to the US, you had wanted very badly for him to marry.

When he had come home to visit, you had set up three meetings with women for him, all of them potential wives. The first meeting went well, and you were happy because your most obstinate son seemed at least open to the idea of marrying this woman.

But according to tradition, before the marriage could be sanctified, a Hindu priest would need to do an astrological reading to make sure Brij and his potential wife were well-matched. You weren't crazy about this idea. Though your values—the priority you placed on duty, the importance of kindness, honesty, even a kind of religious purity—were very much in line with Hinduism, you weren't doctrinaire. You didn't prioritize ritual or dogma. You always honored the individual over a system, the particular over the general. It wasn't the religion you subscribed to that mattered to you, it was what a person did with their religion and belief.

Still, tradition must be followed in these matters, and so the potential bride-to-be's mother had their family's priest do the reading. You felt real disappointment when the mother told you Brij's chart didn't match up with her daughter's, but in your typical fashion, it registered as a problem you could overcome, an obstacle, and not a prohibition. Rather than accept the reading, you hired your own priest to do a counter-reading, and you asked the priest to nudge the outcome toward a more amicable prediction of Brij's union with this woman. You were literally arguing with the stars.

But, alas, you could only do so much. Though your priest's reading was more auspicious, when you gave it to the bride-to-be's mom, she was still stubborn, unwilling to concede. Though the stars may have been beside the point, as Brij would later tell me. "I think her mom was worried that I'd take her daughter to America," and you must have understood this, the desire to keep your own children close.

After the first potential wife fell through, you introduced Brij to the other women you had lined up, but he wasn't interested, and when Brij went back to the US, he was no closer to being married than he was before his visit. This

Above: Rashmi and Arun in Oregon, 1987.
Left: Brij and a friend in Oregon, 1980.

troubled you greatly, and you continued to make attempts to help Brij find a wife. You had some connections to Indian families in the US, and you arranged another meeting with another family, but that one also fell through because Brij ultimately wasn't interested.

This caused you a lot of grief. Brij was like you in so many ways, but he was different, too. I'm thinking again of that period when he had moved to the US and wandered, not just geographically, but in his own mind. I'm thinking of that period in Alaska when he worked as a State Auditor examining books of cities, municipalities, native organizations, any outfit that received money from the state for health and social services, that period when he read voraciously and dove deep into his own psyche.

You didn't share these kinds of internal pursuits.

Again, your practical relationship to your moral obligations and duties, to the concrete business of living, couldn't have been more antithetical to the whole project of existential speculation. This makes sense. So much of your life had been built around solving one problem after another, of tending to basic needs. Camus's problem of "being" is trivial next to the literal problem of living.

More than your other children, who were more practical, more inclined toward tradition, toward building a stable future, you worried that Brij would learn the hard way that when the center gives way, when hardships arise, as they always do, without some support network like family, a wife, security, one is left completely alone. You must have felt that Brij was living something of a fantasy compared to these realities you knew all too well, and your primary concern, not just for Brij but also for all your children, was that they would be okay in the face of difficult realities. This was love for you. And so, however romantic reading Camus in the wilderness may be, it wasn't enough. It wasn't safety and security. Romance would always be secondary to these concerns. And how could it not be. During Partition you had seen the world stripped of romance, of fantasy, of all but the bare bones of living.

Your desire to see Brij married would lead to one of the biggest conflicts you would have with your children. It would also become a point of tension, though shorter lived and less intractable, with Raj. But with Brij, you became so frustrated after your repeated attempts that you gave up on him finding a wife, and you told him this. "I'll never speak with you about marriage again," you said, during one of his later visits. You were trying to wash your hands of the problem. But I see this moment as another point of vulnerability for you. I think because you couldn't protect Brij, because you couldn't find him a wife and rest easy in knowing he would be taken care of, by not speaking to him about marriage, you were also trying to protect yourself.

It's this vulnerability that runs your realism into a kind of idealism that love always runs into. When we love someone—really love someone—we can't help but try to foster the illusion that we can protect them, keep them safe. But we can never fully protect the people we love, no matter how much we want to. To believe otherwise is to believe a fantasy.

So you see, even you, Baij, despite your pragmatism, despite your realism, had a touch of the romantic.

"Make what appears impossible, possible."

Arun and Rashmi in 1992 at Yangon, Myanmar.

Arun with daughter, Aanchal at Yangon, Myanmar, 1992.

6

JOY

And you loved life. You found joy in the mundane. You played. There was something almost childlike in the way you appreciated day-to-day life, despite whatever hardships you confronted.

You were a storyteller, and there was real joy in the way you told stories. Because you were curious and asked about the people you met, you in turn told stories about those people. You told stories about the food vendors who sold you food, and you told stories about the food itself, the different kind of mangoes and where they were grown: the Alphonso mango, golden yellow and so sweet, cultivated in Ratnagiri—long rows of trees yoked with fruit and overlooking the Arabian sea; the Kasar mango from the Girnar hills of Junahadh, the famed land of the lions; and the Dashehari mango, the late season fruit known for its green peel, but more importantly to you, grown just outside of Lucknow, your sweet city, your home, and you would go to those green groves and hand select huge quantities every season to be delivered to your home.

You told stories about your clients and colleagues, the cases you fought and won, and you told stories about your own adventures—little episodes, mishaps and voyages—like the time when you and a friend raced to see who was the faster swimmer, the two of you neck and neck pushing across the Gomti from bank to bank, back and forth, back and forth, in the midsummer heat. You wouldn't stop and neither would he, and so the two of you kept swimming until the heat became too much and you nearly drowned, your friend dragging you out of the water and thumping your chest with his big hands. When you got home to Bhopal House, a half-drowned man, still panting, and Avinash saw you, she made you swear that you would never swim again, and you didn't. You told that story, and you told it well, always arriving with comedic timing at Avinash's demands, how she wouldn't even let your kids near the water.

Then there was the time when you were younger, before Partition, and traveling to see a friend in Afghanistan. You had taken a train all the way, and when you got to his small village it was night, dark, obsidian black. You made your way down the quiet village streets, and as you did you saw what you swore was a jinn, some eerily moving colossal with a monstrous head, weaving toward you. It mystified you to see something so supernatural. Breathless, excited, confounded, when you got to your friend's house you told him what you had seen, and he laughed at you because what you had seen was the town drunk stumbling down the street, his giant hat made of rags and lit with candles floated with a kind of spectral grace. You loved to tell this story because of how funny you found it, the joy in the reveal, of the illusion, of things not seeming as they are. "I thought it was a walking mountain but it was a man!"

And how you loved to tell a funny story, to make people laugh, your own laughter a booming echo, always loud enough to be heard blocks away. You brought laughter to friends and colleagues, but you especially brought it to your own family. I'm thinking of those nights when you all still lived in Bhopal House—all nine of you! Avinash, your mom and dad, your sister Sarla, your four children. All of you slept in the great room, and in the evening, your children waited with excitement for you to finish up work, to shut the door to your small office down the hall, and then join the rest of your family on the charpai and the rolled out dhurrie set just for you. They waited wide-eyed and riveted. "Tell us another one, Daddy. Tell us one more!"

This was a regular affair, but there was one evening that stands out above the others. On this night, you were in rare form, something about the story that you were telling that hit all the right comedic notes, a perfect mix of absurdism and wonder, and it sent your sister Sarla into a fit of laughter so violent that she rolled out of her own charpai and onto the floor. She laid there, laughing hys-

Vandana and Shelly, 1989.

Brij and Ajesh, 1988.

Ajesh, Shelly, Avinash, and Rashmi celebrating Holi, 1998.

LIKE A BANYAN TREE

terically, begging you to stop. But you wouldn't. You had her laughing so hard she eventually wet herself, right there on the floor, and still she couldn't stop laughing.

And now this story itself, how you made your sister laugh until she lost control is its own story, part of your family lore, so comic and absurd, so full of joy that when Raj told it to me, he couldn't help his own fit of laughter, and he shook with mirth in the big leather chair in his office in Atlanta. "He was like that though," Raj said, tears in his eyes. "He was just always a joker. Always ready to laugh."

But it wasn't just stories, it was life. Or maybe more to the point, for you stories and life were connected, and to enjoy the artistry of stories, a turn of phrase, or a minor yet revealing detail is to take joy in life. It reminds me of why I fell in love with reading in the first place, why I wanted to write to begin with. It was the simple fact that I liked how words sounded when they ran into each other in strange ways. And I liked how they didn't just represent the world, but they created it, too. A funny story alive with details can make life more alive and humorous, more livable. There's a vast freedom in this, in the possibility of the creative act.

If there was one thing that I lost when I was sick that caused me the most grief, it was this desire and ability to tell stories, to create and feel the expansive agency in creating. I had become so hemmed in by the singular and all-encompassing narrative of illness that I couldn't find joy in any other stories.

And there was also my ability. In the most literal sense, I couldn't tell the story of my illness even if I did have a clear narrative with which to tell it. My ability to process language, to juggle the necessary syntax and phrases to maintain narrative movement wasn't something I had access to. And this linguistic loss flattened the world. As language became more and more indistinct, the precision and uniqueness of the world also became indistinct. I don't know that I will ever be able to fully explain what it was like to experience that, but what I can say is that as I write your story and find myself swimming in the stories you told, I feel those spontaneous sparks that arise from language coming back to me, and it reminds me that I, too, still know something about joy.

It's telling your son Raj about the various kinds of mangoes and where they

Anuj, Shelly, and Akshay, 1998.

Avinash and Shelly, 1998.

are from. It's me walking on the beach with E. and learning the names of the agates we find—"Carnelian," "Water-Line," "Plume." It's seeing strange men in ominously illuminated hats walking down dark streets and mistaking them for a spectral mountain and then later telling the story of your shock and surprise at learning it was just a man. It's the freedom of language and the curiosity it produces. Joy is in the ability to appreciate craft and artistry wherever it exists and from whatever manner of living it arises.

You had this. I'm thinking now of that time when a traveling gang of pickpockets came to Lucknow. They were on their way to Allahabad for Kumbh Mela where there would be massive crowds of unsuspecting people whom they could take advantage of. They stopped in Lucknow because Prime Minister Nehru was going to deliver a speech and there would also be crowds of people there to see him. This gang of pickpockets planned to stay for a few days, weave through the crowds and furtively take people's things. It was the leader of the gang who came to you to retain your services. He told you that while he and his gang were in Lucknow, they would need a defense attorney if any of them got caught, and you agreed. But then after you had negotiated fees, you became curious.

"So how do you do it," you asked the leader of this traveling pickpocket gang. You stood there in your office and asked him not only how he did it, but how he figured out whose pockets to pick. You were fascinated as this man explained his craft to you. He told you how first he looked for the people who kept touching their pockets. That's how he knew they had something valuable. He explained that once he identified a target, he used a very small razor blade to cut a slit under his victim's pocket, and just like that, the wallet or money clip or whatever was of value slipped out. "If it's on your body I can get it from you without you knowing," he said, flashing the metallic razor he used for dramatic affect, his smile a quick metallic flash of its own.

And it was true; his skills were unrivaled. Though it would happen later in the week that a member of his gang would see a man who kept clutching his pants, and when the pickpocket went up to him to stealthily run his razor along the man's pocket, he will instead slice a gash in the man's testicles, which were engorged with an infection that caused the man to continuously clutch them. The man will die of his wound and the pickpocket will end up in prison, a case that you don't defend. But this man in front of you now, the leader, was a master, and you wanted to know more.

"Is there any place on the body where valuables are safe? Could you really get anything from anyone?"

The gang leader responded quickly. He liked you, surely he did, and he liked this conversation, sharing the tricks of the trade. "Unless it's in your sock and your shoe is on," he said.

You nodded. It made sense. Okay then, so beyond that you could get anything from anyone, you were saying to him, and the pickpocket was nodding, smiling, taking pride in his skill, and you considered this, thinking.

You posed a challenge. If he could really get anything from anyone then get Nehru's pocket watch and wallet. This was the challenge you posed to him. "Show it to me," you said. "And then put it back in his pant pocket."

"Easy," the gang leader said.

And sure enough, the next day, when Nehru was out there giving his speech, members of the Congress gathered around him, this man, this leader of a pickpocket gang who was astoundingly good at what he did, found a way to get close enough to the politician and filch his pocket watch and wallet. And before the gang leader even had a chance to bring it to you, you heard on the radio in the evening news that the Prime Minister's wallet and watch had been stolen. Later, the pickpocket brought it to you.

You were truly impressed. This was criminal and went against your own moral code, but you appreciated the skill, the art of thievery. You used to tell your children that the criminals you defended were just as smart as anyone else, if not smarter. They were resourceful, and you admired this and I can understand why. Their creativity and dexterity. There is real art there, real intelligence.

"Now put it back," you told the pickpocket.

And he did. The next day, another brief article appeared in the Lucknow paper stating that the wallet and the watch had been located in Nehru's pocket, all a misunderstanding.

You loved this, these small fascinations. It reminds me of what I used to tell my Creative Writing students: "Let your characters fall in love with the world and whatever odd thing makes your character tick." You were a character who did fall in love with the world and the joys of simply existing. You lived well and you knew it, relished in it.

Another story was from a stifling hot summer afternoon when Brij was home from The Doon School and Raj was also off for the summer. You sat in the yard of the big house on Pandariba, sitting on the edge of the well, sweating, while your two sons hoisted buckets of water one after the other from the well in the yard. With each new fresh bucket of cold water they dumped on your head, you smiled and laughed, shaking your shag of wet hair, the ice water running down your neck a perfect break from the heat, and your sons smiled, too, a rare and lovely point of eased tension between a father and his adolescent boys.

Even during that difficult period when your days were burdened with your search for S.L., there was one morning during breakfast, when you and Yash Babu, both ravenous, tore through Avinash's first serving of morning puris, ripping at the flakey bread with pleasure. It wasn't uncommon for meals to turn into an eating contest, and you loved these contests. "How many eggs can you eat?" "How many almonds?" "How much lassi can you drink?" But this one stands out to me because it was a difficult period in your life, fraught as it was with the stress and worry over S.L., and yet you still found ways to set this burden aside, to laugh.

Maybe it was you, or maybe it was Yash Babu, but someone at some point proffers the challenge. "How much more puri can you eat?" The question hangs in the air for a moment, your children leaning in, waiting to see where this will go.

You call into the kitchen for Avinash to prepare more puris, another serving, and she does. You and Yash Babu tear through that one just as fast. "Another," you call. And then more after that until your wife runs through all the dough that she has prepared for the day, but you're too deep in the contest to stop now, so Avinash makes more puris, quickly mixing the flour, kneading the dough, frying it in hot oil, and then you and Yash Babu continue on, tearing at the bread and stuffing your mouths, the entire morning put on pause for this child's game, this brief thrill and challenge, Avinash shaking her head and laughing with each new round of fresh puris she prepares. You won. You always did.

There was another time when Raj was just a boy, and you and your family were on vacation in Nainital, a resort town wedged into a deep valley cut through with rivers and lakes in the Himalayas. One morning you went to the market and bought mangoes, of course you did, and you placed the bag in the icy waters of the rushing stream behind the hotel where you all were staying.

When Raj woke up that morning, you said to him, "Babbu, let's go have some mangoes."

Raj followed you down to the stream, the mangoes now chilled, and the two of you sat on a rock, sharing the fruit, finishing one after another and then making the short trip down to the stream for more. It was a warm morning and in the mottled light, the two of you ate, mango juice running down your wrists, the cool babble of the stream steady and even.

As the two of you ate, you pointed out across the valley, indicating a small building where the British had imprisoned Prime Minister Nehru, before Partition, before independence, and you talked about India, your country, your home, and then you moved onto a disquisition on mangoes, an ever-important topic for you, an ever-growing reservoir of knowledge. You told Raj about where each mango was grown and you told him about their defining attributes: the Chausa mango is the sweetest, the Rajapuri mango the largest, and the Totapuri, if looked at from the right angle, resembles a parrot's beak.

As you lazily went on and on, a stranger walked by. An hour later he walked by once again, the pile of seeds in front of you and Raj having now grown into a formidable monument to all that the two of you had consumed. "Baap re Baap," the stranger remarks at the sight. "Oh dear me," and you and Raj laugh, having only now realized how many mangoes the two of you have eaten.

And there was the time when Raj and Rashmi, still little kids, locked themselves in the bathroom in Bhopal House with elaborate plans to make a swimming pool. It was summer and hot, and in their child-reasoning they figured the low, Indian style bathroom with its single faucet, and one drain and a basin was basically already a small swimming pool, so why not add more water, make it deeper, a not entirely irrational premise.

They stuffed towels underneath the bathroom door to block the water—clearly Raj's idea, the little engineer already industrious as ever. The towels were thin but it still only took a few, Raj and Rashmi's small hands diligently rolling the cotton tight, and then working the fabric into the cracks to form a tight seal, stifling their hushed giggles as they did so. Next, they stopped the drain with another washcloth. And then they turned the faucet on and watched the water begin to fill the low basin until it slopped over the sides, and to their great excitement, began to flood around the towels and then inch up the wall.

Their giggles grew louder and soon the water was nearly up to their calves. They stomped around the bathroom, wildly triumphant. But then came the knock on the door. You were at work, but Avinash, suspicious, concerned, stood outside the bathroom, trying to push her way in. "What is going on there?" she asked. "Let me in. Unlock this door."

The children did, and later when Avinash told you this story—of how when Raj opened the door there was all this water, so much water, a great flood deluging the kitchen and the great room—you didn't get angry or frustrated or raise your voice or anything like that.

You laughed.

It's your loud belly-laugh, full of joy and happiness, and Avinash laughed too. The weird and inventive minds of your children seen as a blessing, a marvel.

And there were those afternoons, after work, when you would come home from the courthouse, and stop at the radio repair shop on the bottom floor of Bhopal House, this tiny little store space run by a fellow Punjabi. You would stop in and join him and the other neighborhood men. You would sit there with them, empty-handed while they drank tea—you didn't even drink tea!—and tell stories, hold court. You were in your element then, during these afternoons, the other men asking you about the law, your work, your experiences. You lived for these moments, the ease of conversation, of shared space and fellowship, the warmth of human interaction.

You had Shia Muslim friends too; friends who had been brave enough to stay behind during Partition. You had no antagonisms whatsoever toward Muslims, even after what you had been through. In fact, in some ways, you felt most at home among your Shia friends, especially Mr. Naqvi and Mr. Rizvi, two good friends who spoke Farsi and shared your love of Persian language and art. You appreciated beauty, loved poetry, and with these two friends you would often fall into lengthy conversations about Ferdowsi, the Persian poet, and this made you feel at home as well, to let yourself sink into a language and literary tradition you so admired. There is joy in language, in individual words, in meter and rhyme, and there is joy in sharing this love as you did with Mr. Rizvi and Mr. Naqvi.

But when I think about who you were and how you interacted with people, I always think most about your trip to America. It was May of 1986, and Raj's daughter, Shelly, was four months old. While you were there, every evening you and Avinash would take Shelly on walks around the neighborhood in her stroller, doing slow loops that ran along cul-de-sacs and tree-lined streets.

During these walks, if you happened to run into one of Raj's neighbors, you would always stop and talk. Later in the evenings you would tell Raj what you had learned from these conversations with his neighbors, and you would inevitably have learned more about them than Raj had learned after living next to them for years, sometimes even highly personal information, like family history, or annual income. But this was because you couldn't help but talk to people, and people couldn't help but talk to you, no matter where you were or who you were with.

Ajesh once told me your last name meant "joyful," and that you used to say that this didn't just mean that as an Anand you should be joyful. It meant that as an Anand you should also try to bring joy to others. I think this was true of you. It was all part of this adventure you were on, all part of this strange journey, a journey that no matter where it led, you always made sure it was a journey that included joy. Joy for yourself and joy for those around you. As much as anything else, you understood that there's a joy in living. As much as anything else, you lived for this joy and brought this joy to life for others.

Baij, in 1991, reading his daily papers.

LIKE A BANYAN TREE

*"Never judge people
by how they appear
or worry about
being judged."*

Rashmi and Arun Wedding, 1974.

7

DISCONTENTS AND CONTENT DISCONTENTMENT

In 1974, Rashmi marries Arun, a successful man in the military, and they move to Delhi, where he is stationed. And just like that, your first child is no longer living with you. But she is still in India, another city, yes, but not too far away, a day or so by train. With Rashmi, to have seen her through her education, and then for her to marry a man you respected, even admired, there was a sense of accomplishment, of release. With Rashmi, you couldn't have asked for more.

With your two middle children, Raj and Brij, it was different.

In 1974, Raj was working in sales with Crampton Greaves, but he wasn't entirely content. There was something missing, some unmet desire. It was during this time when Raj had his own experience with a holy man, the one he met in passing when he needed to get some papers delivered. "You will travel overseas," the holy man told Raj. "Your fortune is in another country." It was later that day when you had asked Raj what the holy man had said, when Raj told you and you responded with a rejoinder, a shrug: "You never know if what holy men say is true or influences you for it to be true."

I have thought about your response to Raj because of that rich contradiction between your own ostensible belief in the prophecies your holy man told you

Arun and Rashmi Wedding, 1974.

and the ambivalence with which you greeted the prophecies of the holy man Raj encountered. I do think you understood something about stories, their power, their gravity. I equally believe that because you understood how stories work, how they guide perception, organize meaning, that you did have a complicated relationship with holy men and prophecies.

But the fact remains: You didn't want your son to leave and find his fortune in another country. You loved your children, and you wanted them close, even if that meant pointing out tautologies in a fate you might otherwise be inclined to accept. If there's one thing I've learned about myself and my own thinking, it's how often my intellect is motivated by some deeper, emotional orientation. I think this is true of most of us, at least if we're lucky. It means we care in a way that transcends the theoretical, the logical. Without this, we're hardly human.

And yet, prophetic or not, as so much in your own life felt like fate to you, when Raj received a letter from a friend who was attending Portland State University, in Oregon, a few weeks later, urging him to apply, to come live in the US, to strike out anew, the words of the holy man Raj had seen felt a little like fate to him.

Arun and Rashmi, 1975.

LIKE A BANYAN TREE

There were Raj's other discontents, too, and this was a chance for him to start over, to remake himself. In 1975, your ice cream boy went to America and became a man.

Brij stayed with you for a few more years, living at Pandariba, shadowing you at work. Though he had never seemed that interested, you still hoped that he would take over your practice, or at the very least work for the state, find a stable career, and perhaps strike out on his own, as you did. In 1978, he took his exams, and he passed the first one, but was ultimately uninterested in the life you had hoped he would live. He left for the United States without taking the other parts of the exam.

The time you spent with Brij during those years was nonetheless valuable. Whether you knew it or not, you had an influence on him, perhaps a larger one than even Brij understood at the time. Brij learned to appreciate reading in a way he hadn't known before those years with you. And your indomitable work ethic, just witnessing it, left Brij with an appreciation for persistence and the power of work. Like Raj, however, Brij wasn't entirely content in Lucknow. Though perhaps, unlike Raj, there was something more restless in Brij. Maybe you saw this, maybe you didn't.

In 1979, Raj came home for a visit, and told Brij about living in Portland, Oregon, about his life in the US. It appealed to Brij, the prospects of such freedom. Later that year, your second son packed his bags, and set out on his own. You had overcome so much in your life, met all kinds of obstacles, your will and drive tremendous, truly unique, but there were some things you simply had to accept. There were some things you couldn't argue with or change. The fact that your two sons would leave for America was surely one of the more difficult of those realities. Family meant so much to you and that Raj and Brij would make their homes away from you, in America, must have hurt. It was a hard loss.

But even before Brij left, you were developing a new routine with your third son, Ajesh, who was happily following your career path, and this, in turn, made you happy. It was the 1970s now, and this was a tumultuous decade in India. In 1971, Prime Minister Indira Gandhi signed the Indian-Soviet treaty of friendship, breaking the decade long tradition of non-alignment. And then later that same year, after Pakistan bombed an Indian airbase, India declared war with Pakistan, a war that will end with the creation of a new country: Bangladesh. In 1973 the Bengal Tiger nearly went extinct, and the government inaugurated Project Tiger to save the species from complete annihilation. In 1974, India launched its first satellite into outer space.

The world, and your world in particular, was changing fast.

You were living in an increasingly modernized India and with this came the attendant perils of the 20th century. That same year—1974—India conducted its first nuclear weapon test, a massive underground explosion in Pokhran. By 1975, Fakhruddin Ali would become the second Muslim president of India, and following this were the upheavals of 1975-1977, during "The Emergency," a period of suspended democracy over protests and an ailing economy, and a period of forced sterilization that will remain one of the most controversial periods in India's independent history. By 1978, the Congress had lost its first election since independence, and Moraji Desai of the Janta Party became Prime Minster.

In the early morning light in your Pandariba office, you poured over newspapers and read about all of these events and more. This was still part of your routine, as it had always been. Three newspapers a day. Every day. The house was quiet during these crepuscular hours, and I imagine the sound of pages turning, the creak of the wooden chair in which you sat as you adjusted. Ajesh would rise shortly after you, and go for an early morning jog. As you read, you could hear the first stirring of your wife in the kitchen, making breakfast.

Still, you never drank coffee, not even tea. You had maintained this purity your entire life and you weren't about to change now. Instead, especially during the summer months, you would have a glass of Lassi made from milk curd and spices and sugar. You drank this slowly as you read the local news, then the national news, then the international news.

By 9 a.m. you were in your office with Ajesh, the two of you working. He was still in law school during this time, but you already had him doing tax law, which he didn't need to be licensed to do. But you also went over the cases you were working on at the time with him, and you had your son write the reports. You would dictate cases to him and he would write them freehand—a first draft—and then you would have him type them out on the black Remington Rand typewriter.

As with almost everything you did, there was a method to this: by first writing in freehand and then typing, you were having Ajesh do the work of intuitively revising. As he typed out his own handwritten sentences, he'd pick out the errors he might have otherwise missed if he had transcribed straight to the Remington. You were a meticulous writer, and you wanted this for Ajesh. You wanted him to learn the value of a razor-sharp sentence, a clear argument, the logic of the law free from clutter and excess verbiage.

Around 11 a.m. the two of you would take a break to have a late breakfast of eggs or daal or beans sprinkled with coriander and green chilies, Avinash plating the food and you sitting down at the table with Ajesh. And here you were always your usual jovial self, seamlessly switching out of work mode and the seriousness with which you trained Ajesh into something more playful—little jokes, poetry recitations, the periodic eating contest you couldn't refuse.

After you and Ajesh ate, the two of you would leave for the day. You no longer had a driver now that Ajesh had his license, and as he took you to court, steering the Hindustan Ambassador with ease and precision, you would sit in the passenger seat and go over cases with your son. After Ajesh dropped you off, he would drive himself to law school, where he would study and attend lectures and learn what you had learned in the same classrooms where you had learned.

By late afternoon, Ajesh, finished with his studies, would drive back to the courthouse. If you were in court, he would watch you argue a case, but often you were simply sitting with your colleagues in the bar room, joking and telling stories, as you always had. You were in complete possession of yourself in the company of your colleagues, and I think of this period as the prime of your life. You had proven yourself as more than a competent lawyer. You were a great success by this point. Your children told me you simply wouldn't take a case that you knew you wouldn't win, and this created a reputation that you couldn't lose. You were the The Lion of Lucknow, at least when it came to the law. Your presence swelled those cool halls of the courthouses in which you would argue.

You were in your prime, but at the same time you were preparing your son to take over what you had built, and there was so much you needed to teach him, so much knowledge you needed to impart before Ajesh took over your practice. It's those drives back from court, often stopping at Bhopal House—the old flat where you still had an office, and then back to Pandariba—where I imagine you telling your son stories about past cases, about what you learned from them and what you wanted Ajesh to learn from you now.

Like many skills, being a lawyer is a craft, and you were good at your craft.

This meant knowing the law, sure, but there was also a kind of creativity that you brought to your work, a kind of mental nimbleness that informed how you practiced the law. You were good at finding those small legal loopholes, or logical inconsistencies. It was important to you that you imparted this element of your work, this side of your craft, to Ajesh.

There was the case of the dacoit's wayward wife, for instance, who was married to the leader of a marauding band of thieves but had fallen in love with another member of the same gang. The lovers eloped and moved to Lucknow, far away from the gang. They came to you wanting to get married and start a new life. She wanted to leave her husband, but she knew that this man, who was brutal and severe, would never allow her to get a divorce. She came to you hoping to find a way out.

You knew that if the woman's husband wouldn't allow for a divorce, it likely wouldn't happen. But you told the couple, the woman and the dacoit that she was in love with and wanted to marry, to come to your office every day in the morning and evening at the same time. This was just so you could look at them, figuring that eventually an intuitive solution would arrive. I see an artist's sensibility in this approach, almost relying on the unconscious, letting your mind work on a solution rather than laboring consciously over the problem. It reminds me of my own writing process, those times when I've been stuck and rather than laboring away at the problem, I've taken a walk instead, gone outside, let my mind play. You had this approach with your own work.

The couple came back every day, sat in your office, sometimes for an hour, and you simply glanced at them periodically without saying anything. And then, one afternoon, as intuitive solutions often do, the answer struck you all at once. The woman was young, quite young. "How old were you when you were married," you asked her.

She was fifteen, she told you, which was too young to marry in the State of Uttar Pradesh. Her marriage wasn't legal. It was that simple. You had it annulled. But that it was simple was your point. Just because the answer is simple doesn't mean it isn't the right one. In fact, because it was simple often meant that it was the right one.

There was also the case of the disappearing fraudster. It was 1962, and you were still building your practice, living in Bhopal House. What had happened was this: A conman rented a shop front at Aminabad, the main marketplace in Lucknow. He sold pots and pans and other household wares. During those first few weeks of business, he becomes friendly with the other shop owners, ingratiating himself and charming those who worked in neighboring shops. He gained their trust, and then he enlisted them in an investment scheme, a way to centralize their wholesale purchasing power, or something along those lines, and in doing so he got his fellow shop owners to give him the necessary startup capital.

One morning, a few days after the conman's fellow shopkeepers gave him the startup cash, they found that his shop was closed. It was strange, but not unheard of. Perhaps he was sick? Perhaps there was a family emergency? The next day, however, the shop was still closed. And the day after that, still closed. A week passed. There was still no sign of this man who had taken so much of his neighboring shopkeepers' money. They realized that they have been conned.

They came to you, these shopkeepers, and they were angry. They told you what had happened, how this conman, this fraudster peddling lies, had taken their money under false pretenses and then absconded with it. Hundreds of thousands of rupees, gone. The first thing you told them to do was file a police report. But they doubted the police would do anything to help. They had just lost their livelihood, and they wanted to take matters into their own hands. They wanted revenge, and it was urgent that they get it. You tried to reason with them, explain that you'd have a better chance of solving the case if they didn't interfere, that you'd take care of it. In your office, you eventually calmed them, got them to file the requisite report, got them to wait.

You start working on the case. The first thing you do is hire a private detective, and the two of you begin piecing together possible clues as to where this conman is hiding. The detective finds him in Kanpur, in another town over, about fifty miles away, where he's running the same scheme that he was running in Lucknow, enlisting shopkeepers to invest under false pretenses. It's easy enough to find him, and you tell your clients, the shopkeepers, that you're going to have him arrested. But that he is alive and running another con operation rekindles the anger of these men from whom he has already stolen. What they want is to take matters into their own hands. Again you try to reason with them. Again you try to explain that if they interfere now it will only derail the case.

They don't listen.

Your clients set out on their own. They take a train to Kanpur, seek out the conman at the local market, and find him running a shop like the one he had run in Lucknow. They drag him from his shop, and then take him back to Lucknow on the train. As the train passes over the Ganges, it slows, as it always does, and according to what the shopkeepers tell you later, this is when the conman makes his escape. He tells his captors that he has to use the bathroom on the train, and figuring there is nowhere for him to go, they allow this. But as the train makes its way across the bridge, the conman opens the door of the passenger car they are in and leaps into the Ganges.

Here things get complicated. Your clients return, empty handed, and they tell you what had happened. By this time the conman's wife has already filed a case with the police, falsely claiming that her husband hadn't made an escape, but rather was kidnapped, and then murdered, the motive a business deal gone bad. The police apprehend your clients, all of them, and charge them with kidnapping and murder. You get them out on bail because there is no body, no evidence. It's the conman's wife's word against the shopkeepers'.

Still, your clients are in serious trouble. The wife gets a lawyer, and over the next few months the case progresses. But you're convinced that they didn't kill the fraudster. You believe their story, though you have no way of proving it. You consider this, let it sit with you, and then something occurs to you. You pay a different client of yours to take his case to the conman's wife's attorney, and you pay this client to spend as much time with this attorney as he can, to stay in his office, going over his case, and whatever legal fees he accrues you pay. Weeks go by and your client reports back to you at the end of each day. At first, nothing. He sees the conman's wife a few times come in and out of the attorney's office, but she doesn't say anything revealing.

And then one day, she slips, and your client, the one you are paying to be the wife's attorney's client as well, is in his office and hears everything. Later that afternoon, your client returns to your office and tells you what he's heard: how the wife came in, upset, saying that she and her husband are running out of money, asking how long it would take for her case to come to a close, and she makes a passing reference to how her husband has been masquerading as a holy man, living in a temple, right there in Lucknow. They needed money so he could eat.

She wanted to know how long this case was going to drag out before they could leave.

You send the police to the temple where he is hiding, and they apprehend him, charge him, and your clients, the shopkeepers, are obviously proven innocent, the charges of kidnapping and murder dismissed.

It's a story of resourcefulness, how sometimes your work as a lawyer involved strategy that wasn't about the law, necessarily, but also about a kind of creativity. You wanted Ajesh to understand this, so that he could bring this kind of skill to his work once you retired and once he took over your practice.

There were other cases that you didn't have to tell Ajesh because they were already so well known, cases that you fought in the past and won with what seemed like the flick of the wrist, a simple point made at the right time, in the right way, and the entire edifice a prosecuting attorney had mounted around an argument, just like that, crumbled.

There was the case of the warehouse thieves, for instance, where you sat silently and listened to the prosecutor enlist one piece of evidence after another, building what, to any onlooker, would have seemed like an impervious argument. From an outside perspective it looked like you didn't even have a chance, the case so obviously a win for the persecutor. You just sat there, immovable, waiting until the prosecutor had exhausted himself with a dizzying mountain of evidence.

It was a simple case. A gang of thieves had been breaking into a railway warehouse where goods were stored before being transported. The thieves were caught in the act. But the thing was, the railway networks had their own police, and there was a little-known statute that any railway criminal investigation had to be overseen by the chief inspector of the state police—a different agency—as a kind of safeguard against omissions or corruption. Without this oversight and interagency dependency—signed and sealed by the state chief inspector—no matter how rock solid a case seemed, any investigation would be dismissed out of hand. But this was fine-print stuff, statutes that were easily overlooked in the excitement of a case that seemed like a sure thing. Your attention to detail was phenomenal, however, and your memory of the law books you had read unrivaled. If there was anyone in the courtroom who noted the fine print, it was you.

The chief inspector had never signed off on this investigation, a detail that you kept to yourself throughout the entire duration of the prosecutor's argu-

Avinash and Baij at the Taj Mahal, 1966.

ment. And then when the prosecutor was done, satisfied with himself and the case, you simply walked up the judge, almost casually, and in your deep, clear voice, said: "There is no case here. It was an improper investigation. Under the law the entire case must be thrown out." And then you pointed out the statute, and like that, case dismissed.

Pay attention, you were always telling Ajesh.

Mind the small details.

Notice everything.

Observe. And then observe more.

And read the law carefully and closely.

In your small office in Bhopal House, you would tell Ajesh these things with an intensity and clarity that he would never forget, nor would he forget the stories of your past cases and the wisdom you would use them to impart.

But there was something else that you brought to the courtroom that had nothing to do with the law at all. This was your ability to calm a crowd, your capacity to return people to reason even when tempers were high. One of the most remarkable examples of this took place one night on the roof of Bhopal House.

Raj was eight years old, and it was summer. Like so many summer nights, the residents of Bhopal House spent the evening on the roof where it was cool, telling stories, sharing food, watching movies. As the evening ended and night fell, the women and girls returned to their flats, the daughters resistant as always, wanting to stay and play, and as they protested, you and the other men would go down to your own respective flats and retrieve dhurries and bedding, then return to the roof where you would sleep.

On this night, Raj stayed up late with his cousin, Yash Babu. Like you, Yash Babu was a delightful storyteller, and tonight he entertained Raj with tales of King Kong, his famous wrestling match with Dara Singh. Raj was captivated, as he often was. You sat quietly and listened until Yash Babu had finished up, and then you told Raj it was time for sleep. As always, you fell asleep quickly. It amazes me what you could sleep through, and this night was no different.

You slept through the whole thing. Raj had gotten up around one in the morning to go pee in the grated sewer pipe on the corner of the roof, and while he was peeing, a thief had crept up onto the roof, and began stealthily slipping everyone's shirts and shoes into his big bag. He was silent as he worked, so silent that it wasn't just you who slept, but most of the other men and boys on the roof.

The thief made his way down the row of dhurries, taking what he could. It was Mr. Tandon, a large man who lived in flat number 9 who woke, the thief at his bedside, taking Mr. Tandon's belongings. Mr. Tandon reached for him and yelled, "Chor! Chor! Chor!" but the thief had covered himself in mustard oil, so that he could easily slip away should anyone try to apprehend him, and he did slip from Mr. Tandon's grasp.

You slept through that, too, both you and your own father did. And you slept as the thief sprinted down the roof, the other men and boys waking now, giving chase, and you slept through the moment the thief ran past Raj, who was still standing at the grate, peeing out of his raised pajama pant leg as he was taught to do. Raj tried to grab the thief as he passed, awkwardly, almost losing his balance, but he eluded Raj's grasp. But Raj was a nimble boy, and he quickly ran after the thief. For a brief moment he lead the charge down the stairs and out onto the streets of Lucknow. You slept through that, too.

You slept while under a clear night sky most of all of the men and boys who lived in Bhopal House chased this thief down the streets of Lucknow. The thief ran toward a railway colony and then disappeared into a snarl of bushes. The men and boys stood there, throwing rocks into the brambles where the thief was hiding, Yash Babu, your nephew, leading the assault, hoping to hit him, to draw him out from his hiding.

When a rock did hit him, and the thief made a break from the bushes, it was Yash Babu, muscled and in his prime, who grabbed him and managed to hang onto him when nobody else could, despite the mustard oil and the thief's slick skin. The men and boys returned to Bhopal House, dragging the thief along with them. Back on the roof, they tied him to one of the chimneys and began beating him.

It was then that the commotion woke you. The night sky had given way to dawn's first light, and you heard the commotion, men yelling, the thief crying out with each blow. You and your father quickly made your way over to the crowd, and when you witnessed what was happening, you put yourself between the thief and the men who were beating him.

Crowds don't listen to people. Especially angry crowds when passions are high. But you had this way, this presence, this ability to bring reason to a group of people who had lost their reason. "Nobody is going to beat this man," your voice boomed, your father standing by you, helping you push back the crowd. The crowd submitted. Of course, Yash Babu, your admiring nephew, would have done anything you told him too, and he was one of the leaders of the crowd. But the other men, they didn't have to listen to you, and yet they did. This was one of those ineffable qualities you had. Men listened to you. It was like they couldn't help it. This was known in the courtrooms, part of your reputation, and it was also one of the immaterial skills you had that made you the remarkable lawyer you were.

Naturally, in the way only an admiring son could watch his father, Ajesh witnessed this in you, too, as he worked alongside you.

* * *

But this period in your life wasn't all work, hardly at all. Summer days blended into fall, and the weather cooled, and the rains broke as they always did. Time is a circle, always returning to the echo of where you started. It's true that by 1979, three of your children had left, but there were additions to your family, buffers for the losses to come, and these additions brought you tremendous joy. In 1975, your daughter, Rashmi, had a son, your first grandson, and you couldn't have been happier about this. But that same year there was a loss, too, one that affected you deeply.

Lakhi, your father, passed away shortly after your grandson's birth. You had such different values from your father, and like so many sons with their fathers, yours drove you crazy, at least at times. There was his constant hookah smoking, yes, and there was his distaste for education, but there were also the many ways in which you were more open-minded than your father. He was of a different generation than you and equally so of a different mindset. There was a stubbornness to him. When you moved your family to Lucknow, your father refused to change his traditional Punjabi dress and wore a turban until he died. His inability to change, to adjust to his context, indicated one of the underlying differences between the two of you.

Your father was a proud man, and it's true that he had good reason to be proud. The Anands, your family line, could be traced back to the Khukhrain tribe, a powerful clan in the area of salt mines, on the river Jhelum, in the ancient town of Bhera. In the 11th century, during Mahmud of Ghazni's attacks on India, the Khukhrain's fiercely resisted Ghazni's advances time and time again, but eventually Ghazni overpowered them, and, in defeat, the tribe scattered in exile. Royalty from the tribe ended up in Kala Naur and later Chokkar Kalan, in Pakistan, and it's this royalty in exile to which your own lineage can be traced. This was important to your father. He came from kings, the joke went, and at times there was something comical about this, his regal stubbornness boarding on the pompous.

There was the time you had a Bengali client, whose last name was Banerjee. He came to the house when you were out, hoping to find you. He found your father instead, sitting on the front porch, and Banerjee asked Lakhi to tell you that he had stopped by. Your father gave him a funny look and then later told you a man named Baner came by. You didn't know a Baner, and when Banerjee came by the next day and once again found your father, he asked, once again, that he let you know Banerjee had come by.

Again your father told you a man named Baner came by, and again you said that you didn't know any Baner. "Who is this Baner," you said, and shrugged. It was only later, after you had run into Banerjee in town, that he told you had been coming by, that he had been asking your dad to let you know. That's when you put it together. The term "Ji" is an honorific in Punjabi, a title of respect, and your father wasn't about to bestow an honorific on some young man he didn't know. He had no idea that Banerjee was a Bengali name. If anything, your dad thought that he should be referred to with the honorific Ji. He had come from kings!

And while this stubbornness, this presumption of royalty, this pride, indicated a difference between you and your father, it's also true that it was a point of overlap, one of the places where you and your father were most alike. One afternoon when you and your family were still living in Bhopal House, a rickshawalla had approached your father, who was standing on a street corner, and asked him if he could read him an address and direction. "You idiot," your father snapped at the rickshawalla. "Do I look like an educated man?" But the thing was, your father didn't need an education to be proud. "There is no higher level of confidence than revealing your own ignorance," is how Brij had put it when he recalled this story to me. "And with a tone of reprimand."

It's this confidence that reminds me of you. It calls to mind your certainty that you could send one of your own children to The Doon School, despite your own background. It calls to mind the time you first met Avinash's father, when you were still in the refugee camp, and you were doing dishes in your underwear. You stood up straight and shook his hand without the slightest shame. "You don't have to have anything to be proud," you used to say. "It's what's in your head."

Both you and your father were very much who you were, and though you weren't proud in the same way your father was, you weren't ashamed of anything either. I don't think either one of you ever experienced shame in your lives. There was a kind of presumed dignity that you both shared, even though it manifested in different ways. Your father could only ever be himself, and the same was true of you.

Whatever differences you and your father did have, you loved each other. As you aged and became more and more successful, I think he admired and respected that you were educated. He saw the doors your schooling had opened for you. There was a practical outcome to all your studies, which he appreciated, but I think he also learned to appreciate your education because it made people respect you. In a strange twist of irony, your father's aversion to education came from his sense of royalty. He didn't need to work, to be educated, because he felt entitled to the good life without it. He looked down on education for this reason, and yet, it was your education that helped cultivate the kind of respect he felt entitled too. Toward the end of his life, I think your father began to realize this.

When you and your family moved to Pandariba, there was enough space for your dad to have his own room in the back portion of the house. This was his space, and he spent a great deal of his time there, smoking his hookah, playing chess, flipping through the occasional Urdu newspaper that he could read with his 4th grade education. But even though he had his own room, in the evenings your father would wait up for you. He would refuse to sleep until you came home from court or your office in Bhopal House. He would wait and wait and wait, no matter how late you stayed at work, and then when you came home, always entering through the side door where his room was, he would simply nod his head. "Okay, you have come," he would say. "I just wanted to see that my son is back home." And then he would retire to his room for the night.

This was so important to your dad that there was one night when you came home late and used the front door, since you knew Avinash would have been up waiting for you. Your father didn't see you enter the house. You had gone to bed, forgetting to say goodnight to him. Around one in the morning you woke to your father's voice, thundering downstairs: "Where is Baija my son," he was calling. He was worried because he thought you had not come home. You had to get out of bed and go to the back portion of the house to calm him, reassure him that you had come home, that everything was okay.

There was real love between you two.

You also had a real respect for your father. Despite your differences, he had that self-assurance and strength of will that no doubt wasn't lost on you, but I think you also admired his intelligence, though subtle and different from yours. He was a master at chess, as Brij has attested many times. The games the two of them would play together would last late into the afternoon. When he was a teenager, Brij would try to get the upper hand on his grandfather by cheating. When Lakhi would look away to take a puff on his hookah, Brij would move the pieces to his advantage. Once, when your father caught Brij doing this, he grabbed your son's wrist, furious, and yelled at the boy. There was a severity to your father as there could be a severity to you, too. He shook Brij and the two of them caused such a commotion, yelling at one another, that Avinash, hearing the noise, rushed into the room. Tired of their fighting over chess, she grabbed the board and pieces, rushed them outside, and threw them down the well.

Not that this stopped Brij and Lakhi from playing. They painted squares on a table outside and made their own pieces, resumed their games and were at it again. It's in this, in the love of craft and art of strategy in a game like chess—and how intent your father was on winning—that I see something of you, of your love for the law, the races you would swim against friends in the Chenab, in your competitive edge, your tests of strength. I think you learned this from him and carried on its tradition.

Your father's passing carved an empty space into your life. He died suddenly, and this was part of what was so hard for you about it. You didn't get a real chance to say your goodbyes. You were not prepared for it. He went suddenly, in an hour or two. It was a hot afternoon in 1975, and all morning your father had

Arun, Rashmi, and baby Rohit, 1976.

Rashmi with Aanchal and Rohit, Lucknow, 1979.

Discontents and Content Discontentment

been complaining about pains in his chest. You and your family had decided to take him to the doctor, even though it seemed like a minor problem, whatever it was. Indigestion, perhaps, or maybe finally all that smoke from the hookah was catching up to him; maybe the doctor would tell him to cut out the habit, not that Lakhi would listen.

When you arrived at the doctor's office, your father was lucid. Upon first sitting down with the doctor he carried on a conversation. The impression was that Lakhi would be fine. But then almost immediately after arriving, something happened. Your father fell to the floor. You were there by his side. The doctor rushed to his aid, and you tried to help but there was nothing you could do. Heart failure. It was so sudden. He was there in the morning and then he was gone in the afternoon.

Loss is in the details, the minor absences that point to something much larger that is missing. When you came home from work late in the evening, there was nobody there waiting up for you. In the mornings, there was no longer the smell of smoke and cow dung from your father's hookah. The painted squares on the table outside and the chess pieces lay there, undisturbed.

Brij told me that he had only seen you cry twice in your life.

Your father's passing was the first time.

In 1977, Rashmi had a daughter, Aanchal. She was in Lucknow for the birth, and so you got to be there. "Big daddy," is what your first grandchildren would call you when they were old enough to speak, and when Rashmi would come to Lucknow, visiting from wherever her husband, Arun, was stationed. During these stays you would call your grandchildren your "honored guests."

You loved these visits. There was a game you used to play with your grandchildren when they stayed with you. "My honored guests," you would say to them first thing in the morning when you came downstairs and saw them at the table, waiting for you, and then you would choose one, Aanchal or Rohit, knowing that the next day you would choose the other, and you would sit down and look at them seriously and intently.

"My honored guest," you would say again, now zeroing in on whoever it was today, growing more serious, almost solemn. You would take out a piece of paper and a pen. "My honored guest, what would you like to eat today," you would say. "Whatever you want you will have. I'll make the menu now."

Whoever you chose would shriek with delight and list an eccentric variety of foods that would be impossible to get, but still you wrote it all down, nodding, seriously. "Yes, yes," you'd say. "And what else. What else would you like?" You scribbled any further requests and nodded intently. Even though most of what was on the menu you could never get, you always managed to find one or two items. When you came home later that day, your grandchildren would cry out with excitement, "Big daddy, big daddy, what did you bring?" You would reach into your pockets, as you had done with your own children, and produce some surprise, some treat, some small item from their lists, and hand it over.

You loved doing this, providing, and you loved the eccentricities of children, their little games, but you also loved to find ways to prepare them for the world, teach them what you could. Before they were hardly old enough to hold up their little heads, you were telling them stories, counting on their little fingers. You were ever the teacher and you couldn't resist teaching them everything you could. But these visits were all too brief and infrequent. It wasn't until Ajesh had children of his own that you became a full-time grandfather, with grandchildren living in your house with you.

Ajesh had graduated law school in 1984 and once he was licensed you slowly began his transition to becoming lead attorney. Much of your routine stayed the same after this point. You and Ajesh still rose early and it was still newspapers first thing in the morning. The two of you would still work until 10 or 11 a.m., seeing clients, going over cases, and then you would have breakfast, and after breakfast Ajesh would drive the two of you to court.

But gone were the days when Ajesh would drop you off and then head to school, and gone were the days when you would enter the courtroom alone. Now Ajesh was at your side, and as you walked down halls you would help Ajesh fine-tune the cases that he would argue in your stead. "Are you prepared," you'd ask him, as he kept stride with you, and he would say yes, because he was a quick study, like you, but nonetheless, you would make a point about the legal logic of his argument, the obvious counter argument a prosecuting attorney would make, and the rebuttal Ajesh should make in turn. You'd say these things even though Ajesh had studied hard, knew each case inside and out—you would

Right: Gyan Devi with great grandkids Rohit and Aanchal, 1979.

Below: Gyan Devi at over 100 years old.

LIKE A BANYAN TREE | 211

say these things out of professional concern, of course, but also out of fatherly concern. You wanted Ajesh to do well, to be successful, and to command a courtroom and the cases he argued as you had done. You wanted him to find his stride and confidence, his mastery.

But this required a certain letting go on your part that wasn't always easy. At first, you would enter the courtroom with Ajesh. You would never stand with him, because as the senior attorney, convention dictates that you would have had to make the arguments. So instead, you found a place in the back of the courtroom and watched from there, and you always had something to say after each session. Not criticisms, exactly, but advice.

"Never rely on your memory for legal purposes," you were always telling Ajesh. Even though your own memory was seemingly boundless, your point was about precision. If you're making a legal argument, have the statute in front of you so that you can refer to it. This is what you told Ajesh, and you told him to always quote any statute you referred to in a brief in full. This way, too, you could be explicit, precise.

"And get to know your client." As a lawyer this was another dictum you lived by and you often reminded Ajesh of its importance. You had to know and understand your client as well as possible if you were going to argue on his or her behalf. You had to get into their head, understand their thinking. "Get to know their domestic situation. Get to know every aspect of your client's life," you'd say.

But the most important advice that you gave Ajesh had to do with argumentation style itself. "Go after the grain, not the chaff," you told your son. You had seen too many lawyers try to win cases by building up artifice and stating facts and legal precedents. That was all well and good, but it had a place, and the place for it wasn't at the beginning of an argument. Clarity. A single, effective point. This is how you convince a judge. Don't lose the opening claims to the tangential. Don't even lose the claim to the relevant facts. Make the claim on its own, clearly and with intention. "Hit the nail on the head," you told Ajesh. And then, and only then, develop the case. Go after the grain. Not the chaff.

Over time, you stopped going into the courtroom with him. One day, as the two of you entered those halls, you told him you would wait outside. It was a moment that had been coming for some time, and though it seemed small, a mi-

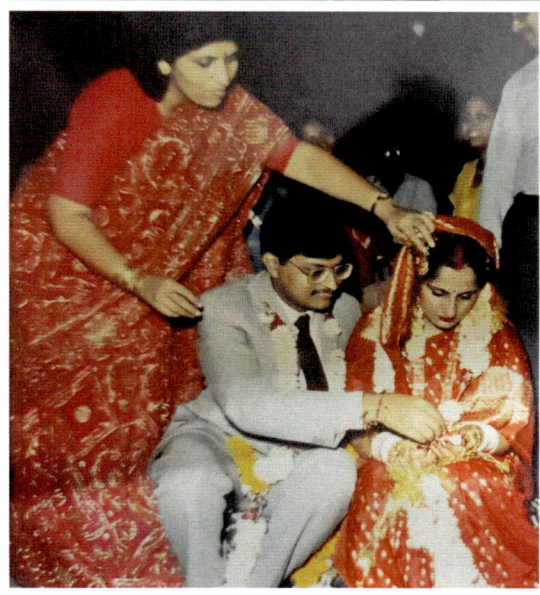

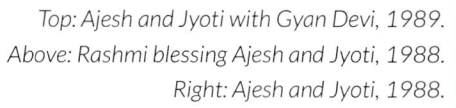

Top: Ajesh and Jyoti with Gyan Devi, 1989.
Above: Rashmi blessing Ajesh and Jyoti, 1988.
Right: Ajesh and Jyoti, 1988.

LIKE A BANYAN TREE | 213

nor variation, it indicated a larger shift. You were handing over more and more responsibility to your son.

But even then, even though you stopped going into the courtroom with Ajesh, you were always sure to send in one of your colleagues to stand in the back and watch and then report back on how he was handling himself. If you didn't do this, if you knew the judge, you would ask him, in passing, after the case had been argued, how your son had handled himself. It made you proud to hear that he was handling himself well.

But just because Ajesh was now arguing cases and taking on more responsibility, you never stopped working. You were always there, at the courthouse, even though you weren't arguing cases. You'd linger with colleagues, discuss developments in the law, and in the late afternoon, when you and your son would leave the courthouse, the two of you would go to Bhopal House together, your office still there, and you were just as active as always, reading cases, writing reports, and seeing clients.

You and your son were increasingly becoming equal partners, but that never once meant that you brought your own workload down. You loved it too much, the challenge of a case, wielding the logic of the law and considering all the different angles from which an argument could be made. And you loved writing and reading too much, too. And again, I see something of an artist's sensibility in you when I consider your passion for your work, the creative play of the mind that this entailed.

You loved it so much, in fact, that even when you were away from your work in Lucknow, you still found a way to engage with the law. To Avinash's consternation, on those vacations that you took with your family to Nainital, you couldn't resist going to the courthouse there and talking with the other lawyers, asking about the cases they were working on. You also couldn't resist troubling over those cases they would tell you about. Sometimes, you would even go so far as taking on a small case while you were on vacation. "Why do you even go on these vacations if you're just going to work," Avinash would ask you. Because you liked it. It was that simple.

This was also true of the time that you visited Raj in Atlanta. When you were there, you had missed working so much that in the mornings you would have Raj drive you to the Dekalb County Courthouse. You would sit in on cases that were being litigated, and afterward you would approach the attorneys and start a conversation with them about the law and their work. It's the kind of thing that under normal circumstances would have just seemed weird, but again, you had this quality where people wanted to talk to you. You became a welcome presence in Dekalb Country Courthouse during your brief stay in the US.

It was four years after Ajesh had graduated from law school that he married, and by 1989, he and his wife, Jyoti, had their first son, Akshay. Your house was filling up again—a daughter-in-law and now a grandson. You were crazy about baby Akshay, and to Jyoti's endless frustration, when you and Ajesh would return in the evening from work, no matter how late it was and no matter how long Jyoti had been trying to put Akshay to sleep, you would wake him just so you could see him and play with him and hear his little laugh.

You would lift him in the air and then hold him to your chest and, as you had always done with your kids and then Rashmi's children too, you would tell him stories, never mind that he was too young to understand them. You would tell him about your day at court, the food you ate, and all the strange things you'd seen out there in the great big world.

Then, when Akshay was a year old, he became ill.

It started with what seemed like a minor incident, the flu, one of the numerous illnesses that children get. But he wasn't getting better. Weeks passed, and his fever would come and go, as would the persistent bouts of vomiting, and each time his fever broke or his stomach steadied, you and Ajesh both would swell with hope, only for your grandson to become sick again.

Ajesh and Jyoti took Akshay to the doctor, and he was prescribed a round of antibiotics. They didn't help. If anything, they seemed to only make Akshay worse, his stomach more volatile now than it had ever been. He was losing weight and he couldn't keep anything down, and on those evenings when you would come home and wake him, he was often too weak to even smile, let alone laugh.

Ajesh took him back to the doctor, and they ran more tests, more antibiotics, but he only worsened still, and so Ajesh took him back to the doctor once again. One month had turned into two and two into three and now four. It would turn out that the antibiotics were what was making Akshay worse. The pills flooded his system, wiped out his intestinal tract, and when the doctor realized this and took him off them, he slowly got better. But I think this experience left you uneasy, with a renewed sense of how precarious life can be.

I'm sure you knew this already, with all you'd been through, but I think it was different this time. You were able to confront your own struggles and even the inevitability of your own passing with such equanimity, though it wasn't so easy to do this with those who were close to you. This must have been compounded by how quickly your own father passed, the suddenness of it driving home how precarious a life could be.

One afternoon, when Jyoti was pregnant with Anuj, your second grandson, you were seeing a client in your office. You spoke freely about your good fortune, how happy you were, a grandfather with another grandchild on the way.

"You already have grandchildren," your client responded, the jealousy in his voice hard to miss. "How could you want more. How could you *need* more."

Your client's response troubled you. "The evil eye," was the expression that came to mind, how having such good fortune can attract bad luck, the jealousy of others. You weren't a superstitious man. You were first and foremost reasonable, rational. But around this time something in you seems to have shifted.

Even though you wanted to celebrate Anuj's birth, for months afterward, you had kept him a secret, not even telling your closest friends. True, you did this to mute your own good fortune, to exercise some sensitivity around those who might become jealous.

But my guess is that Anuj's birth brought back to you the precariousness you were feeling when Akshay became ill, how you almost lost him as well, not to mention how quickly your own father passed. By not talking about Anuj, I don't think you were just trying to prevent others from being jealous. I think you were also trying to protect him—however superstitious that sounds, as if concealing his birth was a way to also conceal him from the world and the possible dangers that are in it. It seems to be one of those rare points in your life when you may have been trying to protect yourself, too.

Part of living is losing what we care about, and learning to accept that fact is very much the work of being here. That's so much easier in theory than in practice. Perhaps, in a way, you were afraid to celebrate Anuj's birth, to name your good fortune, as it would only articulate your attachment to what you loved. It is

Above: Anuj, 1997.
Left: Akshay dressed as Krishna, 1992.

one of the only stories that I've heard about you where you seem to be, however subtly, withholding.

I don't want to read too much into this, but it's almost as if you were weighing the scales, trying to figure out a way that you could cheat the potential of misfortune, a little like how you had tried to argue with the stars with Brij and his potential wife's horoscope. It's these kernels of vulnerability in your life where I find myself relating most to you, and I am especially drawn to the tension and juxtaposition of wanting to protect what you love while simultaneously being so giving, so generous, so open with your life and what you had to offer those who you cared about.

When Anuj was a few months old, you finally let yourself tell your friends and colleagues that you had another grandson. After that, you fell freely into the joys of having two grandsons in your home on Pandariba. Your house was full again and your life, from what I can tell, had become rich and mellow in these later years. You still had your work, but now Ajesh had taken on the more practical side of business. This left you with what you always loved most about working as a lawyer: the cases, yes, reading them and discussing them, but also just simply being in the courthouse and talking with colleagues. Still, you never missed a day of joining Ajesh at the courthouse. While he argued, you enjoy your time in conversation and discussions with your friends there, fellow attorneys and judges as well. And then later in the afternoons, you and Ajesh would work together in your office at Bhopal House.

In those quiet afternoon hours, you brought the same diligence and attention to detail to your work as always, but now you were able to share this with someone, and not just someone, but your own son.

There is an image I have of you as a grandfather during this period in your life that stands out to me. It mirrors an image that you had from your childhood of your own grandfather. During those afternoons when you and Ajesh would finish up early, when the two of you had extra time, Ajesh would drive you to the primary school that your grandchildren attended, and the two of you would wait out front until school ended.

Your pockets were filled with candy and treats. Just like your first memory of what your own grandfather had done for you on your first day of primary school—just as he had reached into his own pockets and with such generosity offered treats to you and all your classmates—now it was your turn to do the same. When school got out, you would call your grandchildren over to you and tell them to go get their friends and classmates, that you had candy for everyone, and when they came running back you would produce sweets from your seemingly bottomless pockets. Your grandchildren and their friends circled around you, laughing.

It strikes me as such a trenchant image to how you celebrated your own happiness: by giving. If you were like a banyan tree that gave and gave and gave, for me it's hard to think of a more innocent and joyful image of that than this. And if your last name means "joy," it's equally hard to find an analogy that so precisely concentrates the joy that passed from generation to generation of Anands than the joy your grandfather brought to you and your classmates and now the joy that you brought to your own grandchildren and their friends.

It's such a small act, and the openhandedness, the love behind it, the happiness, and the desire to give without expectation—as there was nothing to expect in return from the children—feels aspirational. For me, it captures something about the essence of your life that I'd like to carry into my own.

* * *

It's summer now, and I've been thinking about this image of your generosity in relation to those places in my own life where I want to be more giving, but also those places where I feel compelled to do so already.

As I am writing this, a few days ago E. and I celebrated our first anniversary with a weekend out on Port Townsend. We drove from Seattle on a Friday, spent the afternoon on the beach looking for agates, and then afterward had dinner at The Silver Water Café, a small restaurant in an old brick building downtown, that, admittedly, I like more than E. does.

Over dinner we talked about the last year, some of our favorite memories, and for both of us, our favorite times were those less remarkable moments that nonetheless left us feeling a quiet contentment: A Sunday morning lying in bed; those times that I would make her an egg sandwich for breakfast in the morning during the week days that she stayed with me; or waiting for the ferry on a winter's night after spending an afternoon on a beach on one of the San Juan Islands, the rain against the windshield while E. quizzed me on who sings what Beatles songs. "John's voice sounds more metallic and George's sounds more airy! Can't you hear it?" I could hear it, though it took me a while to finally learn the difference.

It's always the small things, isn't it? This is where joy is and I know you understood this. The mangoes, the street vendors, the cadence of a poem in Urdu, your children walking up and down your back, their tiny feet on your spine. It's in these moments that contentment and happiness take hold, and in the same way you also enjoyed the more subtle and quiet moments in your life, I was once again enjoying those kinds of moments in my own.

For dinner E. and I split fish tacos and the salmon. It felt good to recall our shared memories—the one's we both were fond of—especially because, or so it seemed to me, some of the more difficult stages of establishing intimacy were behind us. We had gotten through those first fights, sometimes explosive, that arise from building trust. It finally felt like we had fallen into something reliable, something easier and quieter.

After we ate and ordered desert, I gave E. the gift I bought for her earlier in the week. I was proud of this gift because I felt it was thoughtful and a good indicator of my commitment to her. I pulled a handmade, keepsake box from a small bag I had under the table. It was in the shape of a half moon and had a top, inlaid with copper stars and constellations—the big dipper and the little dipper—that opened to the side on a hinge. I slid it across the table toward her, and explained that I wanted something in which she and I could keep mementos from the coming year.

I wonder if you would have appreciated this kind of a gesture. You weren't a sentimentalist, as I can be, but I do think you were keenly aware of how meaning is something that we bestow onto the world through conscious acts of repetition. Value comes from choosing to value something. That's what this box was for, a repository for the memories in the year to come to give those memories added meaning and significance.

"Provided I can stand you for another year," I joked, "next June we can open the box and go through the reminders of what we had done." The box was meant to be like a time capsule, but and more importantly, it felt like an overt gesture toward acknowledging this was very much a long-term thing for me, or at least I hoped it was. E. seemed genuinely happy and moved by the gift, and over dessert we talked about what kinds of items we would put in it, starting with ferry ticket from this trip.

"I wonder what we would have thought of each other had we met five or six years ago," I said, as we finished dessert.

"I would have hated you," she joked.

"You sort of hate me now."

"True," she said, and took a bite of the chocolate mousse that was between us.

"You know," I said, being serious now. "I am glad we met now and not earlier, when I was younger." I had thought about this, and I had thought too about the ways in which being sick had significantly shifted my priorities, but also how telling your story after my experience with illness seemed to open me up for a relationship in new ways. In my early thirties, my identity was so wrapped up in markers of success, in my work, in my ambition, in being a writer, and I think because of this, I had a very hard time being generous to others, but especially with the people I was close to. Those were the people who could reasonably expect to make demands on my time, but if I felt like these demands interfered with my work or my own ambition, what I hoped to accomplish for myself, I would push people away, even resent them.

What a contrast my old relationship to work is with how you approached your own work. For you, work was the material means to provide. This isn't to say that you didn't enjoy your work. I know you did. But ambition always took a back seat to those you cared for. I understand the value of that more now than I ever did. I simply don't feel the same ambition that I used to. My work is still important to me, and, in fact, has been becoming more important to me, but over the last year it has felt different. I know this is in part because of the perspective illness has given me, but increasingly that perspective feels grounded in reflecting on your life.

What I've come to understand about your own honesty from your children has made me want to be more honest. To write to your children and to their children—rather than to the literary world—has allowed me to prioritize sincerity without all the baggage of trying to be writerly. It's the same sincerity and honesty I want to bring to my relationship with E.

This isn't all to say that I'm glad I got sick. There's still so much in that experience, in those four years of suffering, in the experience of not having a home and the fear and the anguish of feeling like I would never be okay again, experiences that I wouldn't want to have again for anything.

And yet, at the same time, I did experience it. I can't change that. And so the question is what should I do with the fact that I have experienced those things, that it is a part of my life now. In what ways can I still take responsibility for my own life and what has been handed to me while living it? I think the same is true of having to reconcile the death of my own dad and knowing that's a relationship I can never fix. I can't change that I will never know him as I wanted to, but what I do with that is my choice.

I think this is how you thought about your life, your experience with Partition, and the subsequent challenges you had to face. In a way, it's the task of every life. What to do with what we're given? Through illness I was forced to evaluate my own relationship to my ego, what I identified with, my work. Then, in writing your story, I was handed a narrative to think through a new set of values: generosity, sincerity, a different kind of relationship to obligation and duty than I had in the past. I'm not saying I would want to take on all that you did. I don't, and I'm not sure that I could. But, it does make me want to give more to the responsibilities I do take on.

This is what I tried to explain to E. in The Silver Water Café.

I said: "I guess I'm just grateful that we met when I was able to give more than I had been able to in the past. That we met when I'm able to see a little beyond my own immediate wants and needs."

"You're still needy," she smiled.

"I know."

"But I'm glad to be part of those needs."

"So long as I can be part of yours," I said.

Our hotel room that night was one of the worst hotel rooms I've ever stayed in. It had high ceilings that made the space feel cold rather than open, the florescent lighting flickered, and the windowsills were colonized with mold. You've slept in worse places, no doubt. I reminded myself this, as your experience had become another point of reference among many others in my own life now.

We had an early night, and by 10 p.m. or so E. was asleep. I lay awake unable to relax and with my mind running. When I did fall asleep, I had nightmares that I was sick again and that I didn't have a place to live. They're always the same. In them I'm out of money, with no resources to see a doctor, and had to start over. E. was gone, my work was gone, and I was alone and scared. I still have these nightmares once a week or so.

I woke up not feeling great, headachy, and groggy. I showered and then E. and I went to a coffee shop where I bought a newspaper and read some of Nancy Mitford's book, *In Pursuit of Love*, which seemed appropriately ironic, but my eyes were tired and doing that thing they do when I don't sleep well—slipping off the page and failing to track longer sentences. After two cups of coffee we went to the beach to look for agates.

By the time we got out onto the sand, I was starting to feel better, more present. There's something about being by the water that has always put me at peace. I think this is in part because I grew up surfing, and from an early age learned to associate being in or near the water with happiness. I don't surf anymore, but I still find that same sense of ease when I'm near the ocean. The smell of salt and kelp, a strange mixture of brine and something sweeter, hibiscus or watermelon, makes me feel at home, and so too does the way the water, on a windless day, reflects the sky until the horizon collapses the distinction between ocean and clouds, way out there in the distance.

The day was overcast, the water a glassy, almost oily stillness. E. and I separated and as I walked alone, I took deep breaths, trying to find my center, that sense of being okay. Already, the energy of the ocean was calming, making me feel more at peace. We walked for an hour or so down the beach, coming together and drifting apart and then coming together again. Neither one of us had found anything significant—no agates yet—though we still traced the water's edge with great attention, hoping something interesting would turn up. We spent another half hour enjoying our wandering search before turning around to make our way back to the car.

Our fight started twenty minutes or so after we had turned around. We were retracing our steps along the water's edge, hoping to find something we had missed. We were walking side by side and E. had her hand around my arm, leaning into me slightly as we walked. I asked her if she liked the present I had got her—the handmade box—and she smiled and leaned into me further. "It was very thoughtful," she said. My intention hadn't been to start anything, nor did I have an agenda to bring up that I would have liked her to have given me something as well, or at least made some gesture toward that affect, but when she asked me if I was disappointed that she didn't get me anything, I responded honestly, that the thought had crossed my mind once or twice.

"I think it would have made me happy if you had," I said. I could tell that she felt bad right after I said that, and I could also feel a brief jolt of tension in the air. "It's okay though," I said, trying to correct course. "But just something to maybe keep in mind for the future." I looked at her. "But it really is okay. It's not a big deal."

And for a moment, it did seem okay. E. frowned, squeezed my arm tighter and said that she was sorry. In her half-serious, half-joking voice, she then asked if I thought she was a bad girlfriend.

"Yes," I said, relieved to hear the jest in her tone. "I think you're a terrible girlfriend. It's a good thing you can be funny."

"And cute," she said.

"That too," I said. "I guess."

Everything felt fine.

We separated again briefly, tending to our own private search, and everything did feel fine. Ten minutes or so later we came back together, and she told me again that she was sorry. "Are you sure it's okay?" she asked.

You valued peace of mind, Baij. I know this about you, and I know that you probably picked your conflicts wisely because of this. You knew when to let something rest and move on. I have yet to master this skill. If anything, I'm hardly an apprentice at it. So, yes, I wish I wouldn't have said anything and I'm not sure, exactly, why I did. Maybe there was part of me that was more hurt than I wanted to admit, or maybe there was some other motivation that I didn't completely understand.

I said, "I guess I was hoping you were going to give me something today, and when you didn't I was disappointed." As I said this, I could hear the disappointment in my voice, and I realized then that there was truth to it, but I also felt bad wanting and expecting more than what the weekend already was. Why couldn't this be enough? Why the discontent when I already had so much that I wanted?

E. looked at me and I could feel her pull away before she did so physically, letting go of my hand and giving me a little space, which, admittedly, is probably what I would have done had I been in her shoes, too.

"Don't do that," I said. "Don't pull away. That isn't fair. I'm just trying to be honest with you. You asked and so I'm telling you that I would have liked to receive some gesture to indicate that today was important to you too."

I knew that was the wrong thing to say right after I said it. E. obviously thought the day was important, and she had showed me, in her many ways, that she cared.

She threw up her hands and said that she thought this was gesture enough. "We came here to your favorite place, went to dinner at your favorite restaurant," she said. "I wanted to come here to show you how much you mean to me."

From there things began to spin out of control, as they often do when two people who care about each other feel like no matter what they say they keep hurting each other, but there was also an underlying theme that quickly came to the surface. There had been times in our relationship where I had felt like I was making myself more vulnerable than E., putting myself out there more willingly than she was, and generally trying to show up for her in ways that she wasn't doing with me.

In hindsight it seems more obvious to me that this feeling often arose from miscommunications rather than actual ill-intentions, but still it was a feeling that sometimes came up and got the better of me. There was something about this fight, something latent in the idea of me making more of a gesture toward the significance of this last year than she did, that hit those same buttons.

By the time we got back to the car, this was what our fight had become about, with the added layer that because the fights E. and I already had over the past year were about me doing more in the relationship than she was, she would feel like the ways that she was showing up for me, the ways she was making herself vulnerable, in short, all the effort she was making toward the relationship, were overlooked, and that I couldn't see, in this particular case, that her going to

Port Townsend—a place I loved—and that going to dinner at The Silver Water Café—one of my favorite restaurants—was yet another example of how her efforts were being overlooked.

In short, the fight, as most fights often do, perfectly hit all the themes we had fought about in the past, all the tripwires and hot buttons. We each felt like the other person was being the self-centered one and not seeing or hearing what we each were trying to say. And then there was the guilt. I felt like I had ruined the day by voicing my needs and E. felt like she had ruined the day by voicing her feelings about me voicing my needs.

As we eased out of the parking lot at the beach and drove through Port Townsend, how to get things back on track and makes things okay again felt like a complete mystery.

Why are my relationships like this? Why do I become so sensitive and so easily hurt, secretly always weighing who is doing more and who is being overlooked, who is showing up and who isn't, who is making the compromises and who is doing the taking. I hate this feeling, this tallying and keeping track and the awareness of all the subtle shifts of power that arise from who has the moral high ground, from who is right and who is wrong.

I don't think you had this pettiness, and maybe some of this is cultural. Brij has mentioned this before, how there's a resistance among Indian men to getting too hung up on this kind of emotional vulnerability, especially during your time. My guess is that like many of the arguments E. and I had, this one would have also played out with a degree of strangeness and absurdity to you.

But cultural differences aside, there was something here that made me appraise the moment in relation to your generosity. I tend to act selfishly when I'm hurt, and I lose that sense of openness I admire in you.

In that moment, sitting in the car with E., I realized I wanted to break free of this so bad. Yes, in relationships we need things from others, and to pretend we don't is to pretend we are in this world but not of it. Still, I am not content with how I handle these kinds of conflicts and want to be better at it. But more than anything as we got on the highway and Port Townsend grew smaller and smaller in the rearview mirror, I wanted to go back in time 30 minutes and keep to myself what I wished I hadn't said.

Like a child, I brooded in the passenger seat as E. drove. *I was in the laby-*

rinth now. I glanced over at E. She had her eyes forward, hands coldly on the steering wheel.

We drove in silence for a while, and then we tried to talk about what we were feeling, but at this point we were both hurt and resistant. Again, E. told me how it was completely reasonable to want something in return, but that she just wanted also to be clear that she did feel like she was making that gesture by spending time together, spending a day in a town that I loved, eating dinner in a restaurant that I really liked. The entire trip was meant as the very indication that I was looking for. "It's the time that we spend together that matters," she said. "That's how I feel about time. It's the most important thing."

You felt this too. "Time is valuable, don't waste it"—that expression you had hung in your office. And it's true, isn't it. Time is, in a very real sense, all we have. How we spend it is what matters. I unequivocally agree with this. But I was being obstinate, and probably unfair. I was being so unlike you, Baij. I was being petty. I said that time sometimes felt like the minimum thing a person in a relationship could give, that being here, showing up, was the baseline. And then we argued about that, about what the minimum was in a relationship, and then we were right back to the beginning: to tallying of who was doing more. We accused each other of various shortcomings—the shortcomings that we had already been over.

I felt terrible and so did E.

We fell into silence again, a second and deeper silence, the silence of trying to have already broken the silence only to realize it can't be broken because you're back in it, silent again, except now it's doubly silent because you had tried to get out of. It was the silence of being disappointed to be silent again. We were *both* in the labyrinth now.

I sighed, dramatically. "I feel like I ruined everything," I said, looking out the window.

E. gripped the wheel. "That's how *I* feel," she said. "*I* feel *I* ruined everything."

I turned to her then. "You *did* ruin everything," I yelled, but I yelled it in such a way that it sounded funny, a parody of the argument we were having, and it somehow articulated how ridiculous it was, to argue when in fact, we both wanted the same thing, to be with each other and know that that's what the other person also wanted. To know that the time we shared mattered.

E. started to laugh, and then I started to laugh.

"Damn it," I yelled. This time louder. "You always ruin everything." And then we both laughed louder, and somehow the tension in the car broke, and she put her hand in mine.

"I'm sorry," she said.

"I'm sorry, too," I said. "You are a huge pain in the ass."

"At least I'm cute," she said.

I rolled my eyes.

We had been driving for almost an hour by that point, and it felt so good to laugh. But there was something that I was feeling, and it brought me back to thinking about your story, Baij, how you lived, though I'm not sure that I could have articulated it then. But now that I am thinking about it, now that I am writing about this incident and thinking about you, it's that image of you as a grandfather, for some reason, that captures part of what I felt then and part of what I am trying to convey now. The image I have of you in front of your grandson's school, hands out in a gesture of absolute big-heartedness, smile on your face for the joy of giving—I so often felt and do feel that around E., and it's a new feeling for me, something distinct to her and I together. I think it's also a feeling that being sick for four years made more possible. I think being sick opened me up to want to give more.

I turned to E., feeling so ridiculous at having fought about something so trivial in relation to this larger sense of openness I felt around her. Earlier that week, I had driven E. to the airport for a work trip. It was only a day trip, but she left early in the morning, and she came home later that night. The timing of her flight was inconvenient for me. I had to wake up very early to take her and then I had to wait in traffic later that evening to pick her up. But as I was driving to the airport, I felt so happy to be doing that for her, so happy knowing that I was the one who got to do that for her. Looking at E. now, I started listing off the other things I had done for her that week, and at first I think it sounded like I was keeping track so that I could hold it over her head.

At first, it probably sounded like I was saying, look at everything I do for you! What do you do for me? "I make you breakfast every time you stay at my house," I said. "I make you dinner whenever we're together. I go to the store for you. I make sure that you have tea for the morning and bubble water in the refrigerator. I do all this stuff for you," I said. "And it's the first time that I've *wanted* to do these things for anyone, not out of a sense of obligation but of simply wanting to do them. I think that's what love feels like."

But!—there's always a but, isn't there—but it isn't always easy to give, is it? Your two sons still moved away, to start a life somewhere else. Your grandson became sick and it terrified you. S.L. still took and took and took from you. Your father still died suddenly, and it still hurt and the loss was real. And no less true, but on a smaller scale, sometimes E. does drive me crazy, sometimes it does feel like she doesn't give as much as I'd like her too. But in a way, that's the mark of a rich life, isn't it, Baij? To want to give even when the giving can be frustrating, even when it can bring loss with it.

"We should be so lucky," E. says to me sometimes. "We should be so lucky to drive each other crazy." We should be so lucky to love and give—even if it means, in the end, we lose. To lose is what living is, but it's what we do with what we have before we lose it that counts. This is, I think, what it is to be content with our discontentment. To stand with hands open, offering candy—metaphorical and real!—to the people we care about and love, even if they disappoint us…

We should be so lucky to want to give even knowing we might not get what we want in return.

*"First earn it, deserve it,
then desire it."*

8

WAITING AT THE TRAIN STATION

"We should also be so lucky to grow old and get sick and die." That's another thing E. says.

In 1996 you had a health scare, and it was one of the first signs that your own health was fading. Though to call it a health scare maybe isn't quite right. I'm not sure that your health ever scared you. These were the facts of life: The body gets old, it deteriorates. It's just part of nature. "We're like cars," your son Brij says to me periodically. "We can get parts replaced but at some point, the engine is going to break down." I think this was how you thought of it too.

Still, it was a scare, at least for those around you. Ajesh wasn't there, but his wife was. It was night. Fall. Not hot, not cold. There was a pain in your chest, and it grew worse until it became quite powerful. You woke Ajesh's wife, Jyoti, and she acted quickly. You would tell Ajesh, later, that a man's life depends on who is around when he is sick. You were referring to his wife when you would say this, how she saved your life.

She had just passed her driving test, only days earlier, but still she was something of an unsteady driver. She didn't like to drive nor did she have much confidence as a driver yet. She weighed the alternative: Call an ambulance—there was one or two in Lucknow—but it could take hours. You might not even get to the hospital until dawn.

She helped you out into the Hindustan Ambassador, helped you into the passenger seat while you held your chest, and slowly, she made her way down the tangle of streets until reaching the hospital. That night marked the start of your ongoing angina, a condition in which there is an intense localized pain in your chest that you would have to contend with over the years to come. But there's some gray area around what happened during this first visit to the hospital. The doctor kept you there for a couple of days. It wasn't a stroke, but it seems like it was something more serious than just angina pain. It isn't incidental that there is some ambiguity here. You made it a point to keep quiet about your health scares.

Only a day after your stay in the hospital, you went back to court, to work, and when your friends and colleagues asked if you were okay—they had heard it was something with your heart—you waved all their concern away, dismissed it immediately. "Indigestion," you said. "But I feel great now." It was that same day, earlier, when Raj had tried to help you down the stairs outside of the Pandariba house, and you slapped his hand away. "I can do it myself," you said.

You had your reasons for this. Once, Ajesh asked you why, if you're sick, you don't acknowledge that you're sick. You would refuse to rest, even on those days when you felt ill. Ajesh would try to get you to stay home while he went to court, and you would always tell him no, if you stayed home, you'd just feel worse. You wanted to go to court, move around, talk to people. There was something else behind your reasoning too. You explained to Ajesh that as a lawyer, you couldn't let your clients know that you are sick. If they knew, they would find another lawyer. "A client feels no loyalty to his lawyer," you would tell Ajesh. "If a client thinks that his lawyer is sick, he'll find a new lawyer." You were ever the realist about these things.

So part of the reason you veiled your health was professional. But you also believed that you could overcome illness by not acknowledging it, a kind of mind-over-matter willpower. You were like this, always training your body to do what you wanted it to. The way you would eat extremely spicy food because you thought it would help you adjust to the summer heat. Who knows, maybe it did. You did have that startling ability to manifest your will.

When you were sick and you said, "I'm fine," you likely meant it, believed you would be fine. And mostly you were right. Your body had always taken care of itself and it would continue to do so.

Until it didn't, of course. And you knew this, too. At some point, there's no arguing with the body, and it will break down. The tired engine of your heart or whatever it was that finally gave out was the inevitable fact. You accepted this.

You had a saying: "I'm like a passenger with his bags packed, waiting at the train station. The train is going to come and I'm ready to go. But I'm going to enjoy myself while I wait." Your doctor had warned you to change your diet, to eat better, to eat less meat, and for a time, Avinash also tried to get you to eat better. But your point was, when it's your time it's your time. Nothing could change that you were in the twilight of your life. While you were still here, you were going to enjoy it.

You ate freely. If food can be called a vice, food was yours. The periodic eating contests continued. Your famed trips to the open-air market to purchase more mangoes than any one family could ever eat continued. And the stops at food carts to sample all manner of meats also continued. "We are meat eaters," Raj once said jovially to me. "Our whole family." Your bags were packed and you would certainly eat while you waited.

I keep wondering about you though, Baij. Despite your equanimity, despite claiming your bags were packed, despite your comfort with the course of a human life and its inevitable conclusion, I'm not totally convinced that you were ready to go. You had accomplished so much, taken care of so many people, and it's true that your responsibilities, the duties that you were beholden too, had vastly diminished.

Rashmi was married to a successful man, a man you admired. Ajesh was well on his way to becoming the successful lawyer you hoped he would become. He had his own family, his own children. And Raj, though in the US, was also doing well for himself. He was married and had a daughter of his own now. Your own father had passed away, and in 1992, your mother passed as well. She lived to be over one-hundred-years-old, which I still find spectacular, especially given the time. She died on Janamashtami, the day celebrated as Lord Krishna's birthday.

On that day, and in keeping with tradition for Janamashtami, Ajesh and Jyoti dressed their son as a Hindu god, Lord Krishna, as so many other parents dressed their children. Flute in hand and a small crown fitted on Akshay's head,

Jyoti took him to school. At some point during the day, your mom began to feel ill. She was a fit woman, used to gardening every day, and so even then, at her very old age, it seemed possible that this would be just a passing episode. But then she worsened rapidly, and by mid-morning, it became obvious that this was serious. Jyoti rushed to Akshay's school to pick him up. When she got home, your mom was slipping in and out of consciousness. She opened her eyes when her great grandson came into the room.

"Look," Jyoti said. "Akshay is here."

Your mom opened her eyes, briefly, and saw the flashing crown, the flute, the regal costume. "Lord Krishna," she said, thinking that he had come for her, to take her away. "Lord Krishna," she said again, and then closed her eyes and passed.

Both of your parents had left this world. You were no longer responsible for them, either.

Additionally, your sister Sarla had married a man named Moti Lal Chopra, and he also had a good job working for the government. Even your sister Toshi, who you had spent so much time worrying about after S.L.'s disappearance, was doing as well as she could be. You had found her daughters husbands, made sure that they were taken care of and would have a secure future. And your wife, Avinash, so long as Ajesh and his wife were here she would also be well cared for.

You had supported and lifted up so much of your family, made their lives secure. You had done this for friends, too, even strangers. Your responsibility toward those you cared for had diminished greatly over the years, and I think this did free you to accept the inevitability of your own life, that you, too, were getting old, and that it was time for you to start letting go.

But there was a loose thread. Ajesh told me that if there was one thing you worried about in your old age, if there was thing that caused you concern, that preoccupied you, it was Brij. You were so willful in life, and I think that despite what you would say—how your bags were packed, that you were ready to go—you were also willful in your own death. You may have been waiting at the train station, but you didn't leave until you knew Brij would be okay.

It wasn't that Brij couldn't take care of himself. Brij was nothing if not resourceful, and you knew this. In fact, you imparted this quality to him, taught him the skills he needed to be resourceful. After he moved to the US, he quickly began to do well for himself. After Alaska, he began working for Arthur Andersen, a global consulting firm. There's a story Brij told me, how during one of his periods of financial prosperity, he sent you a check because he had more money than he could use. Brij is like you in that way. Quick to generosity. So is Raj, at least in my experience, as I know your sons. But you quickly sent the check back with a note: "I don't need your money."

This is a harsh note to send your son who was being generous, as you had taught him to be. Though I'm not sure that you meant it to be harsh. It wasn't your children's job to take care of you. It was your job to take care of your children. And though Brij was doing well, better than well, at least financially, he wasn't taken care of in that broader sense. He didn't have someone to grow old with. He wouldn't be taken care of in sickness, in sudden bad fortune. Maybe you felt that this was your own failing? You had taken care of everyone you were close with, but you hadn't been able to do so with Brij. I think the right way to read your note is less in terms of what you didn't need—his money—and more in terms of what you did need that money couldn't compensate for. You needed to know that he would be okay in that larger sense, and not that he had money to spare.

For over two decades you worried about Brij.

This wasn't the kind of chaotic and ongoing crisis that your worry over your sister, Toshi, was, nor did it exact the kind of toll that S.L. did on your life. But it was consistent, this low grade, ambient concern, like a slight, sometimes almost imperceptible noise. Even when it seemed to let up, if you listened closely, it was still there.

* * *

In the spring of 2001, Brij came to India. He came to celebrate Rashmi's son's wedding in Delhi. To your surprise, to everyone's surprise, he didn't come alone. He came with his wife, Ann, who he had married three months earlier.

Brij had been living in Portland, Oregon, when he met Ann. Like many things about Brij, his marriage was the least traditional of your children's. Ann isn't In-

Brij and Ann in Hawaii, 2000.

dian. She is from Washington State. She is a painter and a social worker. Not that you necessarily wanted something strictly conventional for Brij. Nonetheless, the marriage was unfamiliar given the marriages of your other children. At the same time, I think there might have also been something familiar to you about Ann. I think she may have, perhaps, reminded you a little of your wife, Avinash.

I first had this thought last November, when I went down to Seaside, Oregon, to spend Thanksgiving with Brij and Ann and a few of his friends—a work assignment, Brij jokingly called it. It was a relaxed two days. Brij had rented an Airbnb near the beach, next to a smaller house he and Ann own, and I had a room on the second floor, with sliding glass doors. Maybe because I was spending more time around Brij than any of your other children, I found myself thinking a lot about Brij in relation to you, noting ways that you two were different but also similar.

Over Thanksgiving, I watched Brij and Ann interact with each other and their guests. It was the first time that I had really seen them together for a sustained period, and it was the first time that I had the chance to really spend much time with Ann. I liked Ann. We had gone for a walk with a larger group of their friends and at one point she and I had split off, and we talked briefly about her work as a painter, and I liked how she talked about her own creative process. There was something quiet in it, not forced or disingenuous. She told me that she painted when she wanted to, when the inspiration to create struck, but that

Top: Avinash, Ann, and Baij, 2001. Above: Brij, Avinash, Ann, and Baij in India, 2001.

it wasn't something toward which she felt an obligation. I admired that kind of honesty around creativity. So many artists aggrandize their work by bracketing it under necessity.

While we all talked over dinner on Thanksgiving, Brij regaled his guests with stories and anecdotes. He was self-possessed in a way that reminded me of how I imagined you, and I started to see Ann, quieter but equally present, equally attentive, as sharing qualities I've imagined Avinash possessed. As your wife's kind but reserved bearing served as a counterbalance to your loquaciousness and openness, so, too, did Ann's thoughtful but quieter presence begin to strike me as a sort of equalizer to Brij's charisma. And then there was that passing comment Brij had once made about his mom—that he had never heard her say a stupid thing in her life. I had that same feeling with Ann. It was hard to imagine her saying something that she hadn't first given serious thought. I'm not sure if we become our fathers to find our mothers all over again. Maybe we do. Maybe we don't. But I do think there are ways in which we gravitate toward those personalities that balance our own. This is how I think of you and Avinash, two counterbalances steadying each other. Over Thanksgiving I began to think of Brij and Ann in a similar way.

Perhaps you noticed the same thing when you met Ann, too. I can't know for sure. I can't ask you. But I do know what Ann first thought of you: She told me that you had a seriousness, a confidence, that you were very much a man in charge. She also told me that she could tell right away that you weren't a bullshitter. "He wanted to talk about real things," Ann said, and this makes sense, squares with how I've imagined you over this last year. You wanted to find that intimate connection. You weren't interested in small talk. "I could tell he really wanted to know who I was as a human being," Ann told me, which also makes sense. You had this capacity for sincerity.

But Ann also said that you had a willingness to be vulnerable, and I think this is one of those subtle points about your life that I keep coming back to, though it's easy to overlook. As inviolable as you seemed, as in control and capable of dealing with any number of challenges, for all your optimism and all that you overcame, there is nonetheless a deep vulnerability that I think ran through your whole life. It is most salient in how you cared for and loved your children.

Rashmi, all your children have agreed, was your favorite. But I see you at your most vulnerable with Brij. You were endlessly hard on him, endlessly severe with him. The two of you had more conflict than you had with any of your other children, but you also worried more about him than you did any of your other children. That's where the conflict arose. We worry about what we love.

You didn't attend Rashmi's son's wedding in Meerut, so it wasn't until after the wedding, when Brij and Ann flew up from Delhi, that you met Ann for the first time. Your health was precarious and had been for some time. Ever sensitive about being a burden to others, the reason you didn't attend the wedding was because you worried that if you got sick away from home other people would have to take care of you. How exactly like you, to be concerned about others even while you were sick.

From the Lucknow airport, Brij and Ann came straight to your house on Pandariba. You had mentioned to Brij that you wanted to tell Ann about your past, your story, the history of how you and your family got to India, but you weren't pushy about this when they arrived. You were gracious, offering drinks, food, those indicators of caring you have always offered to those people in your life you cared about.

There is so much about this reunion with Brij, about meeting Ann, which I can't know. I don't know what you thought of her, and I don't know what your first words to your son were after such a long absence, nor do I know what your first words were to Ann, your new daughter-in-law. I don't know where you stood in the house, as you made your guests feel welcome, or what the lighting was like coming through the windows. I don't know what the first exchanges were, who said what, but I do know that you were a father who worried about his son, as all good fathers do, and what you worried about most was that Brij would never marry, never find someone to grow old with, and now here he was, with his wife. I know that this mattered to you, and I know that it allowed you to release something, to let go of something. And I know it must have made you happy, to have them there, with you, together.

You talked briefly, small pleasantries, introductions, but you weren't one for small talk, and Brij knew this. Perhaps in consideration of you, of what he knew of his father, he said, "Did you want to tell Ann your story?"

What is it about opening up, telling someone what we've been through, who we are? It's such a radical gesture of connection, such absolute vulnerability. You sat them down across from you in the sitting room. It was just the three of you. You had grown old. You were in your eighties.

You were tense as you started to relate what had happened to you, and you related it without preamble. "Hit the nail on the head," as you would tell Ajesh to do in his professional writing. Now you followed your own rule as you began retelling your own story.

You wanted Ann to know all of it, what happened during Partition, and what happened those years following. You told her how you and your family were living in Gujranwala, and you told her about the fires you saw from the roof of the building in which you lived. You told her about the train station, the water tower, what it was like hiding in there. You told her about the gunshots and massacres at Gujranwala station, and while you talked she and Brij listened.

Avinash and Baij, 1998.

You told of your narrow escape and of each narrow escape that followed, the train stations in Gujrat, Kuthala, Wazirabad, Ghaukal, Ghakhar, Kamoke, Muridke, and Shahdara, and you told of what you saw there, and with each word I imagine you letting go of something new, giving something away, one word at a time. Your voice was steady and deep as it always was. There was the fear you and your family shared and then the relief you felt once you reached Haridwar—"God has saved us"—you had said on that night as the train pulled into the station, and then you told about the refugee camps, living with nothing. But it wasn't until you reached the point where your mom had to sell her last possessions, her gold bangles so that you and your family could eat that your voice began to shake.

Detail by detail you described that scene, what it was like for your family. And then, finally, as your mom parted with her last possession, your voice broke, and you wept.

"That was the only other time I had seen my father cry," Brij told me.

Like so much about that afternoon, I can't know your reasons for crying. But what I do know is that your entire life was built around caring for others. You had lifted your family up one by one, and Brij was the only one left who hadn't reached safety. But he had now, and you could finally let go of him. It was the second time Brij had seen you cry but I think it was the first time you had told your story without worrying about someone else in it. Perhaps it was the first time you let yourself realize what you had been through. Perhaps it was the first time you cried for yourself.

Three months later, on July 23, 2001, you passed away. It was a Monday, and you went to court with Ajesh the Friday before. Of course you did. There are certain moments in your life that seem emblematic of who you were, small dramas that indicate something much larger about your character: When you went back into Pakistan to save your sister; when you invited a thief into your house and when you forgave him after he stole from you; all those times that you bought piles upon piles upon piles of mangoes only to share them with everyone around you; each time you reached your hands into your pockets to produce a piece of candy, a small treat. It's these moments and moments like these where I have gotten to know you, but the fact that you stayed engaged with your work up until the very end seems to me especially like you. You couldn't be here, in this world, and not engage. That was just as much who you were as anything else.

That Friday at court, three days before you passed, there happened to be a small gathering with your colleagues, not a party, exactly, but most of the people you worked closely with. All your lawyer friends from over the years happened to be there. You ate, told stories, joked. It was a simple occasion, just you being yourself among friends.

The next day, Saturday, you fell unconscious. You were in your house in Pandariba, and it was Jyoti who found you. She ran to Ajesh, who was taking a bath.

"Dad is unconscious," she yelled. "He isn't responding."

Ajesh rushed out of the bath and ran to you. He called the doctor and hurried you to the hospital. You were unconscious the whole way there. You came to that evening in the ICU. You were lucid, almost strangely so. You sat up in bed and you asked for something small to eat. Ajesh and Jyoti, as well as your own wife, were there with you.

You slept, and by Sunday morning, you seemed fine. You asked for a glass of milk when you woke, and then you ate. The doctor talked with you, explained that he wanted to keep you under observation for a few more days, do a CT scan to be on the safe side and make sure that there was no clotting in your brain. Ajesh went with you to the CT scan.

Everything seemed fine. Back in your room you rested in bed. You were weak. You could feel it, something unsteady, and Ajesh could tell, but by Monday evening, you told him he should go to the office, take care of any work that needed to be done while you stayed in the hospital.

"I'm fine," you said. "There's nothing to worry about."

It was six in the evening, and Ajesh agreed. He left you there, and then drove half way to work. For some reason he turned around. He wanted to be with you. When Ajesh returned, his wife was there. She brought you dinner, soup. After you ate, Ajesh told his wife she could leave.

It was 7:30 p.m. or so, and now it was just you and your son. It's strange, how the mundane enters into death, the absolutely normal, the almost trivial.

You told your son that you had to go to the bathroom, and so he passed you the bedpan, and you urinated. You needed Ajesh's help after you were finished.

You wanted to adjust in bed and you needed him to steady you because you were still weak.

"I would like to sit up," you said to him.

Ajesh moved toward you, put his arm around your backside, cradled you and then he lifted you slightly, almost like a child. You moved in his arms, and then you moved toward him. Then, very suddenly, you inhaled, deeply, almost as if a shock had passed through you. And then you were gone.

"I lost him," Ajesh told me. "When he was still in my arms."

It was so fast. Here. Then gone.

For centuries your family's priests have lived in Haridwar. This is the same lineage of priests who gave you and your family shelter during Partition, the same lineage of priests who have kept a record of the male side of your ancestry line. There had always been a symbiotic relationship between your family and these pandits. The record they kept of each male passing was, in turn, compensated by donations your family would make at the time of each death they recorded. Now it was your sons' turn to make the journey to Haridwar, to have your passing entered into the register.

Raj, Ajesh, and your nephew Yash Babu boarded the train in Lucknow with your ashes. "Flowers," is the euphemism used in Hindi to refer to remains. You had been cremated the day after your passing, in accordance with tradition, and your flowers were gathered in a white cloth, and then placed in an urn. The color white, in your culture, is absence of color, and this absence of color signifies sorrow.

It's true that in Haridwar, Ajesh knew where to go to find the Anand family priests, but had he not, your sons would have simply said to someone, a stranger, anyone passing at the train station, as you had said during Partition: "We are Anands from Kalanaur," and they would have been directed to your family priests.

Haridwar is in the foothills of the Himalayas and there the Ganges is cold and runs fast and powerful, not yet the open and slow-moving river it becomes when it reaches the plains. There are chains anchored into the walls and rocks at its banks, and after the head priests greeted your family, after your sons and Yash Babu showered and then changed into the white clothes appropriate for mourning, they waded out into the current. They gripped the chains to brace themselves against the icy waters, and there they opened the urn and unfolded the white cloth and then loosed your flowers into the current.

Afterwards, the head priests brought out the register, and in it were the entries that preceded yours, entries from when your father in his early twenties made the journey from Chokkar Kalan to spread his brother's flowers into the Ganges, and there was the entry you made of your own father, and behind these entries were those of the generations before: your father's father, and his father's father before.

A modern day map showing Baij's birthplace, Chokkar Kalan, his adult home in Lucknow, and his final resting place in Haridwar.

Your own entry, the one that Raj and Ajesh wrote, was simple, as they were supposed to be. It indicated the date of your passing, the family members who survived you, a note or two about your life. Your entry wasn't your story—how could it be—but it denoted the time in which your life was lived, that space within which your story took place.

In Hinduism the atma is attached to the body. Once the body is cremated, there is no longer a physical attachment to this world. But there is an emotional attachment to the loved ones that are still here. "The atma doesn't want to leave," Raj explained to me. So there is a ceremony on the fourth day after passing, called Choutha. In part this ceremony is meant to honor the reality of death, as well as the good deeds of the soul that has passed. But it's also meant to help the atma detach from those loved ones who are left behind so that it can travel across the ocean of consciousness and eventually find a new body for rebirth.

When I think of you, Baij, having to finally leave behind those you loved, I can't help but think of that paradox by which you lived, that paradox Brij has summed up well with the phrase "one foot in the world, and one foot out." You were so attached to the people you cared about, so committed to them. And yet, at the same time, you had this distance, this remove from the things of this world.

This is paradoxical, but at the same time, there's something coherent in it, something that makes sense: Our time here is short, and so we should enjoy the things of this world not despite the ephemeral nature of being here, but because of it.

I think for you, the joy of life arose from the transitory nature of things. I think this was part of your optimism. Everything changes. The good, yes, but also the bad. So do your best, do your duty, be good and honest, and enjoy.

Thirteen years after your passing, on July 17, 2014, your son, Raj, had a grandson. As you were a grandfather, now it's his turn. I've gotten to know Raj over this last year, and I've come to understand him as generous, and very kind and very thoughtful. When I think of him as a grandfather, it's hard not to think of you, and how you were with your grandchildren. There are certain qualities all your children have that seem to have come directly from you. I don't know why, but it's as a grandfather that I see Raj stepping most into your shoes.

But here's the strange thing—as there was always a strange thing with you. The day after Raj's grandson was born, he called Rashmi, excited to tell her. When she picked up, he told her the good news. "A grandson," he said.

"I know," Rashmi said.

Raj was puzzled. How do you know, he asked.

And Rashmi told him. Because last night you had to come to her in a dream. "I heard dad's voice," she told Raj.

And what did you say?

You said, "I have come."

The End.

Paintings of Baij and Avinash by Ann Anand.

LIKE A BANYAN TREE | **247**

Painting of Lakhi by Anjali Dhillon, 2021.

Anand Family Tree

Originally from Bhadravati area (has salt mines) now called Bhera, moved to Kala Naur around the 11th century after defeat of Raja Jai Dev Anand by Mahmud of Gazhni.

Anand

- Kaval Nain, est. birth 1740
- Amar Chand, est. birth 1765
- Bhavani Das, est. birth 1790
- Ratan Chand, est. birth 1815
- Budamal, est. birth 1840
- Radha Kishan, est. birth 1865
- Lakshmi Das, est. birth 1895-1975, (m. Gyan Devi, b. 1892-1992)
  - Prakash (Suri), est. b. 1912; Rambheji (Sethi), est b. 1929; Toshi (Chadha), est. b. 1935; Sarla (Chopra), est. b. 1938 *(Baij's siblings)*
  - Baij Nath Anand, 1917-2001 (m. Avinash Chadha, 1931-2014)
    - Rashmi Anand, b. 1951 (m. Arun Chopra, b. 1946)
      * Aanchal Chopra, b. 1977
      * Rohit Chopra, b. 1975 (m. Vibhuti Thapa, b. 1975)
        - Lyra Chopra, b. 2007
        - Shiv Chopra, b. 2009
    - Rajesh Anand, b. 1953 (m. Vandana Chopra, b. 1955)
      * Shelly Anand, b. 1986 (m. Eric Erzinger, b. 1988, USA)
        - Narayan Anand Erzinger, b. 2014
        - Uma Anand Erzinger, b. 2017
    - Brijesh Anand, b. 1956 (m. Ann Glick, b. 1961)
    - Ajesh Anand, b. 1959 (m. Jyoti Marwaha, b. 1966)
      * Akshay Anand, b. 1989 (m. Rachita Khanna, b. 1991)
      * Anuj Anand, b. 1994

Arun and Rashmi, 2022.

Aanchal, 2022.

Rohit with Lyra, Shiv, and Vibhuti, 2022.

Raj and Vandana, 2022.

Shelly with husband Eric and children, Uma and Narayan, 2022.

Brij and Ann with Max (3) and Pippin (7) in Seaside, Oregon, 2022.

Ajesh and Jyoti, 2022.

Akshay and Rachita at their wedding with Anuj, Delhi, 2022.

253

"Low aim is a crime."

- Baij, p. 38 -

"He had one overarching belief, a belief in which he never wavered in his life; it was a belief in his own ability to accomplish whatever he set his mind to."

- Raj about Baij, p. 10 -

"If you can stay this healthy after six months as a refugee and you also have an education, you're hired."

- Baij's first boss in Lucknow, p. 49 -

"This wedding would have been a grand show if we were in our own country. Huge gathering of our city's best, our celebrity would have been different. The music and song which sound hollow, would have a different tone. The whole occasion would be so different if this city was Lahore."

- Khushal Chand Chadha, Father of Avinash, p. 55 -

"Craft your life."

- Brij, p. 63 -

**"You never know if what holy men say
is true or influences you for it to be true."**

*- Baij to Raj, after a holy man told Raj
his fortune was in another country, p. 191 -*

"To this day, I'm suspicious of windfalls.
I don't like it when a business opportunity
yields more money than I've worked for."

- Raj, p. 129 -

"You'll have enough time in life to ruminate
and now isn't it. As a young man
you should be immersed *in* life."

- Avinash to Brij, p. 165 -

"That was the only other time I had seen my father cry."

- Brij as Baij tells his story to Ann, p. 241 -

"Time is valuable, don't waste it."

- Sign in Baij's office, p. 64 -

Glossary of Non-English Terms

Angithi: Indian charcoal/coal/wood burning brazier | 45

Atma: The core consciousness of all living beings, loosely translated as soul | 245

Baap re baap: A term of surprise | 187

Barfkhanna: Ice factory | 155

Bhindi: Okra | 75

Daal: Lentil | 75

Daayan: An alluring female evil paranormal entity, she sucks life out of humans to get powerful, her feet are backward, she has lustrous hair where her power resides | 72

Dhurrie: A woven thin rug, easily rolled up and laid on the floor for sitting and sleeping | 64

Dukana: Shops | 155

Dupatta: A multipurpose shawl like scarf worn by Indian women | 145

Ji: A term of respect | 205

Khua: Water well | 155

Lassi: Yogurt based drink | 186

Mama: Uncle | 155

Milni: Meeting | 53

Nokar: Servants | 155

Pani: Water | 155

Puri: Indian fried bread | 186

Rickshaw: A three wheeled carriage for hire, where a person pedals to transport customers | 73

Rickshawalla: The person who pedals a rickshaw | 73

Subzi Baghicha: Vegetable garden | 155

Shiksha: Lesson, learning | 53

Thafter (Duftar): Office | 155

These words are from the languages of Hindi, Urdu, Punjabi.

Photo Index

63 Pandariba, Lucknow, Anand Family residence since 1968 | 88
A Father's Words (original letter) | 54
Ajesh and cousin Anita in 1963 | 90
Ajesh and family in 2022 | 253
Ajesh and Jyoti in 1988 | 213
Ajesh with Jyoti and Gyan Devi in 1989 | 213
Akshay dressed as Krishna in 1992 | 217
Anuj in 1997 | 217
Arun with Aanchal at Yangon, Myanmar | 178
Arun with Rashmi at Yangon, Myanmar | 178
Avinash, in 1984 | 152
Avinash and Shelly in 1988 | 183
Avinash celebrating Holi with family | 181
Avinash in 2010, 2013 | 156
Avinash with Ajesh and family in 1997 | 159
Avinash with Akshay in 1991 | 159
Avinash with Ann in 2011 | 156
Avinash with Rashmi and Raj, 1955 | 77
B.N. Anand Complex blueprints | 270
B.N. Anand Complex Illustration | iv
Baij, in 1988 | 140
Baij and Avinash at Taj Mahal, 1966 | 201
Baij and Avinash in 1998 | 240
Baij and Avinash with Ann and Brij | 237
Baij and family at Taj Mahal, 1966 | 82
Baij reading his newspaper in 1991 | 189
Baij with Ajesh and Brij in 1966 | 130
Baij's sisters in 1960s | 80
Baij's three eldest children in 1958 | 62
Bhopal House and Sharma Chai House | 98
Brij and Ajesh in 1988 | 181
Brij and Ann in Hawaii in 2000 | 236
Brij and family in 2022 | 252
Brij as a baby in 1957 | 80
Brij in 1982 | 112

Photo Index Continued

Brij in Oregon in 1980 | 176
Brij official Doon School photo in 1968 | 136
Certificates from University of Panjab | 16
Chadha Ice Factory sketch | 155
Gyan Devi at over 100 years old | 211
Hindustan Ambassador Car | 106
Keshav and Rashmi, 1955 | 74
Khushal Chand, Avinash's Father (1950) | 53
Lakhi's hookah base | 65
Lucknow Lawyer Association protest march in 1960s | 121
Lucknow Lawyers' Association, 1960s | 121
Map of Baij's birthplace | 244
Map of India and surrounding countries | 31
Maps from Chokkar Kalan to Lucknow | 22
Official documents and letters | 46-48
Painting of Lakhi by Anjali Dhillon | 248
Paintings of Baij and Avinash by Ann | 247
Raj and family in 2022 | 251
Raj and Rashmi boating with Gyan Devi | 82
Raj and Vandana Wedding, 1982 | 142-143
Rajesh Anand, President & CEO | vi
Raj in Portland, 1977 | 165
Raj official photos in 1969 and 1975 | 136
Raj with Vandana and Brij in 1982 | 165
Rashmi and Arun at their wedding, 1974 | 190
Rashmi and Arun's wedding | 192
Rashmi and Arun in 1975 | 193
Rashmi and Arun in Oregon in 1987 | 176
Rashmi and family in 2022 | 250
Rashmi in 1967 | 90
Rashmi with Aanchal and Rohit in 1979 | 208
Rashmi with Arun and Rohit in 1976 | 208
S.L. with Rashmi and Raj, 1954 | 77
Shelly, Akshay, and Anuj in 1988 | 183
Train stations of Lahore and Lucknow in the 1920s and 1950s | 43
Vandana and Shelly in 1989 | 181

AFTERWORD

What did I learn from Baij? Though not in these exact words, this is a question that Brij has often asked me over the last year, and in some ways it's a difficult question to answer. I worry about reducing the complexities of a life lived into something more pedantic, a means to teach. Baij, just like any one of us, was more than a means or a lesson. And yet, at the same time, I think the spirit of Brij's question is in service of enlarging Baij's life, not narrowing it. It's a question meant to denote learning in that broader sense, aimed to articulate points of connection with another person, the kind of connection that I think many of us feel are lacking in our current cultural moment.

Ultimately, there's a lot to say about what I've personally taken from Baij's life. I've often thought that I'd like to write a book about writing *Like a Banyan Tree* to further expand on this. Telling Baij's story turned into a dialogue, one in which, sometimes implicitly and other times explicitly, I considered my own story next to his. I believe that we only know who we are through the stories we tell about ourselves, but our stories are never truly our own. They are always in relation to other people's stories.

Part of writing *Like a Banyan Tree* was my own attempt to address this relational aspect of how we know ourselves, and my hope is that those places where

I do have a narrative presence mark directly some of the insights I've arrived at through considering Baij's life. I'm thinking here about Baij's spirit of generosity and the way he related to others on a personal level, as an individual among individuals. I'm also thinking about his sense of duty to family. In a time when family itself has become an increasingly attenuated idea, the sense of obligation to those with whom we are close, despite the many ways close relationships can be difficult and messy, has served as a foil for me to rethink my own obligations.

But beyond all of this, I want to talk about another aspect of Baij's life that feels especially relevant to my own: This is his optimism and unshakable faith in his own trajectory and future. This kind of optimism and hope in the future was something I would have related to before I got sick, but my experience with illness greatly changed that. I was thirty-three years old and teaching when I became ill. I had been on my own trajectory before then, and it very much felt like one of my own making. I had worked hard for the last ten years or so, and it was starting to pay off. I was publishing my own fiction at a good rate, and I had landed a job teaching. It wasn't permanent, but it felt to me it would open the door to more. I wanted to write and I wanted to teach, and I was moving in that direction. In narrative terms, that was the story I had been telling about who I was, and it was the story I used to understand myself. I believed it was true and because of this, like so much belief, it was a kind of existential anchor.

There's still some mystery around the exact cause of my illness, but the year before I had gotten sick, I lived in Portland, Maine. Lyme disease tests tend be equivocal—I had two negative tests and one positive—but many of my neurological symptoms indicated tick-borne illness. There's a lot of stigma and competing narratives around chronic health conditions, and this has always intrigued me from a narrative perspective, and frustrated me from a personal one. Not being able to find a definite diagnosis has only contributed to my frustration. Though I periodically still feel the lingering effects, my health has recovered markedly from what it was, but beyond that, I often find myself conflating a full recovery with narrative mastery, with finally being able to tell the story of my experience with illness in a coherent way.

The problem is that I don't have access to a coherent narrative. This is part of the reason I haven't written about it. I think it's also part of the reason it still sometimes feels present, like I'm still in the process of recovering rather than fully recovered. It's only in writing about Baij's life that I've even begun to touch on what the experience was like for me. Still, so much about it remains not just unsaid but illegible, the very nature of it resistant to my attempts to put it in story.

What I can say about it is this: to have been sick for four years has been the most formative and significant event of my life. I hope that changes. I hope it isn't always so defining, and in some ways, I can already see new events, significant in themselves, taking shape and edging some of the more salient features of illness out of the picture. My relationship with E. is one of these events. Our relationship has created a story that challenges the narrative around illness I had been telling myself—that life wouldn't revert to normal, that illness would forever be isolating. While I still hold that narrative mastery over difficult events is part of healing, my relationship with E. has also convinced me that part of healing is letting new stories take root, as it's new stories that make room for alternative interpretations of events.

Nonetheless, the fact remains that illness fundamentally altered the course of my life. After I became sick, I tried to continue teaching, but by that spring I could no longer grade papers effectively, could no longer break down a complicated lecture into digestible parts. By summer, I had very little money, and I had no job and no way to provide for myself. I saw one relationship after another dissolve. Sickness, I learned quickly, is a burden, and it frightens people around you. It is a reminder of what is true for all of us: So much of what we identify with—our accomplishments, physical and mental prowess, even our own will—is contingent, vulnerable, and eventually we have to let go of identifying with any of it.

But far more significant was that I couldn't read and I couldn't write. As I've mentioned in this book, my vision was hugely impacted by being sick. My field of vision in my right eye was narrowed greatly, and this made reading difficult, though manageable. The real problem was that my verbal processing skills were slipping. What this was like is hard to explain. As language vanishes the world seems to vanish as well, or so it did for me. It was hard to recognize words, and in this I felt a deeper unraveling, a fraying of the larger tapestry of meaning. It was scary, and it would have been even if I wasn't a writer, but I had built my life around words. The way I experience the world was very specific not just to language—that's true of us all—but to reading, to the cadences of poetry and prose. I think for people who aren't especially interested in reading as an activity, it can seem like a retreat from the world. But for me—and I think many readers feel this way—it was the thing that connected me to the world, the thing that enriched my experience. This is what illness took from me.

Early in my illness, my inclination was to try to write about this very thing, to document it, to use writing, however difficult it had become, to tell the story of how I could no longer write, how I could no longer tell stories. I couldn't quite let go of the writerly side of myself, and this was the side of me that had always been drawn to these kinds of narrative contradictions: stories about stories that can't be told. I still feel those are the ones that are most worth telling. So I attempted to write about it. I would sit at my computer, wait out one migraine after another, struggle through the lack of hand-eye coordination that made typing difficult, and I would try to string sentences together. I couldn't do it. It just wasn't available to me anymore, and after a year or so, I couldn't argue with that reality. It was the single biggest loss I had ever experienced. It also completely unmoored my sense of self. I was, in short, no longer a writer. I felt like I was primarily an illness.

But in letting go of who I thought I was, my experience with illness burned away a lot of what my ego had been built around. What was left behind after that was all this space and room to reconsider how I thought of myself, as well as what my priorities were. Even in sickness, there is relief in this. The palliative effects of letting go were an important lesson for me.

I don't know how you have that kind of experience and return to who you were. I know that I haven't been able to. Though I have just spent a year writing, it's still very hard for me to think of myself as a "writer." It's very hard for me to think of myself as anything at all other than what I happen to be doing in the moment. What I've learned is that to identify with something is only to identify with the contingent, the fleeting. I recognize the proximity of this to spirituality and revelation, and though I don't have any specific spiritual orientation, I have noticed the parallels between my own illness-born insights and some of Baij's beliefs. I think this would be rich terrain to explore, and maybe down the road I will.

But spirituality aside, it's Baij's experience in Partition that I found myself thinking most about. While of course our experiences couldn't be more different—culturally and politically—what I related to was the extremities of personal loss. I also felt sympathetic to the ways Partition created a loss that might be hard to explain, ambiguous, and therefore hard to understand. It seems to me that this kind of loss leaves existential wreckage in its wake because it resists a tidy narrative. It's true that there are political explanations, particularly within the context of colonialism that do help illuminate Partition, the violence Baij witnessed, how quickly people regress not just to force but cruelty—this must have left a mark. And how could this mark not shake the foundations of what seemed possible and within reason? In living through Partition, I think there must have been some rerouting of meaning for Baij, some foundational rupture. And this isn't even to mention in concrete terms what he lost: his home, his country, everything he owned. In a way he also lost his cultural bearing. Though there would be many Punjabi refugees who would settle to Lucknow, Baij nonetheless had to adjust to another culture, another way of doing things. In fact, part of what I find so remarkable about him is his ability not just to adapt to this change, but to thrive in doing so.

So, I see Partition marking a distinct before and after in his life. In essence, yes, he was still generous, still duty bound, still all of the things that seem constitutive of his character, but I can't help but think of his life as split. There's before that August of 1947, and then there's after. I connect with this sense of split. My own life is very much organized around a distinct before and after, too. Before illness, and now this, after.

But Baij was different than me. He was able to do something during his own experience with loss and upheaval that I was not able to do with mine. Judging from the stories I've heard about him and judging from the way I have come to understand his character, I think he was able to stay optimistic during Partition and those years he lived as a refugee. He seemed to always believe that there would be an afterward to what he was going through, and he never stopped planning for that afterward. That he intended to send one of his children to The Doon School while living in a refugee camp couldn't be a clearer indicator of this. I think Baij always believed that he would be okay, no matter what kind of difficulty confronted him.

I didn't have this faith when I was sick. I think I began to lose it sometime around the third year. I could only handle so many false promises and diagnoses, false starts of optimism, only to find myself in the clutches of another neurological storm, the rapid and electric clenches of muscle spasms so intense my whole body would shake for days on end. In my own story, I had gone from protagonist to an apostrophe character, a quickly fading footnote to other people's lives. It felt to me that there would be no afterward, only illness, only more suffering. And for a while, I was right. I watched more weeks turn into months and then months turn into another year, and I was still sick. I could no longer find myself, and the belief that I never would became a kind of organizing principle.

And yet, here I am, writing about my own "afterward."

This is actually a hard thing to come to terms with. Looking at the belief I held then, while I was sick, that I would always be sick, and now living in an afterward that is different presents a kind of disjointed self that feels distinctly incompatible. They are beliefs that can operate only in two different people. And yet, these people are, as far as I can tell, both me.

I can't say exactly what one thing precipitated my recovery. Sometime in the fall of 2020 I found a doctor who was able to identify and treat a series of systemic bacterial infections, and this helped. But the recovery was bumpy, with ups and downs that were hard to trust. In hindsight, when I really look at the last five years, I think it wasn't until the summer of 2021 that things began to really turn around for me. What exactly happened? What precipitated my healing? There are two pieces that feel instrumental to me. The first was the project and work of writing this book. The second was meeting E.

I took on this project with real doubt. Uncertain about my own ability as a writer and feeling out of practice combined with the general idea of rendering something true and essential about a man's life that was so different from my own. I found myself moving forward very slowly, one sentence at a time, but moving forward nonetheless. There was something about tending to language again, one day after another, that felt restorative. It was a reminder of the agency we have in creativity, and I needed this reminder. That I had the resources and time to do this work I owe to Brij and Raj. People come in and out of our lives at strange times, and I will forever be grateful for the intersection of my own life with theirs and with the opportunity they presented. They took a chance and trusted me with their own stories, and for this they will both remain significant people in my own story.

I happened to meet E. around the same time that I started this project. Building a relationship is not the same thing as writing a book, but they are not entirely dissimilar either. Both require attention to detail and narrative awareness. If you spend enough time with someone, the question inevitably arises: Where is this going? What is the narrative trajectory with this person? What are we trying to build? And like writing a book, that question can't be answered without the day-to-day work and minutia, without working with the metaphorical page or scene in front of you.

There is uncertainty in this and uncertainty is difficult for me, but what I learned is that over time I began to trust in the process. With careful attention, this trust became something I learned I could rely on. With each problem that arises, there's a choice to scrap the entire project, or to rework it, revise, and figure out a way to keep moving forward. Each time E. and I chose to move forward, I came to believe more and more that this work was something we both cared a lot about, and that we both cared a lot about each other. This, too, was restorative.

I do think that we all have the capacity to heal alone, but it helps to be able to do it with someone. My last year with E. has been no less healing than writing itself. And the overlap of writing about a man whose generosity and openhandedness touched so many lives around him while wanting to be more generous and openhanded in this new relationship with E. created a kind of thematic resonance between my own life and Baij's. In short, what I found in all of this is an "afterward" to my illness, and a restored belief that life does go on, that time moves forward, that I'll be okay.

I had lost this belief when I was sick, but the way Baij lived as an undeterred optimist reminded me that I wanted to believe again. That he was able to rest in knowing he would be okay during the darker episodes of his life—like Partition, his conflicts with S.L., the loss of his own father—is something that I admire greatly. His trust in his own life reoriented obstacles and loss from potential roadblocks to something that can be worked with, even learned from. This is what I am learning to do, and over this last year I have taken Baij as a guide. It was a chance meeting between the two of us, but that we met at all says something about what's possible, that good things can arise when we least expect them to.

* * *

Writing this has called to mind a different "afterward," but one that feels nonetheless relevant. I grew up surfing and I'm thinking about an afternoon when I was seventeen years old. I'm sitting on the floor at my best friend Jake's place reading "Surfer Magazine." It's early afternoon, summer, and we had just surfed that morning, which means the kitchen at Jake's mom's house is still messy with the aftermath of our feverish, post-surf eating.

This was part of our routine. We would surf in the morning and then afterward clear out the cupboards at Jake's mom's house, eating whatever was easy and quick: cereal, chips, burritos, smoothies, sometimes all of the above. I remember that on this day, it was sunny, though not hot, as it was almost never hot in the small, Northern California town where I grew up. Jake is sitting next to me with his own issue of the same magazine I'm reading in front of him. We are content.

I remember this day because of the article I was reading. The author was a surfer who had grown up in Hawaii and surfed for most of his life. He had, however, recently moved to Kansas for reasons that were outside of his control. The article was a dirge, a torch song, a letter of mourning because the writer could no longer surf, and I remember well the despair I felt on this writer's behalf. I imagined the claustrophobia of endless rows of corn, the flat monotony of a Midwest horizon, and the dry, dry air, with no ocean or sweet-smelling southerly wind to cool it. Surfing was my life, and I could feel this other surfer's suffering at being land locked.

I felt then that I would rather die than not surf. I'm not being dramatic. This was my sincere and I think honest reaction to this article. If I were put in that man's shoes and had to live in Kansas and I couldn't do what I loved, what animated everything about my life, if I couldn't surf, I simply wouldn't want to be here, in this world. That's how much surfing meant to me. As a teenager and into my early twenties, it was the single most important thing to me.

A few years after I had read that article, I quit surfing. I quit willingly, however complicated my reasons were. I was twenty-two years old, had just gone through my first difficult break up, and went to South America to surf, but I felt such despair over the loss of this relationship that I couldn't surf. In fact, surfing itself made things worse, as it only served as a reminder of what I had lost.

So I gave away my surf equipment and went into the mountains of Argentina. There I thought about what I would do, and I realized that I couldn't go home, back to California, where everything reminded me of this relationship that had just ended. So instead of going home, I went to Alaska, and then Canada, and then, two years later, I moved to Washington, and I went back to school. During my travels I had fallen in love with reading and felt the first inclination to write. It would become a passion that I would pursue with a single mindedness that wasn't dissimilar to the passion with which I pursued surfing.

It was years later, when I was living in Idaho, an obviously landlocked state, and going to graduate school, that I found myself thinking of that article I had read when I was seventeen. I remember I had gone for a hike at Kamiak Butte, a trail that ascends a couple thousand feet, and at the top offers a view of vast fields of wheat, a view that isn't dissimilar to how I've always imagined Kansas.

It hit me then that my own life had taken a turn that wasn't that different from the surfer who had to relocate to a landlocked state. Here I was, in Idaho, with no ocean in sight. And yet, I was living a deeply fulfilling life as a writer, a teacher, and a student. I looked out at the flat expanse below Kamiak Butte, at the wheat fields golden and parched, and the juxtaposition between my certainty as a seventeen-year-old that there would be no "after" surfing, and my life then, at thirty, as a writer, very much living an afterward without surfing, couldn't have been more pronounced.

The irony of it took my breath away. But this is living, the strange and unforeseen turns a life can take. As I watched the wheat below me gather and roll with the wind in patterns that looked like waves, I realized that I was happier in that moment than I had ever been as a surfer, or at least more fulfilled with my work as a writer.

I still dream about surfing. They are mostly frustrating dreams where I am hurrying to put my wet suit on before the sun goes down, hoping to catch just one last wave. Or worse, I am paddling for a wave, steadily gaining velocity, readying to jump to my feet, and then, when I do, I wake up. I can still feel it, almost twenty years later—the glide and the flight, what it's like to cut through water. But if I hadn't quit surfing, I wouldn't have had that moment on Kamiak Butte. I wouldn't have felt and experienced all those things that came after. I may not have started writing.

What I'm trying to say is that life's afterwards come in surprising forms, and sometimes what is birthed from loss can be something deeper and more gratifying than what we are afraid of losing.

I do still miss parts of my life before I got sick, the confidence, the almost blind trust in my ability, the feeling nothing bad could happen to me. But this, here, this afterward that I believed would never come, I wouldn't trade it for who I was then, and I wouldn't want to go back, even if I could. Because it was the sickness and loss that lead to this, to my life in Seattle, to this book, to walking on the beach with E. and looking for agates. And in saying yes to this afterward, I also have to say yes to all that came before it.

To me, this is optimism: to find in life's afterwards the desire to embrace even the most difficult circumstances that lead to them. I think this kind of thinking is something that Baij would have understood.

~Eric

Eric Severn is a writer from Arcata, California. His writing has appeared in ZYZZYVA, New England Review, Michigan Quarterly Review, and numerous other journals. His short story McGuffin was 2020 notable Best American Short Story. Eric received his MFA in Creative Writing from The University of Idaho and currently lives in Seattle, Washington. To see more of his work, visit EricSevern.weebly.com.

*"Anand means 'joyful.'
As an Anand, this doesn't just mean
that you should be joyful. It means
that as an Anand you should also
try to bring joy to others."*

~ Baij to his children, p. 189 ~

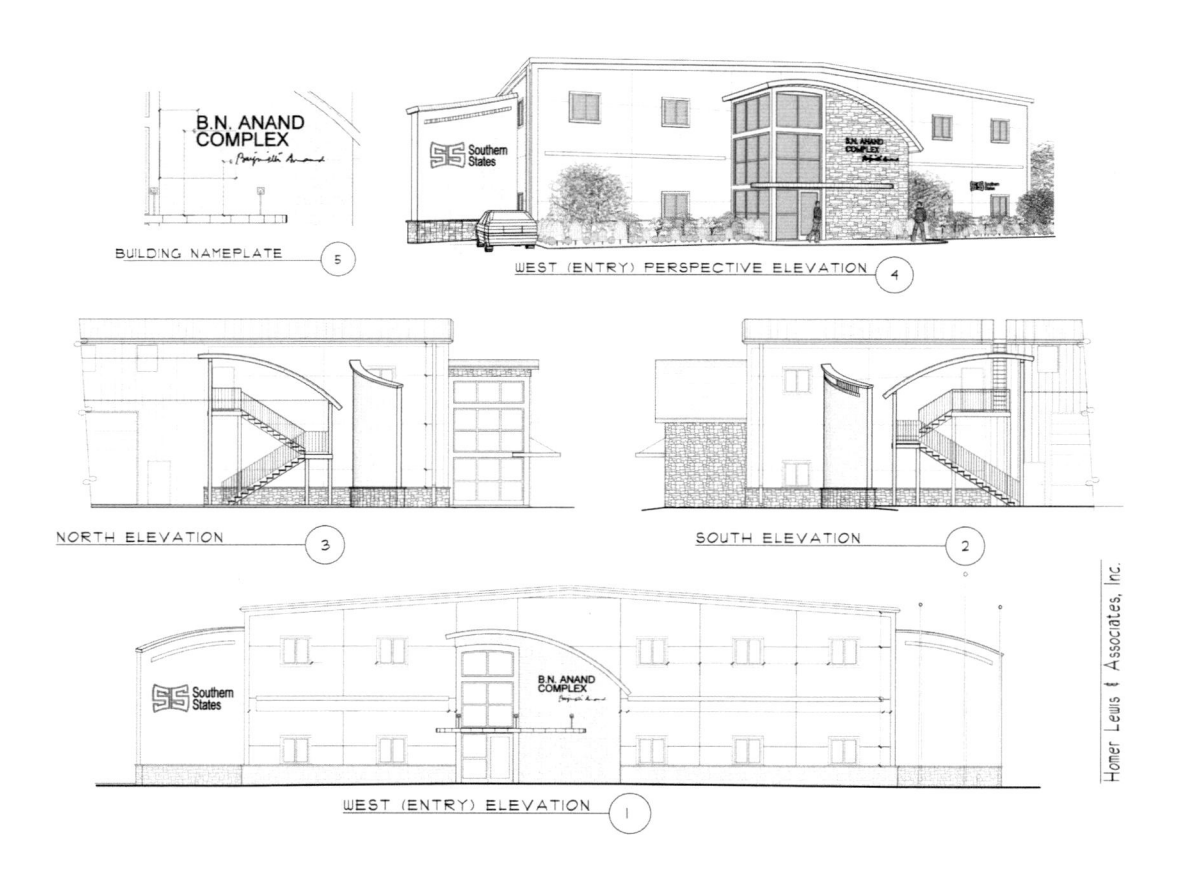

This book is dedicated to Baijnath Anand and his optimistic disposition and exemplary life.

~ Rashmi, Rajesh, Brijesh & Ajesh

Made in the USA
Columbia, SC
26 September 2024

8505a953-876f-4ca4-8ce7-3646086abdb7R01